VACATION ON *Location*
MIDWEST

EXPLORE THE SITES WHERE YOUR FAVORITE MOVIES WERE FILMED

JOEY GREEN

CHICAGO
REVIEW
PRESS

Copyright © 2017 by Joey Green
All rights reserved
Published by Chicago Review Press Incorporated
814 North Franklin Street
Chicago, Illinois 60610
ISBN 978-1-61373-725-5

Library of Congress Cataloging-in-Publication Data
Is available from the Library of Congress.

Cover design: Andrew Brozyna
Cover photos: Unless otherwise indicated, cover photos are copyright © 2016
by Jerome Pohlen. Used with permission. (front, clockwise from upper left)
The Bridges of Madison County, "Roseman Covered Bridge." *Field of Dreams*,
"Field of Dreams" copyright © 2016 by Iowa Memories, LLC, d.b.a. Field
of Dreams Movie Site. Used with permission. *Breaking Away*, "Rooftop
Quarry" copyright © 2016 by Lynae Sowinski, *Limestone Post Magazine*.
Used with permission. www.limestonepostmagazine.com. *The Dark Knight*,
"Chicago Board of Trade Building" copyright © 2010 by Antoine Tavene-
aux. Used with permission. *A Christmas Story*, "Leg Lamp." (back, left to
right) *The Blues Brothers*, "Pilgrim Baptist Church." *8 Mile*, "Cow Head." *A
League of Their Own*, "Huntingburg Stadium." *The Shawshank Redemption*,
"Mansfield Prison."
Interior design: Jonathan Hahn

Printed in the United States of America
5 4 3 2 1

For Debbie

CONTENTS

INTRODUCTION

*W*HILE STAYING AT AN AUSTRIAN GUESTHOUSE thirty years ago, I bicycled into downtown Salzburg on a hot summer afternoon, happened upon the stunning Mirabell Palace and Gardens, and felt overcome by déjà vu. I suddenly realized I was standing in the midst of the beautifully manicured garden seen in the 1965 movie *The Sound of Music*, where Maria (Julie Andrews) leads the Von Trapp children to dance around a fountain, singing "Do-Re-Mi." Awestruck and dumbfounded to find myself on a real-life movie set, I patted the same dwarf gnome statue on the head that the Von Trapp children did, pranced through the same pergola tunnel covered with vines, hopped up and down the same terrace steps, and skipped across the same pedestrian Mozart Bridge.

I explored Salzburg, determined to visit all the locations seen in *The Sound of Music*, becoming truly immersed in the city. I discovered that the Von Trapp home seen in the movie is actually a composite of three different Salzburg locations. Maria gets off the bus and sings "I Have Confidence" on her way down a tree-lined lane along Hellbrunner Allee. The courtyard and front of Frohnburg Palace starred as the front of the Von Trapp home. The back of Leopoldskron Castle in Salzburg was used as the back of the home, where the children are seen boating on Leopoldskron Lake and falling into the water. In reality, the Von Trapp family lived in Villa Walburga, a mansion in Aigen, a suburb of Salzburg.

Enchanted by these pop culture icons, I danced around the gazebo in which Liesl sings "Sixteen Going on Seventeen" (now located at Hellbrunn Palace), visited the Salzburg festival hall where Captain Von Trapp sang "Edelweiss" and the Von Trapp family sang "So Long, Farewell," and toured Nonnberg Abbey, where the nuns wonder how to solve a problem like Maria. I paid homage at the Collegiate Church of St. Michael in nearby Mondsee, where Maria's wedding took place in the movie, and I spun around in the green meadow where Maria sings that "the hills are alive with the sound of music" and then, hearing the ringing bells of the convent, runs down to Nonnberg Abbey in minutes. In real life, however, the meadow sits in Marktschellenberg, Germany, approximately twelve miles south of the abbey, meaning Maria could not possibly hear the ringing bells or run to the convent in less than two hours. The real wedding also took place at Nonnberg Abbey, not eighteen miles to the west in Mondsee.

That experience forever changed the way I travel. From then on, I did extensive research to plan my travels and our family vacations around towns off the beaten trail where Hollywood producers filmed classic movies. We've toured the prison used in *The Shawshank Redemption* (Mansfield, Ohio), visited the island seen in *Jurassic Park* (Kauai, Hawaii), and celebrated Groundhog Day in the very town where Bill Murray relives February 2 over and over in *Groundhog Day* (Woodstock, Illinois). We've cruised the streets from *American Graffiti* (Petaluma, California), dined in the college cafeteria where John Belushi unleashed a food fight in *Animal House* (Eugene, Oregon), and stayed in the foreboding and grandiose hotel in *The Shining* (Timberline, Oregon). We've gone white-water rafting down the same raging river depicted in *Deliverance* (Tallulah Gorge, Georgia), played golf at the country club used in *Caddyshack* (Davie, Florida), and run up the same 72 steps and raised our arms in triumph at the same museum seen in the Rocky movies (Philadelphia, Pennsylvania).

But it seemed unfair to keep all my homemade maps and plans for movie-inspired pilgrimages to myself. After all, visiting these places brought my family and me tremendous joy and a deeper insight into the films we love. But now, with this book as a guide and the detailed maps I've created inside, everyone can—and should—make these excursions as full-scale vacations or quirky side trips to enhance their appreciation of their favorite movies and the magic of filmmaking.

Stepping into the landscapes and cityscapes of your favorite movies really makes you feel like you're meeting the unsung stars in the film or starring in the movie yourself. To make things simple I've listed the locations in the order they appear in each film. So you can sit at home in a comfy chair and discover where the most memorable scenes from your favorite movies took place or hit the road and see them for yourself. Either way you're a step closer to bringing the magic of Hollywood to life. Sure, planning your vacations around movie locations may qualify as obsessive behavior. But you're unlikely to be toted away in a straightjacket unless you show up in Salzburg wearing a nun's frock and habit, playing a guitar, and singing "Climb Ev'ry Mountain." On second thought, you might actually get away with that—unless you're trailed by seven children dressed in play clothes made from curtains.

ILLINOIS

The Blues Brothers

In 1973, comedian Dan Aykroyd, who had been performing with the comedy troupe Second City in Toronto, introduced fellow comedian John Belushi, a Second City alumnus visiting Toronto to recruit talent for *The National Lampoon Radio House*, to the blues. Five years later, as cast members on *Saturday Night Live*, Belushi and Aykroyd performed a sketch as the Blues Brothers.

After Belushi's success in *National Lampoon's Animal House* and the Blues Brothers' 1978 hit album *Briefcase Full of Blues*, Universal agreed to make the *Blues Brothers* movie, from a script written by Aykroyd and *SNL* writer Mitch Glazer.

Both Belushi and Aykroyd envisioned shooting the entire movie on location in Chicago, the home of the blues and where Belushi had performed in Second City. Chicago, however, had been off limits to Hollywood filmmakers throughout Richard J. Daley's 21-year reign as mayor. In 1979, three years after Daley's death, a nervous John Belushi met with Chicago mayor Jane Byrne to request permission to shoot the Blues Brothers movie in the city in exchange for a $200,000 donation to Chicago orphanages.

As a fan of Belushi's work, Byrne immediately said fine.

"He said, 'Wait,'" recalled Byrne in the *Chicago Tribune*. "We also want to drive a car through the lobby of Daley Plaza. Right through the window.' I remember what was in my mind as he said it. I had the whole 11th Ward against me anyway, and most of Daley's people against me. They owned this city for years, so when Belushi asked me to drive a car through Daley Plaza, the only thing I could say was, 'Be my guest!'"

In the *Chicago Tribune*, movie critic Gene Siskel called *The Blues Brothers* "the best movie ever made in Chicago."

1. JOLIET CORRECTIONAL CENTER
1127–1299 Collins Street, Joliet, IL 60432

At the start of the movie, Jake (John Belushi) is released from the Joliet Correctional Center. Built in 1858 with 20-foot-high limestone walls and neo-Gothic guard towers on historic Route 66, the Joliet prison became one of the nation's largest maximum-security prisons. The facility has sat abandoned and unused since its closure in 2002. The City of Joliet has yet to reach an agreement with the Illinois Department of Corrections to turn the prison into a tourist attraction by offering tours led by former guards.

2. EAST 95TH STREET BRIDGE
3259 East 95th Street, Chicago, IL 60617

Elwood (Dan Aykroyd) demonstrates the power of the new Bluesmobile (a 1974 Dodge Monaco) by driving it west over an open drawbridge across the Calumet River, at Calumet Harbor.

3. ST. HELEN OF THE BLESSED SHROUD ORPHANAGE
West 18th Street at South Normal Avenue, Chicago, IL 60616

Although the Blues Brothers drive toward Calumet City, they visit Sister Mary Stigmata (Kathleen Freeman) at the orphanage, no longer standing, at the end of a street lined by seedy warehouses.

4. TRIPLE ROCK BAPTIST CHURCH
Pilgrim Baptist Church, 3235 East 91st Street, Chicago, IL 60617

Inside this church, Reverend Cleophus James (James Brown) belts out the gospel song "Let Us Go Back to the Old Landmark," prompting Jake to see the light. The interior scene was filmed on a soundstage at Universal Studios in Los Angeles.

5. THE TRAFFIC LIGHT
Intersection of South Cumberland Avenue and West Talcott Road, Park Ridge, IL 60068

At this intersection, the Bluesmobile runs through a red light as the Blues Brothers head north on South Cumberland Avenue.

6. THE COPS
Private Residence, 729 Gillick Street, Park Ridge, IL 60068

Jake and Elwood make a right turn onto Gillick Street and pull over for the police in front of this house. Elwood insists, "The light was yellow, sir." Please be respectful and do not loiter or disturb the residents.

7. THE CHASE
Intersection of Glenlake Avenue and Courtland Avenue, Park Ridge, IL 60068

The Blues Brothers head east on Glenlake Avenue, make a left turn to head north in the wrong lane on Courtland Avenue, and go into a spin in the intersection at West Talcott Road and Devon Avenue. "They're not going to catch us," says Elwood. "We're on a mission from God." They continue west along Devon Avenue.

8. DIXIE MALL
15201 Dixie Highway, Harvey, IL 60426

The police corner the Blues Brothers in the parking lot of the Dixie Mall, which had gone out of business and been abandoned before filming began. The filmmakers dressed the stores for the movie. The Blues Brothers drive through a Toys R Us store, through the middle of the mall, and back out through the J. C. Penney. "This place has got everything," observes Jake. After filming, the sprawling building stood derelict until 2012, when it was demolished.

9. TRAILWAYS BUS TERMINAL
West Randolph Street and North Wabash Avenue, Chicago, IL 60601

The Blues Brothers drive west on Randolph Street, passing the Trailways Bus Terminal (demolished) and the Oriental Theater, a 2,253-seat theater in a renovated historic movie theater built in 1926.

10. PLYMOUTH HOTEL, FOR MEN ONLY
22 West Van Buren Street, Chicago, IL 60605

Elwood parks the Bluesmobile behind the Plymouth Hotel by a CTA transformer. The hotel, the shops along Van Buren Street, and the transformer have since been demolished. Although the Mystery Woman (Carrie Fisher) destroys the hotel in the movie, the filmmakers achieved that special effect by destroying a large photograph of the building adhered to polystyrene blocks. A small park behind the El sits where the buildings once stood.

11. AEROSOL CAN FACTORY
1 West Hegeler Lane, Danville, IL 61832

The factory where Elwood works, originally known as CCL Custom Manufacturing, was acquired by KIK Custom Products in 2005.

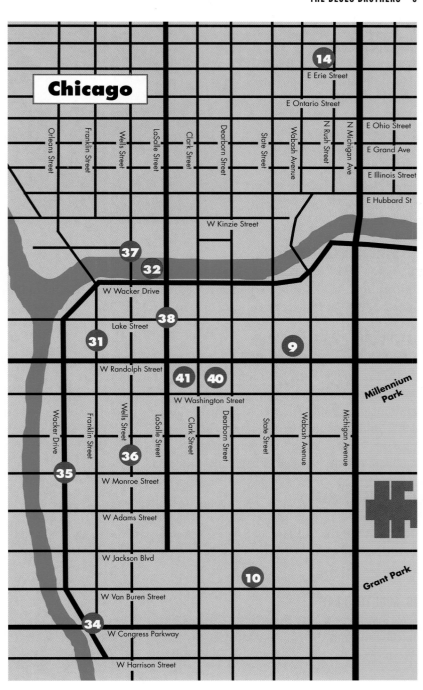

12. MRS. TARANTINO'S BOARDING HOUSE

1623 South 51st Court, Cicero, IL 60804

Jake and Elwood visit this quaint home to look for former band members Tom "Bones" Malone and Blue Lou Marini. "Are you the police?" asks Mrs. Tarantino (Toni Fleming). "No ma'am," says Elwood. "We're musicians."

13. HOLIDAY INN EXTERIOR

Quality Inn O'Hare Airport, 3801 Mannheim Road, Schiller Park, IL 60176

Murph and the Magic Tones perform "Quando, Quando, Quando" in the music lounge of this seedy Holiday Inn. The Armada Room was a set.

14. THE CHEZ PAUL RESTAURANT

660 North Rush Street, Chicago, IL 60611

At this upscale French restaurant, the Blues Brothers recruit horn player Mr. Fabulous (Alan Rubin), who works as the maître d' and whose wait staff includes Paul "Pee-Wee Herman" Reubens. The restaurant closed in 1995, and the building now houses office space. The interior was filmed on a set. "Give us a bottle of your finest champagne, five shrimp cocktails, and some bread for my brother," says Jake.

15. THE NAZI PARADE

Junction of Columbia Drive and Science Drive, Jackson Park, Chicago, IL 60637

Just south of the Museum of Science and Industry, the Nazis hold a rally in the park and jump from the bridge into the East Lagoon. "I hate Illinois Nazis," says Jake.

16. SOUL FOOD CAFE

Nate's Delicatessen, 807 West Maxwell Street, Chicago, IL 60608

In the center of the bustling Maxwell Street flea market, where waitress Aretha Franklin sings "Think" and John Lee Hooker performs in the street, the Blues Brothers find Matt Murphy and Lou Marini. The buildings have since been torn down, and the area was redeveloped as a part of the University of Illinois at Chicago campus.

17. CURL UP & DYE BEAUTY SALON
8500 South Burley Avenue, Chicago, IL 60617
This beauty salon, where the Mystery Woman works, now stands empty.

18. RAY'S MUSIC EXCHANGE
Shelly's Loan Company, 300 East 47th Street, Chicago, IL 60653
The band buys their equipment from Ray Charles and then dances in the street in front of the store as Ray sings "Shake a Tail Feather." The mural of music stars (Muddy Waters, B. B. King, and Ray Charles) still graces the western wall of the store along South Prairie Avenue.

19. HOWARD JOHNSON'S
Des Plaines Tollway Oasis, 1960 South Mt. Prospect Road, Des Plaines, IL 60018
The hotel where the band stops so Jake can make a phone call has since been demolished.

20. WRIGLEY FIELD
1060 West Addison Street, Chicago, IL 60613
The dim-witted Nazis pay a visit to the Blues Brothers at this address, which, to their dismay, turns out to be Wrigley Field. To plan your visit, see http://chicago.cubs.mlb.com/chc/ballpark/.

SHOT ELSEWHERE

BOB'S COUNTRY BUNKER

This country bar, where the Blues Brothers perform "Gimme Some Lovin'," "Theme from *Rawhide*," and "Stand by Your Man" on a caged stage, existed on the lot of Universal Studios in Universal City, California, and has since been demolished. The Good Ole Boys, driving a Winnebago, chase the Blues Brothers through Griffith Park in Los Angeles.

21. THE SCHOOLYARD
Oscar Meyer School, 2250 North Clifton Street, Chicago, IL 60614

The Blues Brothers steal the speaker from the playground of this school, but the tower no longer exists.

22. THE ORPHANS
116 North Main Street, Wauconda, IL 60084

Along this street, Curtis (Cab Calloway) hands out flyers to the orphans to hang up around the city.

23. THE BLUESMOBILE PUBLICITY ROUTE
127 North Main Street, Wauconda, IL 60084

With the giant horn roped to the roof of their car, the Blues Brothers drive south along North Main Street, Wauconda, and along Phil's Beach on Bangs Lake. "And it's Ladies' Night tonight!"

24. LLOYD'S TIRE CLINIC
Illinois Route 59 and Garys Mill Road, West Chicago, IL 60185

At this empty gas station, Jake and Elwood wait for a delivery. The service station, built especially for the movie, was destroyed for a scene deleted from the movie, and only the foundation remains.

25. THE PALACE HOTEL BALLROOM
South Shore Cultural Center, 7059 South Shore Drive, Chicago, IL 60646

The Blues Brothers play their first gig "up north on Lake Wazzapamani" some 106 miles from Chicago, but the exterior shot of the Palace Hotel Ballroom is actually this 1916 Mediterranean-style building on Chicago's

South Side. The South Shore Cultural Center sits on more than 65 acres of parkland and includes a theater, stables, nine-hole golf course, formal dining hall, a private beach, a nature sanctuary, a butterfly garden, and the Washburne Culinary Institute and its elegant restaurant, the Parrot Cage. The center was added to the National Register of Historic Places in 1975. For more information, visit www.chicagoparkdistrict.com.

The filmmakers shot the interiors at the Hollywood Palladium, an Art Deco theater at 6215 Sunset Boulevard, Hollywood, California, where Cab Calloway sings "Minnie the Moocher," and the Blues Brothers play "Can't Turn You Loose," "Everybody Needs Somebody to Love," and "Sweet Home Chicago."

26. TUNNEL SHOOTOUT
Unknown location

The Blues Brothers escape through the service tunnel. The Chicago Tunnel Company operated an underground electric narrow-gauge railroad to move coal, merchandise, and mail in and out of Chicago for many downtown businesses. The Bluesmobile exits from a tunnel under the Grant Memorial in Lincoln Park.

27. THE GOOD OLE BOYS CHASE
7751 West Higgins Road, Chicago, IL 60631

The Good Ole Boys race along this road after exiting the westbound Kennedy Expressway at the Canfield exit. They crash their Winnebago into the lake on the Universal Studios backlot in Universal City, California.

28. TWIGGY'S MOTEL
West Wind Motel, 28W721 Roosevelt Road, West Chicago, IL 60185

A chic woman (Twiggy) waits fruitlessly for Elwood outside this motel.

29. POLICE CAR PILEUP
US 12 (South Rand Road), north of the intersection with Illinois 176, Wauconda, IL 60084

When Elwood pulls over, the police cars go flying over the embankment.

30. TRUCK
US 12 (South Rand Road), south of the Barrington Road Overpass, Wauconda, IL 60084

Police Car 55 goes sailing into a northbound truck, prompting Correctional Officer Burton Mercer (John Candy) to take the one-way radio and announce, "We're in a truck."

31. MOUNTED POLICE
North Franklin Street and Couch Place, Chicago, IL 60606
Police on horseback head south on Franklin Street, with the Merchandise Mart behind them.

32. POLICE BOATS
Chicago River, LaSalle Street Bridge, Chicago, IL 60654
Police boats head east along the Chicago River.

33. THE CHASE SCENE
2301 South King Drive, Chicago, IL 60616
The Blues Brothers drive east through the police roadblock at East 23rd Street (the bridge was demolished to build the McCormick Place complex), and then turn left to head north on South Lake Shore Drive.

34. WACKER DRIVE ENTRANCE
Intersection of West Congress Parkway and South Franklin Street, Chicago, IL 60607
The Bluesmobile appears across town, enters the south entrance to Lower Wacker Drive at West Congress Parkway, and heads north.

35. POLICE CAR JUMP
Intersection of South Wacker Drive and West Monroe Street, Chicago, IL 60606
The Bluesmobile, previously heading north, speeds south on Lower Wacker Drive and jumps over a police car at the top of the ramp leading up to West Monroe Street.

36. HEADING SOUTH
South Wells Street and West Arcade Place, Chicago, IL 60602
The Bluesmobile appears two blocks east and one block north of its previous location, driving south on South Wells Street at West Arcade Place.

37. HEADING NORTH
Wells Street Bridge, Chicago, IL 60606
The Bluesmobile appears some ten blocks north, driving south across the Wells Street Bridge. At North Wells Street and West Washington Street, the Blues Brothers nearly miss a group of bicyclists.

38. SQUAD CAR PILEUP
Intersection of West Lake Street and North LaSalle Street, Chicago, IL 60601
At least 10 police cars pileup at this intersection.

39. NAZIS IN THE ALLEY
915 West Jackson Boulevard, Chicago, IL 60607
As the Blues Brothers head east on West Jackson Boulevard near South Peoria Street, the Nazis emerge from an alley at 915 West Jackson Boulevard, turn right, and follow after them. The Blues Brothers turn right into an alley at 855 West Jackson Boulevard (between South Peoria Street and South Green Street), exit the alley at 860 West Van Buren Street, turn right, and head west. The Nazis run out of road in a scene shot at a highway construction site near the Hoan Bridge on Interstate 794 in Milwaukee, Wisconsin. The filmmakers used a helicopter to drop the Ford Pinto 1,400 feet over Chicago and into a vacant lot. The car falls into a hole filmed on the Universal Studios backlot in Universal City, California.

40. RICHARD J. DALEY CENTER PLAZA
50 West Washington Street, Chicago, IL 60602
The chase scene culminates at this building named for Mayor Richard J. Daley, who served for 21 years and died in 1976. The steel sculpture in the south plaza, standing 50 feet tall and weighing over 160 tons, is an untitled work created by Pablo Picasso in 1967 and given by the artist as a gift to the city. Jake and Elwood use the cubist head as a landmark. Director John Landis obtained permission to land a helicopter in the plaza and crash the Bluesmobile through the Daley Center windows.

41. CITY HALL–COUNTY BUILDING, CHICAGO
118 North Clark Street, Chicago, IL 60602
The Blues Brother drive through the Daley Center and across Clark Street, and park on the sidewalk, where the Bluesmobile falls apart. The duo barricade themselves inside the building, and as the Chicago police, firefighters, and National Guard troops charge the building and a four-man SWAT team rappels down the columns, Jake and Elwood hand their payment to the Cook County clerk (Steven Spielberg).

Other Feature Attractions

VOLO AUTO MUSEUM
27582 Volo Village Road, Volo, IL 60073

See the original Bluesmobile with the oversized loud speaker mounted to the roof. "It's got cop tires, cop suspension, cop shocks," says Elwood Blues. "It's a model made before catalytic converters so it'll run good on regular gas." For more information, visit www.volocars.com.

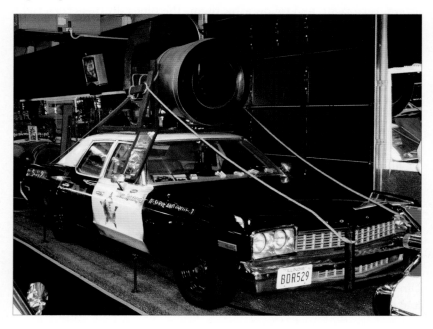

The Breakfast Club

After the success of the 1983 movie *National Lampoon's Vacation*, based on his short story first published in *National Lampoon*, John Hughes wrote the script for *The Breakfast Club*, a film about a group of widely dissimilar high school students serving detention together on a Saturday in the school library. A graduate of Glenbrook North High School in Northbrook, Illinois, Hughes set the film in fictional Shermer, Illinois, a town he created. Northbrook was originally named Shermerville. In fact, Glenbrook North High School is located on Shermer Road.

Hughes shot his film about "a brain, an athlete, a basket case, a princess, and a criminal" in Chicago because he was a native of Northbrook who still lived there. He felt that living in the Chicago suburbs helped keep him in touch with young people.

"Many filmmakers portray teenagers as immoral and ignorant with pursuits that are pretty base," Hughes told *Chicago Tribune* movie critic Gene Siskel in 1985. "They seem to think that teenagers aren't very bright. But I haven't found that to be the case. I listen to kids. I respect them. I don't discount anything they have to say just because they're only 16 years old. Some of them are as bright as any of the adults I've met; all they lack is a personal perspective."

"John Hughes lets the kids challenge, taunt, and confront each other as if this were *Twelve Angry Men*," wrote *New York Times* film critic Janet Maslin. "Personalities are dissected; tears are shed. The kids, each representing a different teen stereotype, come to understand each other."

1. SHERMER HIGH SCHOOL

Illinois State Police, 9511 Harrison Street, Des Plaines, IL 60016

This police station was formerly Maine North High School, which opened in 1970 and closed in 1981 due to a decrease in the student population.

Director John Hughes used the outside of this futuristic concrete building as the exterior of the high school, shot scenes in the hallways, and built a replica of the library in the gym for use as a set. The filmmakers decided that the actual library was too small for their purposes. A plaque commemorating the movie production hangs on a wall in a hallway just outside the library.

2. SHERMER HIGH SCHOOL HALLWAYS
Glenbrook North High School, 2300 Shermer Road, Northbrook, IL 60062
Director John Hughes shot some of the interior hallway scenes inside this school, which was his alma mater.

3. FOOTBALL FIELD
Illinois State Police, 9511 Harrison Street, Des Plaines, IL 60016
After Claire (Molly Ringwald) hands her earring to him, John Bender (Judd Nelson) walks across the football field and raises his clenched fist in the air in triumph as we hear the song "Don't You (Forget About Me)" by Simple Minds. The football field stood on the east side of the school, and the bleachers behind Bender stood on the west side of the field.

The Dark Knight

In this 2008 sequel to *Batman Begins*, Batman (Christian Bale) joins forces with Lieutenant James Gordon (Gary Oldman) and district attorney Harvey Dent (Aaron Eckhart) to fight the Joker (Heath Ledger).

Director Christopher Nolan used Chicago rather than New York as Gotham City, showcasing the cinematic versatility of Chicago's architecture and skyline. Why? "Well, I grew up partly in Chicago," Nolan told *Newsweek*. "And when Nathan Crowley, my production designer, first set up here in my garage, putting together composites of what Gotham might be, we started imagining a city with all these layers, with bridges and subterranean streets and tall skyscrapers. And at a certain point I said to him, 'I know where this is. This is Chicago.'"

While many Batman fans equate Gotham City with New York, veteran Batman illustrator Neal Adams believes Gotham shares more in common with the Windy City. "Chicago has had a reputation for a certain kind of criminality," Adams told the Associated Press. "Batman is in this kind of corrupt city and trying to turn it back into a better place. One of the things about Chicago is Chicago has alleys (which are virtually nonexistent in New York). Back alleys, that's where Batman fights all the bad guys."

The Dark Knight "avoids such familiar landmarks as Marina City, the Wrigley Building or the skyline," observed *Chicago Sun-Times* film critic Roger Ebert. "Chicagoans will recognize many places, notably LaSalle Street and Lower Wacker Drive, but director Nolan is not making a travelogue. He presents the city as a wilderness of skyscrapers, and a key sequence is set in the still-uncompleted Trump Tower."

1. GOTHAM NATIONAL BANK
Chicago Post Office, 404 West Harrison Street, Chicago, IL 60607

The Joker (Heath Ledger) and his gang, wearing clown masks, rob this building, which doubles as the Gotham Police Department. Says the Joker: "I believe whatever doesn't kill you simply makes you stranger."

2. ROOF OF GOTHAM CITY POLICE STATION
200 West Randolph Street, Chicago, IL 60606

From atop this parking garage, Lieutenant Gordon (Gary Oldman) sends the Bat Signal. Inside the garage, Batman (Christian Bale) arrests the Scarecrow (Cillian Murphy) and an assortment of other villains, including several Batman imitators.

3. POLICE COMMISSIONER'S OFFICE, HARVEY DENT'S OFFICE, MAYOR'S OFFICE, AND WAYNE ENTERPRISES INTERIORS
IBM Building, 330 North Wabash Avenue, Chicago, IL 60611
This monolithic black glass building, built in 1971, was designed by German American architect Ludwig Mies van der Rohe, a pioneer of modern architecture. The Joker hangs a phony Batman outside the building.

4. BRUCE WAYNE'S BEDROOM
Wyndham Grand, 71 East Upper Wacker Drive, 39th Floor, Chicago, IL 60601
From Bruce Wayne's penthouse bedroom in the former Hotel 71, we see spectacular views across the Chicago River.

5. BATMAN'S LAIR
1623 South Lumber Street, Chicago, IL 60616
At this spot, Alfred enters a dumpster that leads to an underground facility where Bruce Wayne stores his Bat gear.

6. COURTROOM AND WAYNE ENTERPRISES
Richard J. Daley Center, Daley Plaza, 50 West Washington Street, Chicago, IL 60602
Built in 1965 and named after Mayor Richard J. Daley, who served for 21 years, this building can also be seen at the climactic end of *The Blues Brothers*. Inside is the courtroom where District Attorney Harvey Dent (Aaron Eckhart) prosecutes Maroni (Eric Roberts).

SHOT ELSEWHERE

LIKE A BAT OUT OF HELL
The Criterion Restaurant, where Bruce Wayne meets Rachel Dawes (Maggie Gyllenhaal) dining with Harvey Dent, is an upscale eatery in London. Built in 1874 in neo-Byzantine style, the Criterion is located at 224 Piccadilly, St. James, London W1J 9HP, United Kingdom.

---

7. BANK OF GOTHAM BUILDING
Federal Reserve Bank of Chicago, 230 South LaSalle Street, Chicago, IL 60604
James Gordon (Gary Oldman) and a SWAT team descend on this bank to find the safe empty. One of 12 banks that control the money supply of the

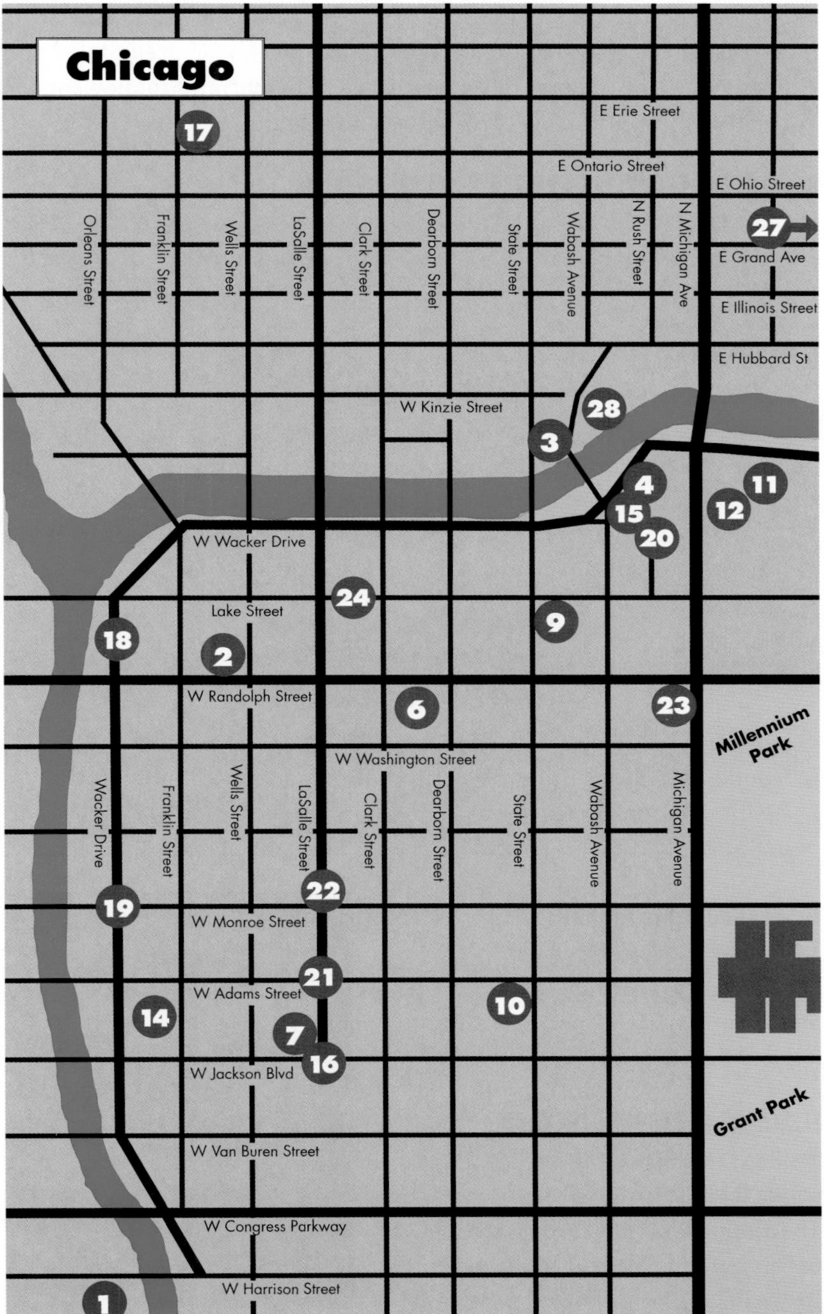
Chicago
17
E Erie Street
E Ontario Street
E Ohio Street
Orleans Street
Franklin Street
Wells Street
LaSalle Street
Clark Street
Dearborn Street
State Street
Wabash Avenue
N Rush Street
N Michigan Ave
27
E Grand Ave
E Illinois Street
E Hubbard St
W Kinzie Street
28
3
4
15
20
11
12
W Wacker Drive
24
Lake Street
9
18
2
W Randolph Street
6
23
Millennium Park
W Washington Street
Wacker Drive
Franklin Street
Wells Street
LaSalle Street
Clark Street
Dearborn Street
State Street
Wabash Avenue
Michigan Avenue
22
19
W Monroe Street
21
W Adams Street
10
14
7
16
W Jackson Blvd
Grant Park
W Van Buren Street
W Congress Parkway
W Harrison Street
1

United States, the Federal Reserve Bank of Chicago houses a fascinating museum that displays all the currency issued by the United States and explains how the Federal Reserve manages the nation's money supply. For more information, visit www.chicagofed.org.

8. WAYNE ENTERPRISES APPLIED SCIENCE DIVISION
Convention Hall of the West Building, McCormick Place, 2301 South Lake Shore Drive, Chicago, IL 60616

In this enormous warehouse, built inside the convention hall, Lucius Fox (Morgan Freeman) provides Batman with an assortment of gadgets.

9. GOTHAM BALLET
Chicago Theatre, 175 North State Street, Chicago, IL 60601

Harvey Dent and Rachel Dawes show up to attend an evening at the ballet but discover the performance has been canceled. Originally known as the Balaban and Katz Chicago Theatre, this lavish landmark theater opened in 1921 and was added to the National Register of Historic Places in 1979. For more information, visit www.thechicagotheatre.com.

SHOT ELSEWHERE

THE PEARL OF THE ORIENT
Lucius Fox meets with financier Lau (Chin Han) in the tallest building in Hong Kong, Two International Finance Centre, from which Batman takes flight.

10. BERGHOFF RESTAURANT
17 West Adams Street, Chicago, IL 60604

Lieutenant Gordon arrests Maroni at this historic German restaurant, housed here since 1905.

11. WAYNE PENTHOUSE INTERIOR
One Illinois Center Building, 111 East Wacker Drive, Chicago, IL 60601

The filmmakers transformed the lobby of this building into the living room of Bruce Wayne's penthouse apartment,

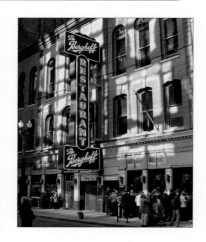

using green screens so the special effects team could later add panoramic views of the city.

12. HARVEY DENT'S FUNDRAISING EVENT
Two Illinois Center, 111 East Wacker Drive, Chicago, IL 60601

The Joker crashes a fundraising cocktail party at this office complex designed by German American architect Ludwig Mies van der Rohe. Harvey Dent asks Alfred, "Any psychotic ex-boyfriends I should be aware of?"

13. JUDGE SURRILLO'S HOUSE
Private Residence, 1910 North Hudson Avenue, Chicago, IL 60614

At this address, Judge Surrillo gets into her car and opens the envelope. Please be respectful and do not loiter or disturb the residents.

14. WILLIS TOWER
233 South Wacker Drive, Chicago, IL 60606

Standing atop the skyscraper best known as the Sears Tower, Batman surveys Gotham City. While tourists cannot stand atop the building, you can see four states from the Skydeck on the 103rd floor. To plan your visit, see http://theskydeck.com.

15. 8TH & ORCHARD

801 East Wacker Place, Chicago, IL 60601

The Joker sends police to this apartment to find the bodies of two people named Harvey and Dent.

16. MEMORIAL SERVICE

Chicago Board of Trade Building, 141 West Jackson Boulevard, Chicago, IL 60604

The parade starts at the intersection of South LaSalle Street and West Monroe Street and heads south to the Chicago Board of Trade Building for the memorial service for the police commissioner. Visit the CME Group Visitor Center from Monday to Friday (8 AM to 4 PM). To see the trading floor, book a group tour in advance. For more information, visit www.cmegroup.com.

17. THE DISCO

Sound Bar, 226 West Ontario Street, Chicago, IL 60654

Inside this club with nine bars and a 4,000-square-foot dance floor, Batman chases after Maroni.

18. THE CHASE

Lower Wacker Drive, Chicago, IL 60606

The Batmobile chases after the Joker's truck.

19. BURNING FIRE TRUCK

Intersection of South Wacker Drive and West Monroe Street, Chicago, IL 60606

The police head north on South Wacker Drive.

20. EXITING THE TUNNEL

Intersection of Lower Wacker Place and North Garland Court, Chicago, IL 60601

The police trucks turn south onto North Garland Court.

21. THE HELICOPTER CRASH
Intersection of South LaSalle Street and West Adams Street, Chicago, IL 60604

The helicopter flies north above LaSalle Street and then crashes to the street at this intersection.

22. THE TRUCK FLIPS
39 South LaSalle Street, Chicago, IL 60603

In front of this building, the Joker's truck flips in the air, and the Joker walks south, firing his machine gun as Batman rides the Batpod north on LaSalle Street.

23. SHOPPING CENTER
Millennium Station, 151 East Randolph Street, Chicago, IL 60601

Batman rides through this shopping mall on the Batpod to rescue Harvey Dent's convoy.

SHOT ELSEWHERE

HOLY EXPLOSION!

To create the massive explosion for *The Dark Knight*, the film crew blew up London's abandoned Battersea Power Station in the dead of the night on October 11, 2007. Neighbors held parties on their balconies to witness the event, but other residents flooded emergency services with telephone calls reporting a terrorist attack. The explosion created a 200-foot fireball and columns of gray smoke, which could be seen for miles across London. The defunct power plant is located at 188 Kirtling Street, London SW8 5BN.

---

24. BRUCE WAYNE IN THE LAMBORGHINI
Lake Street and North Franklin Street, Chicago, IL 60601

Bruce Wayne drives his Lamborghini along Lake Street beneath the tracks of the El, between North Franklin Street and North Michigan Avenue.

25. GOTHAM GENERAL HOSPITAL
Brach's Candy Factory, 401 North Cicero Avenue, Chicago, IL 60644

Blown up in the movie by the Joker, this building was demolished in 2014 and replaced with a warehouse and distribution center.

26. BAR
Twin Anchors, 1665 North Sedgwick Street, Chicago, IL 60614

Harvey Dent (Two Face) confronts Detective Wuertz at this bar founded in 1932 and frequented by Frank Sinatra.

27. EVACUATION OF GOTHAM
Navy Pier, 600 East Grand Avenue, Chicago, IL 60611

The citizens evacuate Gotham City by boarding ferries at this 3,000-foot pier built in 1916.

28. CLIMACTIC FIGHT SCENE EXTERIOR
Trump Tower, 401 North Wabash Avenue, Chicago, IL 60611

Batman and the Joker fight at the construction site of this building. The interior fight scenes were shot on a set built inside Shed 2, one of two airship hangars at Cardington, England.

Other Feature Attractions

HISTORIC AUTO ATTRACTIONS
13825 Metric Road, Roscoe, IL 61073

At this museum, you can see an original Batmobile from the 1960s television series, the Bat Car from the 1989 movie *Batman Returns*, and the Batman costume wore by George Clooney in the 1997 film *Batman and Robin*. For more information, visit www.historicautoattractions.com.

VOLO AUTO MUSEUM
27582 Volo Village Road, Volo, IL 60073

See the 18-wheeler semitrailer the Joker drove in *The Dark Knight*, the Batmobile from the 1989 movie *Batman Returns*, and an original Batmobile and the Batcycle from the 1960s television series. For more information, visit www.volocars.com.

Ferris Bueller's Day Off

Director John Hughes, who grew up in Chicago, worked as a copywriter at Leo Burnett Advertising, and lived in Highland Park, called his 1986 movie *Ferris Bueller's Day Off* "sort of my love letter to the city."

In the movie, Ferris Bueller (Matthew Broderick) plays sick to skip one of his last days of high school and borrows a Ferrari to spend the day exploring downtown Chicago with his girlfriend, Sloane (Mia Sara), and best friend, Cameron (Alan Ruck), pursued by the school's dim-witted principal Edward Rooney (Jeffrey Jones). "Life moves pretty fast," says Ferris. "If you don't stop and look around once in a while, you could miss it."

Hughes set the film in the fictitious Chicago suburb of Shermer and filmed the high school scenes at his alma mater—Glenbrook North High School. Northbrook, Illinois, the community where Hughes grew up, had been named Shermerville until 1923.

"I really wanted to capture as much of Chicago as I could," said Hughes. "Not just in the architecture and landscape, but the spirit." Hughes claimed the scene at the Art Institute of Chicago was "a self-indulgent scene of mine—which was a place of refuge for me. I went there quite a bit. I loved it. I knew all the paintings, the building. This was a chance for me to go back into this building and show the paintings that were my favorite."

At the 2010 Oscar tribute to Hughes, actor Matthew Broderick said, "For the past 25 years, nearly every day someone comes up to me, taps me on the shoulder and says, 'Hey, Ferris, is this your day off?'" In 2014, the Library of Congress selected the film for preservation in the United States National Film Registry.

1. SHERMER HIGH SCHOOL

Glenbrook North High School, 2300 Shermer Road, Northbrook, IL 60062

Ferris Bueller (Matthew Broderick) plays hooky from this high school, which director John Hughes attended in real life. Hughes had previously shot scenes from his earlier film *The Breakfast Club* in these same hallways. The entrance to the high school's center for the performing arts at the back of the school was used as the front of the high school, where Ferris picks up Sloane (Mia Sara) by pretending to be her father.

FERRIS BUELLER'S HOUSE

You may be disappointed to learn that the Bueller family's house, which looks like a typical North Shore home, sits in Southern California. This private residence, located at 4160 Country Club Drive, Long Beach, CA 90807, was one of the few locations John Hughes used outside of the Chicago area.

In addition, Sloane's house, where she and Ferris enjoy the hot tub while Cameron tumbles into the pool, is also a private residence in California: 340 South Westgate Avenue, Los Angeles, CA 90049. If you visit either house, please be respectful and do not loiter or disturb the residents.

The interior of the police station where Jeanie (Jennifer Grey) converses with a punk teenager (Charlie Sheen) was shot in a warehouse at 635 South Mateo Street, Los Angeles, CA 90021.

And defeated Principal Rooney (Jeffrey Jones) climbs aboard the school bus in Long Beach at 3833 Country Club Drive, near Los Cerritos Park. "Gummi bear?" asks a student. "They've been in my pocket. They're real warm and soft."

2. CAMERON'S HOUSE
Private Residence 370 Beech Street, Highland Park, IL 60035

In one of two steel-and-glass buildings cantilevered over the ravines and designed by A. James Speyer, a protégé of Ludwig Mies van der Rohe, Cameron's (Alan Ruck's) father houses his pristine 1961 Ferrari 250 GT California. Please be respectful and do not loiter or disturb the residents.

3. KATIE BUELLER'S OFFICE
583 Chestnut Street, Winnetka, IL 60093

Ferris's mother, Katie (Cindy Pickett), works in the offices of real estate company Koenig and Strey.

4. TOM BUELLER'S OFFICE
333 West Wacker Drive, Chicago, IL 60606

This tall glass office building where Tom Bueller (Lyman Ward) works overlooks the Chicago River.

5. A1-EZ OK PARKING GARAGE
WMW Self Park, 172 West Madison Street, Chicago, IL 60602

Ferris drives south on Clark Street and turns left onto Madison Street, heading east. He then turns right into this parking garage. The attendants drive the Ferrari right on Madison and then make a left, heading south on Wells Street under the El.

6. WILLIS TOWER
233 South Wacker Drive, Chicago, IL 60606

Ferris, Sloane, and Cameron go to the top of the tallest building in the United States (at the time), best known as the Sears Tower, for panoramic views of Chicago. "Anything is peaceful from 1,353 feet," says Ferris. You too can visit the Skydeck on the 103rd floor. To plan your visit, see http://theskydeck.com.

7. CHICAGO BOARD OF TRADE
141 West Jackson Boulevard, Chicago, IL 60604

While overlooking the trading floor of the Chicago Board of Trade, Cameron practices the hand signals that the traders use and Ferris proposes to Sloane. To book a tour of the building, visit www.architecture.org/experience-caf/tours/detail/chicago-board-of-trade-building/.

8. CHEZ QUIS
Private Residence, 22 West Schiller Street, Chicago, IL 60610

This building, since remodeled, served as the exterior of the upscale French restaurant where Ferris passes himself off as Abe Froman, "the sausage king of Chicago." Please be respectful and do not loiter or disturb the residents. The interior was shot at L'Orangerie at 903 North La Cienega Boulevard in West Hollywood, California, which has since been remodeled and renamed Nobu. "I weep for the future."

9. THE PIZZA PLACE EXTERIOR
Corner Cooks, 507 Chestnut Street, Winnetka, IL 60693

Principal Rooney (Jeffrey Jones) searches for Ferris inside the Pizza Palace, the interior of which was shot at Regular Jon's Pizza, 11645 San Vicente Boulevard, Brentwood, California—now the Coral Tree Café.

10. WRIGLEY FIELD
1060 West Addison Street, Chicago, IL 60613

Principal Rooney misses seeing Ferris, Sloane, and Cameron on television at Wrigley Field, home to the Chicago Cubs. The baseball game shown on the television took place on June 5, 1985, between the Chicago Cubs and the Atlanta Braves. The filmmakers shot the scene with Ferris, Sloane, and Cameron in the left field stands on September 24, 1985, at a game between the Cubs and the Montreal Expos. To plan your visit, see http://chicago.cubs.mlb.com/chc/ballpark.

11. THE ART INSTITUTE OF CHICAGO
111 South Michigan Avenue, Chicago, IL 60603

The three friends explore this world-class museum and each stand before his or her own Picasso painting: Sloane studies *The Red Armchair*, Ferris admires *Portrait of Sylvette David*, and Cameron considers *Seated Woman*. Ferris and Sloan kiss in front of *America Windows* by Marc Chagall, and Cameron becomes mesmerized by *A Sunday on La Grande Jatte* by French impressionist Georges Seurat, the inspiration for the 1984 musical *Sunday in the Park with George* by Steven Sondheim. To plan your visit to this museum, see www.artic.edu.

12. THE PARADE
North Dearborn Street and West Calhoun Place, Chicago, IL 60602

Ferris lip syncs "Danke Schoen" by Wayne Newton and "Twist and Shout" by the Beatles during the Von Steuben's Day parade, heading south along Dearborn Street, intercut with scenes restaged on the following Saturday.

13. THE FLAMINGO SCULPTURE
Federal Plaza, 230 South Dearborn Street, Chicago, IL 60604

Cameron and Sloane walk south along Dearborn Street, passing *Flamingo*, a sculpture by Alexander Calder that stands 53 feet tall, completed in 1973 and unveiled in 1974.

THE ART OF *FERRIS BUELLER*

The artwork in the Art Institute of Chicago featured in the movie includes:

- *Paris: A Rainy Day* by Gustave Caillebotte
- *Nighthawks* by Edward Hopper
- *Improvisation 30 (Cannons)* by Wassily Kandinsky
- *Painting with Green Center* by Wassily Kandinsky
- *Nude Under a Pine Tree* by Pablo Picasso
- *The Old Guitarist* by Pablo Picasso
- *The Child's Bath* by Mary Cassatt
- *Jacques and Berthe Lipchitz* by Amodeo Modigliani
- *Day of the Gods (Mahana No Atua)* by Paul Gauguin
- *Tanktotem No. 1* by David Smith
- *Greyed Rainbow* by Jackson Pollock
- *Bathers by a River* by Henri Matisse
- *UNESCO Reclining Figure* by Henri Moore
- *Portrait of Balzac* by Auguste Rodin
- *The Equestrienne* by Toulouse Lautrec
- *The Red Armchair* by Pablo Picasso
- *Portrait of Sylvette David* by Pablo Picasso
- *Seated Woman* by Pablo Picasso
- *America Windows* by Marc Chagall
- *A Sunday on La Grande Jatte* by Georges Seurat

14. DANCING SPECTATORS

Exelon Plaza, 31 South Clark Street, Chicago, IL 60603

On these steps, a group of spectators dance to "Twist and Shout."

15. SAVE FERRIS WATER TOWER

Corner of 1st Street and Center Avenue, Northbrook, IL 60062

From this spot, Jeanie (Jennifer Grey) views the water tower painted with the slogan "Save Ferris."

16. MICHIGAN AVENUE
Intersection of South Michigan Avenue and East Washington Street, Chicago, IL 60604
While driving south on Michigan Avenue, Cameron realizes how much mileage is on the odometer and goes berserk.

17. THE BEACH
Glencoe Beach, 1 Park Avenue, Glencoe, IL 60022
Ferris sits atop a bench while Sloane tries to comfort a catatonic Cameron.

18. JEANIE NEARLY HITS FERRIS
460 Berkeley Avenue, Winnetka, IL 60093
Jeanie drives the car south on Berkeley Avenue and turns right onto Cherry Street.

19. THE STOP SIGN
Intersection of Ash Street and Hibbard Road, Winnetka, IL 60093
Jeanie drives east along Ash Street, runs the stop sign in front of a police car, and turns right, heading north on Hibbard Road.

20. OBLIVIOUS TOM BUELLER
Intersection of Glendale Avenue and Cherry Street, Winnetka, IL 60093
While driving south on Glendale Avenue, Tom Bueller stops at the intersection and reaches into the glove compartment for a mint, failing to notice that his daughter, Jeanie, passes him, followed by a police car.

21. FERRIS RUNS
2105 Butternut Lane, Northbrook, IL 60062
Mr. Bueller drives north and passes a running Ferris, failing to identify his own son.

22. THE NEIGHBOR'S HOUSE
2067 Butternut Lane, Northbrook, IL 60062
Ferris runs through this house and tells the woman cooking in the kitchen, "Smells delicious."

The Fugitive

In this movie based on the 1960s television show starring David Janssen, Chicago surgeon Dr. Richard Kimble (Harrison Ford) flees from the law after being wrongly convicted of murdering his wife. Deputy United States Marshal Sam Gerard (Tommy Lee Jones) relentlessly pursues Kimble across Chicago while the fugitive tries to find the one-armed man who killed his wife. "Both stars have toughness and restraint that make their characters' battle of wits truly hypnotic," wrote film critic Janet Maslin in the *New York Times*.

In the television show, Kimble travels the country searching for the one-armed man. In the movie, he rents a ramshackle basement apartment, doctors an ID to work undercover as a janitor at Cook County Hospital so he can search through the prosthetics lab records, and crisscrosses Chicago to investigate these one-armed men—one by one. In the process, we get a tour of Chicago—from its seedy underbelly to its lavish ballrooms.

Film critic Peter Travers wrote in *Rolling Stone*, "As Gerard chases Kimble through tunnels and streets, evocatively shot by the great cinematographer Michael Chapman (*Raging Bull*), it's not a stretch to think of Victor Hugo's *Les Misérables*, in which Inspector Javert shadows the blameless Jean Valjean."

Born and raised in South Chicago, director Andrew Davis and native Chicagoan actor Harrison Ford enjoyed working in their hometown. The film opens with aerial shots of Chicago's skyline because, says Davis, "We wanted to have this tiny little character lost, running away, trying to hide in this incredible fabric."

1. THE KIMBLE HOME
Private Residence, 342 West Wisconsin Street, Chicago, IL 60614

In this townhouse, a one-armed man murders Helen Kimble (Sela Ward), and her husband, Dr. Richard Kimble (Harrison Ford), fights the assailant. Please be respectful and do not loiter or disturb the residents.

2. FUNDRAISING DINNER
Four Seasons Hotel, 120 East Delaware Place, Chicago, IL 60611

The Kimbles attend a dinner and fashion show for the Children's Research Aid Foundation in the Grand Ballroom of this hotel.

3. JAIL

Ariel Community Academy, 1119 East 46th Street, Chicago, IL 60653

In the back of this building, Richard Kimble and other convicts are loaded on a bus headed to Menard Correctional Center. In the basement of this former grammar school, the filmmakers built sets for the jail, hospital, and police interrogation room.

SHOT ELSEWHERE

THE TRAIN CRASH AND THE DAM ESCAPE

The succeeding scenes aboard the bus were filmed in Dillsboro, North Carolina, where the bus tumbles down a ravine and into the path of an oncoming train, alongside the Tuckasegee River. The bus and the train cars sit alongside the tracks opposite Tunnel Mountain Road and Fugitive Run, at 1148 Haywood Road, Sylva, NC 28779. If you ride the Great Smoky Mountains Railroad's Tuckasegee River Excursion (from Bryson City to Dillsboro), you'll pass by the crash site. For more information, visit www.gsmr.com.

"The guy did a Peter Pan right here off of this dam," says Marshall Sam Gerard (Tommy Lee Jones). Kimble jumps off Cheoah Dam over the Little Tennessee River in Robbinsville, North Carolina. The 225-foot tall dam, completed in 1919, was listed on the National Register of Historic Places in 2004. The tunnels seen in the movie were filmed on a soundstage.

---

4. COPELAND'S HOUSE

4512 South Halsted Street, Chicago, IL 60609

Gerard and his team track down Copeland (Eddie Bo Smith Jr.) at this house, which has since been demolished.

5. WELLS STREET BRIDGE

275 North Wells Street, Chicago, IL 60606

After dying his hair and hitch-hiking back to Chicago, Kimble calls his lawyer from a payphone at the Wells Street Bridge and asks for help.

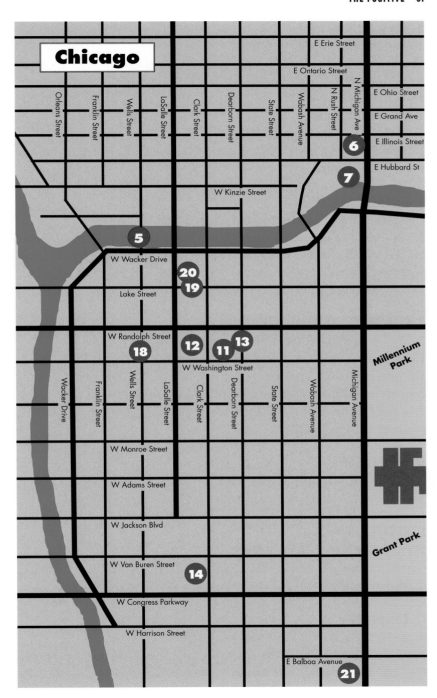

6. MARSHALL'S OFFICE
444 North Michigan Avenue, Chicago, IL 60611

The fictitious US Marshal's office offers sensational views of Michigan Avenue, the Wrigley Building, and the Chicago River.

7. NORTH BANK CLUB
400 North Michigan Avenue, Chicago, IL 60611

Kimble finds Dr. Charles Nichols (Jeroen Krabbe) at his tennis club and requests some cash.

8. BASEMENT APARTMENT
Private Residence, 9000 South Houston Avenue, Chicago, IL 60617

Kimble rents a basement apartment in a house owned by a Polish woman and her son. The back of the house remains identifiable as the film location, despite the fact that the house has been refurbished. Please be respectful and do not loiter or disturb the residents.

9. COOK COUNTY HOSPITAL EXTERIOR
1830 West Harrison Street, Chicago, IL 60612

Kimble pays a visit to the prosthetics and orthotics wing at Cook County Hospital and steals a janitor's identification card for future use. Later he returns to the hospital to get a list of patients who received a prosthetic arm and attends to a boy who survived a bus crash. The historic building has been vacant since 2002.

10. THRIFT SHOP
8949 South Commercial Avenue, Chicago, IL 60617

Kimble buys clothes from a thrift shop and runs across this street.

11. GARAGE
50 West Washington Street, Chicago, IL 60602

Gerard and his team leave this garage in a car though the exit on North Clark Street.

12. CHICAGO JAIL
Chicago City Hall, 118 North Clark Street, Chicago, IL 60602

Kimble walks from Daley Plaza across Clark Street and goes upstairs to the "jail" to question a one-armed prisoner who might be the killer. He walks through the lobby and halls, and Gerard chases him down the stairs. In reality, Chicago City Hall does not contain a jail.

13. ST. PATRICK'S DAY PARADE
Intersection of North Dearborn Street and West Randolph Street, Chicago, IL 60602
Kimble runs across Daley Plaza, grabs a green hat from a trash can, and joins the St. Patrick's Day Parade, heading south on North Dearborn Street in a scene reminiscent of Alfred Hitchcock's 1935 movie *The 39 Steps*.

14. HOTEL MEN ONLY
426 South Clark Street, Chicago, IL 60605
After fleeing his basement refuge, Kimble resides here.

15. THE BAR
Pullman's Pub, 609 East 113th Street, Chicago, IL 60628
From inside this bar (now closed), Kimble telephones the apartment of a one-armed man named Sykes (Andreas Katsulas), who isn't home, then walks across the street and climbs onto the roof of the building.

16. SYKES'S APARTMENT
Private Residence, 11217 South St. Lawrence Avenue, Chicago, IL 60628

Kimble breaks into Sykes's apartment and discovers that Sykes is both the killer and connected to the Devlin McGregor pharmaceutical company, whose fundraiser Kimble had attended the night of the murder. Please be respectful and do not loiter or disturb the residents.

17. CHICAGO MEMORIAL HOSPITAL
John Crerar Library, 5750 South Ellis Avenue, Chicago, IL 60637

Kimble visits Chicago Memorial Hospital (played by the John Crerar Library at the University of Chicago).

18. SYKES SPOTS KIMBLE
125 North Wells Street, Chicago, IL 60606

Briefed by Dr. Nichols, Sykes spots Kimble emerging from an alley and walking south on Wells Street.

19. BALBO CTA STATION
Clark/Lake Station, 124 West Lake Street, Chicago, IL 60601

Sykes follows Kimble, now walking east on Lake Street, up the stairs to an El station. Kimble rides the train and pulls the emergency brake, breaks a window, and exits at this station.

20. MAILBOX
203 North LaSalle Street, Chicago, IL 60601

Kimble drops the gun into a mailbox at this building.

21. CHICAGO HILTON AND TOWERS
720 South Michigan Avenue, Chicago, IL 60605

Earlier in the film, Gerard and his team speak with Dr. Nichols in the presidential suite and the halls outside the ballrooms. Later, Gerard and his agents converge at the International Association of Cardiologists' Chicago Conference in the Grand Ballroom while Nichols delivers his keynote address, which Kimble interrupts. Kimble and Nichols fight in a smaller ballroom and on the roof, fall through a glass window (built by the filmmakers), tumble down an elevator shaft, and continue fighting in the hotel's massive laundry room in the basement.

Groundhog Day

In this 1993 movie, cynical WPBH-9 television weatherman Phil Connors (Bill Murray), news producer Rita Hanson (Andie MacDowell), and cameraman Larry (Chris Elliot) drive from Pittsburgh to Punxsutawney, Pennsylvania, to cover the annual Groundhog Day festival held on February 2. Each year, a groundhog nicknamed Punxsutawney Phil, "the seer of seers, prognosticators of prognosticators," emerges from his home in Gobbler's Knob to look for his shadow. If he sees it, winter last six more weeks. For Phil Connors, winter lasts an eternity because he gets stuck in time, reliving the same day over and over again.

Although the story takes place in Punxsutawney, approximately 85 miles northeast of Pittsburgh, the producers did not film this classic movie in Punxsutawney but rather in Woodstock, Illinois, roughly 50 miles northwest of Chicago and some 600 miles from the real Punxsutawney.

Director Harold Ramis decided against filming the movie in Punxsutawney because that town lacked a quaint, photogenic town center. Ramis and his crew scouted all over southern Wisconsin and northern Illinois in search of the ideal small town. The instant they drove into the town square of Woodstock, the crew realized that this small hamlet—with its majestic courthouse, restored opera house, and handsome central square—was the perfect, idealized version of Punxsutawney. Many local Woodstock residents appeared in the movie as extras.

The City of Punxsutawney did send delegates to make sure Ramis and his crew portrayed the groundhog ceremony accurately. "They were very jealous that the movie wasn't shot in Punxsutawney," recalled Ramis, "but when they saw Woodstock, they thought it looked better than their town."

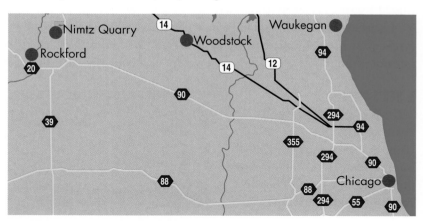

35

1. PENNSYLVANIAN HOTEL

Woodstock Opera House, 121 Van Buren
Street, Woodstock, IL 60698

When Phil Connors (Bill Murray) and his crew first enter the town, the van drives south along Main Street, turns right on Cass Street, and then circles the square, stopping in front of the Pennsylvania Hotel, which Phil describe as "a fleabag." Rita (Andie MacDowell) and Larry (Chris Elliot) stay here. Much later in the film, Phil does a swan dive from the tower.

2. CHERRY STREET INN

The Royal Victorian Manor, 344 Fremont
Street, Woodstock, IL 60698

"Okay, campers, rise and shine!" Phil stays at this bed and breakfast, a beautiful Victorian gingerbread house. Every morning, he looks out the north-facing window toward South Madison Street. At the time of filming,

this 114-year-old Queen Anne Victorian house was a private home. Now it's a genuine bed and breakfast, where you can actually stay. "And don't forget your booties 'cause it's cold out there!" The filmmakers shot the interiors scenes on a soundstage in a warehouse in nearby Cary, Illinois.

3. NED'S CORNER

100 Cass Street (corner of Benton Street),
Woodstock, IL 60698

"Bing!" Every morning, Phil bumps into insurance salesman Ned Ryerson (Stephen Tobolowsky) on the northeast corner of Woodstock's town

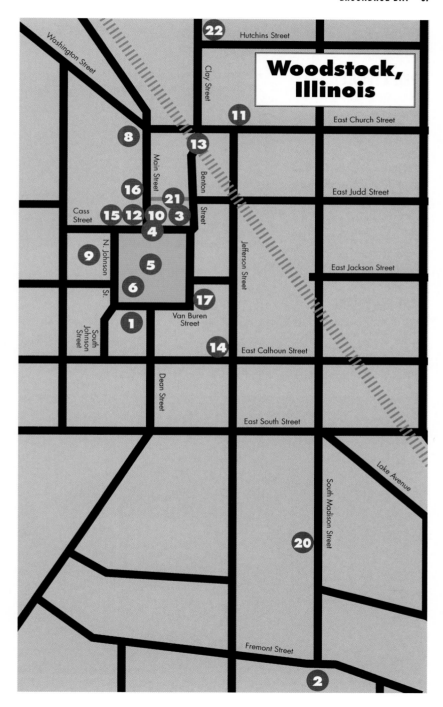

Woodstock, Illinois

square, and they walk west along Cass Street together. "Am I right or am I right or am I right?"

4. PHIL'S PUDDLE

108 Cass Street (curb at the corner with Main Street), Woodstock, IL 60698

"Watch out for that first step," says Ned. "It's a doozy!" A plaque on the ground marks the spot where Phil Connors accidentally steps into the same puddle every day. It reads: "Bill Murray Stepped Here."

5. THE BANDSTAND

Center of Woodstock Square Park, Woodstock, IL 60698

Under this bandstand, locals sing and dance to "The Pennsylvania Polka," and later Phil dances with Rita during a snow flurry. Nearby, Phil and Rita build a snowman together, and Phil carves an ice sculpture.

6. GOBBLER'S KNOB

Town Square, Woodstock, IL 60698

In the real Punxsutawney, Gobbler's Knob is a little spot on Woodland Avenue, about a mile southeast of the city, where a groundhog makes its annual appearance and prediction. In the movie, Punxsutawney Phil makes his prediction at Gobbler's Knob in the southwest corner of Woodstock's Town Square, surrounded by town elders and the citizens of Punxsutawney. The film crew built a replica of the real Gobbler's Knob, and after shooting the film, dismantled it.

7. STRANDED ON THE HIGHWAY

Amstutz Expressway, south of the Mathon Drive overpass, Waukegan, IL 60685

In an attempt to get out of Punxsutawney before the blizzard hits, Phil, Rita, and Larry drive north on the Amstutz Expressway.

8. THE GAS STATION

Gas Depot, 151 Washington Street, Woodstock, IL 60698

Inside this gas station, Phil makes a telephone call to an operator. "Don't you have some kind of a line you keep open for emergencies . . . or for celebrities?" He then gets hit in the head with a snow shovel.

9. THE BAR

The Public House, 101 North Johnson Street, Woodstock, IL 60698

At the bar inside this restaurant, Phil orders "sweet vermouth, rocks, with a twist"—Rita's favorite drink—and toasts to "world peace." A plaque marks the spot.

10. TIP TOP CAFÉ

Taqueria La Placita, 108 Cass Street, Woodstock, IL 60698

In this restaurant, Phil, Rita, and Larry get coffee and breakfast, Phil gorges himself on doughnuts and pastries, and a waitress drops a tray of dishes every morning. The producers built the set for the Tip Top Café in an empty storefront, and when production ended, locals turned the phony restaurant into a genuine Tip Top Café. Over the years, ownership of the restaurant has changed several times. In the movie, stopped clocks decorate the interior walls of the restaurant.

11. BOWLING ALLEY
Wayne's Lanes, 109 East Church Street, Woodstock, IL 60698
Phil drowns his sorrows with two locals, Gus and Ralph, at the bar in the bowling alley, before they stumble outside and pile into a red Buick convertible for a reckless ride along the railway tracks.

12. CRASHING INTO THE MAILBOX
Northwest corner of Cass Street and Main Street, Woodstock, IL 60698
On this spot, Phil drives the red Buick south on Main Street, makes a right turn into a mailbox, and continues along Cass Street, making a left turn onto South Johnson Street.

13. THE RAILROAD TRACKS
Benton Street Crossing, Woodstock, IL 60698
Phil backs the red Buick onto the railroad tracks at this spot and then proceeds to drive southeast along the tracks followed by a police car, its sirens wailing.

14. THE CRASH INTO THE GROUNDHOG SIGN
131 East Calhoun Street, Woodstock, IL 60698
Phil drives west on Calhoun Street and crashes into a groundhog sign standing in an empty lot. "Too early for flapjacks?" he asks the police officer. An office building now stands on the empty lot.

15. THE ARMORED TRUCK HEIST
Chase Bank, 118 Cass Street, Woodstock, IL 60698
In front of the Northern Federal Savings Bank, Phil grabs the bags of money from the parked Keystone armored truck while security guards Herman and Felix scramble to pick up a spilled roll of quarters.

16. ALPINE CINEMA
Woodstock Theatre, 209 Main Street, Woodstock, IL 60698
Dressed like Clint Eastwood in *The Good, the Bad, and the Ugly*, Phil takes his date, dressed as a French maid, to see *Heidi II* at this movie theater.

17. CHOCOLATE SHOP

Ethereal Confections, 113 South Benton Street, Woodstock, IL 60698

Phil buys chocolates for Rita in this chocolate shop and café, known for its world-class handmade truffles, chocolate bars, infused olive oil melt-aways, and ambrosia.

18. GERMAN RESTAURANT

The Bad Apple, 4300 North Lincoln Avenue, Chicago, IL 60618

While having dinner with Rita in Heidelberger Fass, a German restaurant that closed in 2009, Phil recites a French poem written by screenwriter Danny Rubin, based on the lyrics of "Bachelor's Dance" by singer-songwriter Jacques Brel. In English, the poem reads: "The girl I will love / is like a fine wine / that gets a little better / every morning." In this same restaurant, Phil performs the Heimlich maneuver on Buster (Brian Doyle-Murray). "If you're going to eat steak," admonishes Phil, "get some sharper teeth."

19. NIMTZ LIMESTONE QUARRY

5300 Nimtz Road, Rockford, IL 61111

Desperate to break the cycle of repeating the same day over and over again, Phil kidnaps the groundhog Punxsutawney Phil, steals a red pickup truck, and drives off a dirt road into this limestone quarry. To follow the route Phil takes, start on the west side of Woodstock Square, head south on Johnson Street, make a left onto Van Buren Street, make a left onto Benton Street, turn left onto Church Street, and continue as it turns into Washington Street. Then abruptly appear heading northwest on Lake Avenue and make a right going around Hunts Service Station onto East South Street. Go under the viaduct and then cut to the quarry—35 miles west of Woodstock.

20. PIANO TEACHER'S HOUSE

Private Residence, 348 South Madison Street, Woodstock, IL 60698

In this quaint house, Phil takes piano lessons for $1,000 per lesson. Please be respectful and do not loiter or disturb the residents.

21. OLD MAN'S ALLEY

Benton Street at East Judd Street, Woodstock, IL 60698

In the alley on the west side of this intersection, Phil attempts to revive the elderly homeless man who panhandles for spare change every morning on Ned's Corner (#3).

22. THE GROUNDHOG DAY DANCE
Woodstock Moose Lodge, 406 Clay Street, Woodstock, IL 60698

Phil plays the piano onstage inside this lodge and gets auctioned off to Rita in the big bachelor's auction.

COMING ATTRACTIONS

GROUNDHOG DAYS

At the beginning of every February, the town of Woodstock, Illinois, hosts an annual Groundhog Days festival, with the annual Groundhog Prognostication with its own groundhog, Woodstock Willie, a descendant of the original animal actor seen in the film. The schedule of events features a pancake breakfast, a free showing of the movie, a walking tour of the film sites around town, and an annual dinner/dance at the Woodstock Moose Lodge. Past celebrity guests have included actor Stephen Tobolowsky (Ned Ryerson), director Harold Ramis, location manager Bob Hudgins, and screenwriter Danny Rubin.

Home Alone

"I was going away on vacation and making a list of everything I didn't want to forget," writer/director John Hughes told *Time* magazine. "I thought, 'Well, I'd better not forget my kids.' Then I thought, 'What if I left my 10-year-old son at home? What would he do?'" Hughes stopped packing and wrote eight pages of notes that turned into the screenplay for the 1990 smash hit *Home Alone*.

In the movie, eight-year-old Kevin McCallister (Macaulay Culkin) accidentally gets left behind when his family flies to Paris for their Christmas vacation. Kevin celebrates the disappearance of his big family—until two burglars (Joe Pesci and Daniel Stern) threaten to break into his house, compelling Kevin to lay a series of booby traps to thwart them.

John Hughes set the movie on Chicago's North Shore, and director Chris Columbus, who grew up in nearby River Forest, shot most of the scenes at a historic, five-bedroom house in the upper-class suburb of Winnetka. Columbus said his production team spent weeks searching the North Shore for the appropriate house.

"We knew we were going to shoot in the North Shore, so we were in the Wilmette, Winnetka, Glencoe, Lake Forest area, so we basically drove around for several weeks until we found the right house," Columbus told *Entertainment Weekly*. "And then when we found the house, I took some pictures and sent them over to John, and I remember John saying, 'This is perfect. This is exactly how I imagined the house.'"

Although critics assailed the sadistic violence (Kevin hits the criminals in the face with paint cans, triggers a blowtorch to the head, sears a hand on a red-hot doorknob, impales bare feet on shattered Christmas ornaments, and shoots a BB gun at the crotch), the movie became the number-one box office hit for 12 consecutive weeks, grossing more than $285 million. "Keep the change, ya filthy animal."

1. KEVIN'S HOUSE
Private Residence, 671 Lincoln Avenue, Winnetka, IL 60093

Inside this gorgeous house that starred as the home of the McCallister family, Kevin (Macaulay Culkin) tells his mother, "I don't want to see you again for the rest of my whole life." Several scenes were shot in the kitchen, main staircase, and foyer of this residence, while other interior scenes were filmed on a set built inside New Trier High School at 385 Winnetka Avenue. The filmmakers built a tree house in the backyard specifically for the movie and dismantled it when production finished. Please be respectful and do not loiter or disturb the residents.

2. OLD MAN MARLEY'S HOUSE
Private Residence, 681 Lincoln Avenue, Winnetka, IL 60093

Home of the "South Bend Shovel Slayer." According to Buzz McCallister (Devin Ratray), back in 1958 Marley "murdered his whole family and half the people on the block with a snow shovel." Please be respectful and do not loiter or disturb the residents.

3. CHICAGO AIRPORT
O'Hare International Airport, 10000 Bessie Coleman Drive, Chicago, IL 60666

At this airport, the McCallister family runs through concourse K in terminal 3 to "Run Rudolph Run" performed by Chuck Berry and accidentally departs without Kevin. O'Hare International Airport also supplied the interiors for the Paris airport.

4. THE WET BANDITS' LAIR
656 Lincoln Avenue, Winnetka, IL 60093

Harry (Joe Pesci) and Marv (Daniel Stern) operate from the empty Murphy house across the street from Kevin's home, where they flood the basement and hang Kevin up on a door hook. Please be respectful and do not loiter or disturb the residents. The filmmakers used only the exterior of this house and built sets of the interior inside New Trier High School. They built the basement in the indoor swimming pool of the high school so they could flood it.

5. HUBBARD WOODS PHARMACY
940 Green Bay Road, Winnetka, IL 60093
The pharmacy where Kevin asks, "Is this toothbrush approved by the American Dental Association?" is now a Panera Bread restaurant.

6. THE GREEN
Hubbard Woods Park, intersection of Green Bay Road and Gage Street, Winnetka, IL 60093
Pursued by a police officer, Kevin runs across this village green and its ice skating rink and then runs across the bridge over the Metra railroad tracks.

7. CHURCH EXTERIOR
Trinity United Methodist Church, 1024 West Lake Avenue, Wilmette, IL 60091
Kevin hides in the nativity scene in front of this church.

8. GROCERY STORE
The Grand Food Center, 606 Green Bay Road, Winnetka, IL 60093

In this supermarket, Kevin goes grocery shopping and asks, "Are those microwave dinners any good?"

9. SANTA CLAUS VILLAGE
810 Chestnut Court, Winnetka, IL 60093

Kevin visits the cottage housing Santa Claus, standing in front of Winnetka Village Hall. "Will you please tell [Santa] that instead of presents this year, I just want my family back."

10. FAMILY GATHERING
Private Residence, 306 Laurel Avenue, Highland Park, IL 60035

Kevin walks southwest along Laurel Avenue and watches a family gathering to celebrate Christmas in their home illuminated with holiday lights. Please be respectful and do not loiter or disturb the residents.

11. CHURCH INTERIOR
Grace Episcopal Church, 924 Lake Street, Oak Park, IL 60301

Inside this church, Kevin has a heart-to-heart talk with Old Man Marley. Grace Episcopal Church, one of the best examples in America of the Gothic Revival movement, opened in 1905.

My Best Friend's Wedding

Julianne Potter (Julia Roberts) and her best friend, Michael O'Neal (Dermot Mulroney), agreed they would marry if they were still single by age 28, but three weeks before that birthday, Michael telephones Julianne to tell her he's marrying someone else—bubbly 20-year-old heiress Kimmy Wallace (Cameron Diaz)—in just four days. Julianne flies to Chicago to sabotage the wedding and win back Michael. While taking a boat tour of Chicago, Michael tells her, "If you love someone, you say it. You say it right then, out loud." But Julianne can't bring herself to speak up.

Australian director P. J. Hogan filmed the 1997 movie *My Best Friend's Wedding* entirely in Chicago. "Chicago's center is a show room for the world's great architects," said Hogan. "It is a great metropolis, charged with excitement. It represents Julianne's challenge. Its grandness is a symbol for what she's up against."

"Chicago is a character in the film," explained production designer Richard Sylbert. "The action begins when Julianne arrives at massive O'Hare Field, one of the biggest airports in the world. This is a gigantic windmill the lady is attacking. The city grows ever bigger as her task turns more difficult and she gets more desperate, until it becomes almost surreal with the wedding and reception."

Ultimately, Julianne's editor, George Downes (Rupert Everett), tells her the truth: "Michael's chasing Kimmy, you're chasing Michael. Who's chasing you? Nobody. Get it?"

1. THE NEW YORK RESTAURANT

Charlie Trotter's, 816 West Armitage Avenue, Chicago, IL 60614

Food critic Julianne Potter (Julia Roberts) lunches with her editor, George Downes (Rupert Everett), at this Chicago landmark, named the fifth-best restaurant in the United States by *Restaurant* magazine in 2007. Charlie Trotter himself plays the chef who yells to his assistant, "I will kill your whole family if you don't get this right!" Trotter closed the restaurant in 2012, a year before his death.

2. NEW YORK AIRPORT AND CHICAGO AIRPORT

O'Hare International Airport, 10000 Bessie Coleman Drive, Chicago, IL 60666

Julianne leaves New York from near gate M3 in terminal 5 and arrives in Chicago near gate C17 in terminal 1 to be greeted by her best friend, Michael O'Neal (Dermot Mulroney), and his fiancée, Kimmy Wallace

(Cameron Diaz). Later in the movie, Julianne drops off George in front of terminal 1.

3. DRESS SHOP
Saks Fifth Avenue, 727 North Rush Street, Chicago, IL 60611
Having been completely remodeled, the facade is no longer recognizable as the same building.

4. HOTEL
Conrad Hilton Suite, Chicago Hilton and Towers, 720 South Michigan Avenue, Chicago, IL 60605
Kimmy stops the elevator, triggering Julianne's claustrophobia, and they get out at the penthouse.

5. COMISKEY PARK
U.S. Cellular Field, 333 West 35th Street, Chicago, IL 60616
Julianne meets Michael's billionaire future father-in-law (Philip Bosco), owner of the Chicago White Sox baseball team, at his box in their home stadium and announces, "I've got moves you've never seen." At the end of the film, Julianne locates Kimmy in one of the women's restrooms. Comiskey Park, home of the Chicago White Sox, opened in 1991 and was renamed U.S. Cellular Field in 2003.

6. DONNIE'S
75 East Lake Street, Chicago, IL 60601
Sadly, the karaoke bar where Julianne persuades Kimmy to sing karaoke to "I Just Don't Know What to Do with Myself" by Burt Bacharach and Jeff Bova, no longer exists.

7. THE EL STATION STAIRS
Intersection of State Street and Lake Street, Chicago, IL 60601
Julianne and Michael sit on the steps just inside the entrance to this El station and have a heart-to-heart talk.

8. MARSHALL FIELD'S DEPARTMENT STORE
Macy's, 111 State Street, Chicago, IL 60602
While walking through the china department of Marshall Field's, Julianne convinces Kimmy that Michael thinks his reporting job isn't good enough for her family. In 2005, this Marshall Field's store became Macy's.

9. THE CLUB

Union League Club, 65 West Jackson Boulevard, Chicago, IL 60604

Inside this exclusive club, founded during the Civil War to promote loyalty to the Union and President Abraham Lincoln, Kimmy asks her father to give Michael a job.

10. JULIANNE'S HOTEL ROOM

Drake Hotel, Room 703, 140 East Walton Place, Chicago, IL 60611

In this suite, Julianne attempts "death by mini-bar" and makes plans to sabotage the wedding. Observes George, "It's amazing the clarity that comes with psychotic jealousy." Later, in the hallway, the bellman (Paul Giamatti) tells Julianne, "My grandmother always said, 'This too shall pass.'"

11. THE CLOTHING STORE

77 East Adams Street, Chicago, IL 60604

"Guard this with your life," says Michael, handing Julianne a box containing the wedding ring he bought for Kimmy. In this clothing store, Julianne attempts to tell Michael she loves him and introduces him to her "fiancé," George.

12. THE CHURCH

Fourth Presbyterian Church, 126 East Chestnut Street, Chicago, IL 60611

"Love the bag, love the shoes, love everything!" says George, after Julianne introduces him to Kimmy and her mother inside this church, where the wedding later takes place. Dedicated in 1914, Fourth Presbyterian Church was designed by Ralph Adams Cram, America's leading Gothic Revival architect, best known for his work on the world's largest Gothic cathedral, the Cathedral of St. John the Divine in New York City.

13. BARRY THE CUDA'S SEAFOOD RESTAURANT

Joe's Crab Shack, 745 North Wells Street, Chicago, IL 60654

In this restaurant, all the patrons join together to sing "I Say a Little Prayer," written by Burt Bacharach and Hal David for Dionne Warwick. Unfortunately, you can no longer do the same because the restaurant closed and is now a furniture store.

14. CHICAGO RIVER CRUISE

Chicago River, Chicago, IL 60606

Julianne and Michael spend the afternoon together on a cruise along the Chicago River from the bridge at North Dearborn Street to the bridge at North Columbus Drive. A number of companies offer boat tours of the Chicago River, including Chicago's First Lady, Wendella Boats, Chicago Line Cruises, and Seadog Chicago.

15. WALLACE COMPANIES BUILDING

77 West Upper Wacker Drive, Chicago, IL 60601

In Walter's office, Julianne types up and saves a fake e-mail to get Michael fired from his job as a sports reporter.

16. THE WALLACE FAMILY ESTATE

Cuneo Mansion and Gardens, 1350 North
Milwaukee Avenue, Vernon Hills, IL 60061

"Crème brûlée can never be Jell-O," says Julianne. At this elegant 100-acre estate with its rose-colored villa, the Wallaces host a lavish rehearsal brunch by the pool. On the tennis court filled with helium balloons, boys sing "Annie's Song (You Fill Up My Senses)" by John Denver, and at the gazebo, Julianne reveals her true feelings to Michael.

Built in 1914 for Thomas Edison's partner, Samuel Insull, the mansion was purchased by Chicago businessman John Cuneo in 1937 and remained his family home until 1990. The Cuneo Foundation gave the estate, including the museum's extensive collection of fine art and furnishings, to Loyola University Chicago in 2009. Cuneo Mansion and Gardens are open to the public, and you can find more information at www .luc.edu/cuneo/visitorinformation/.

17. UNION STATION

210 South Canal Street, Chicago, IL 60606

Julianne steals a bakery truck, drives south on Michigan Avenue to Canal Street, and finds Michael in the magnificent Great Hall of Chicago Union Station. "I'm pond scum," she tells him. "Well, lower, actually. I'm like the fungus that feeds on pond scum."

Planes, Trains and Automobiles

Uptight executive Neal Page (Steve Martin), trying to fly home from New York to Chicago in time for Thanksgiving dinner with his family, winds up diverted to Wichita, Kansas, and reluctantly teams up with fellow traveler Del Griffith (John Candy), a jolly chatterbox and shower curtain ring salesman. "The last thing I want to be remembered as is an annoying blabbermouth," says Del. "You know, nothing grinds my gears worse than some chowderhead that doesn't know when to keep his big trap shut."

"Del isn't just a guy with questionable taste: He's way beyond that," wrote film critic Hal Hinson in the *Washington Post*. "He's a guy who revels in tackiness. He's hugely, grandiloquently gauche. But, however bumbling, the guy's a mensch—a kind of double-knit hero."

As the two mismatched traveling companions struggle to get home, everything that can go wrong does. Writer/director John Hughes, who started his career as an advertising copywriter at the Leo Burnett agency in Chicago, once flew to New York on a Wednesday morning to meet with a client at 11 AM and planned to fly back to Chicago at 5 PM. Due to winter winds, the airline canceled all flights to Chicago, forcing Hughes to spend the night in a hotel. The next day, his plane to Chicago was diverted to Denver and then rerouted to Phoenix due to a snowstorm. Hughes did not get back home to Chicago until Monday, and the experience inspired him to write the script for his 1987 movie *Planes, Trains and Automobiles*.

While the majority of the road trip takes place in Kansas and Missouri, Hughes shot most of the film in the greater Chicago area. A lack of snowfall forced the filmmaker to shoot some scenes in South Dayton, New York.

SHOT ELSEWHERE

NEW YORK CITY

Seeking a taxi, Neal Page (Steve Martin) races fellow businessman (Kevin Bacon) west along 54th Street, from Madison Avenue to Park Avenue. On the southwest corner of Park Avenue and East 52nd Street, Del Griffith (John Candy) grabs the taxi, and Neal Page runs south after it and miraculously catches up with it two blocks north, at 54th Street.

1. THE PAGE FAMILY HOUSE

Private Residence, 230 Oxford Road, Kenilworth, IL 60043

In this six-bedroom house built in 1916, Neal's wife and three kids wait for him to show up. Please be respectful and do not loiter or disturb the residents.

2. INTERIOR AIRPORT

St. Louis Lambert International Airport, 10701 Lambert International Boulevard, St. Louis, MO 63145

This international airport in St. Louis, Missouri, plays the parts of the Mid-Central Airlines gates at both LaGuardia airport and Wichita airport.

3. THE BRAIDWOOD INN IN WICHITA, KANSAS

Sun Motel, 140 South Hickory Street, Braidwood, IL 60408

"Those aren't pillows!" When their plane is diverted to Wichita, Kansas, Neal and Del take Doobby's Taxiola—a 1968 Pontiac Bonneville—to this fleabag motel, share room 114, and experience homosexual panic the following morning. Edelen's Braidwood Inn is now the Sun Motel.

SNOW JOB

Facing insufficient snow in Illinois, director John Hughes shot the scene at the Stubbville train station outside South Dayton, New York, approximately 45 miles south of Buffalo. Tobacco-chewing Owen and his pregnant wife drive Neal and Del in the back of their pickup truck southeast on Pine Street, make a left turn on Railroad Street, and drop off the duo at the South Dayton Train Station (112 East Railroad Street). Neal and Del catch the "Contrack" train, whose smoking diesel engine comes to an unexpected halt, forcing all the passengers to alight in a desolate field.

4. BUS OVER BRIDGE

Eads Bridge, St. Louis, MO 63102

As the Trans-Missouri bus crosses the Mississippi River, Neal tries to lead the passengers in a sing-along of "Three Coins in the Fountain." When no one else knows the lyrics, Del rouses the crowd by singing the theme song from *The Flintstones*.

5. THE ST. LOUIS BUS STATION

Wabash Randolph Self Park, 20 East Randolph Street, Chicago, IL 60601

In this bus station, Del sells shower curtain rings to raise some quick cash. "This is Czechoslovakian ivory," he says. The bus station was torn down after the movie was made, and a parking garage stands in its place.

6. MARATHON CAR RENTAL PARKING LOT AND DESK

St. Louis Lambert International Airport, 10701 Lambert International Boulevard, St. Louis, MO 63145

In a parking lot (no longer identifiable due to extensive renovations) near the Renaissance St. Louis Airport Hotel, Neal fails to find the car he just rented. At a rental car counter supposedly in this airport (but filmed on a set in a soundstage), exasperated Neal explodes a soliloquy peppered with 18 f-bombs. Outside the terminal, a taxi booth operator punches out Neal—just as Del pulls up in his rented green, wood-paneled convertible. The filmmakers modified a 1986 Chrysler LeBaron Town and Country.

7. EL RANCHO MOTEL

River Trail Gardens & Inn, 36355 North
Highway 41, Gurnee, IL 60031

After the rental car bursts
into flames 102 miles from
Chicago, Neal drives the
incinerated car to this motel
and attempts to book room 6
with $17 "and a helluva nice
watch." In the morning, Del
backs the car into the motel
room.

8. OLD WOODSTOCK COURT HOUSE

Old Courthouse Arts Center, 101 North
Johnson Street, Woodstock, IL 60098

A police officer impounds the
burned-out car outside the old
Woodstock courthouse, the
site of the bar in *Groundhog
Day* where Phil Connors (Bill
Murray) toasts to world peace.

9. THE TRUCK

209 Main Street, Woodstock, IL 60098

The Oshkonoggin Cheese truck, heading south on Main Street, stops
just past the same movie theater that Phil Connors frequents in
Groundhog Day.

10. THE LASALLE–VAN BUREN EL STATION

121 West Van Buren Street, Chicago, IL 60605

At this El station, Neal boards the train and then returns to this spot to
find Del sitting by his lonesome in the station.

11. THE WALK HOME

Warwick Road, between Woodstock Avenue and Oxford Road, Kenilworth, IL 60043

Neal and Del carry the trunk down Warwick Road to the Page family house.

Risky Business

When his parents leave him home alone for a week in their upper-class house on Chicago's North Shore, high school senior Joel Goodsen (Tom Cruise) hires a prostitute named Lana (Rebecca De Mornay) who extracts $300 for her services by stealing his mother's Steuben crystal egg from the mantel. After Joel accidently lets his father's Porsche roll into Lake Michigan, he agrees to let Lana turn his parent's house into a brothel for one night to raise enough money to cover the repairs and buy back the glass egg. Afterward, he has sex with Lana on an El train.

Risky Business writer/director Paul Brickman, who graduated from Highland Park High School and grew up three minutes from Joel's house, set out to make a film that he would want to see if he were in high school. "Chicago is a set up well for *Risky Business*, because you have the relative safety of the North Shore and you have the train line connecting to adventure and darker elements in the city," Brickman told *Salon*. "That's the journey Joel takes. So it was an exploration of things not only geographically, but an exploration of the darker side of himself."

Jon Avnet, a producer on the film, told the *Chicago Tribune* that Highland Park dovetailed with the movie's depiction of privileged lifestyles. "This is where it was always set. It was basically white boys off the lake," said Avnet. "The chase, the locations, the houses we used—they were the perfect settings for this to come to life."

Brickman shot many of the scenes at locations in Highland Park where he had a personal connection. "Shelton's Ravinia Grill, where Joel and his friends talk about their futures, is where I used to hang out after walking home from school in the eighth grade," he said. "We'd go there and throw French fries at each other. Part of the car chase sequence with Guido, the killer pimp, goes by the Highland Park Movie Theater where I saw movies as a kid."

1. JOEL'S HOUSE, 345 REMSON, GLENCOE, IL
Private Residence, 1258 Linden Avenue, Highland Park, IL 60035

Although Joel Goodsen (Tom Cruise) lives in Glencoe, the actual house seen in the movie resides four miles north in Highland Park. The iconic scene where Joel dances in his underwear to the rock song "Old Time Rock 'n' Roll" by Bob Seger and the Silver Bullet Band was shot onstage in a schoolhouse in Skokie. Please be respectful and do not loiter or disturb the residents.

POKER HOUSE
Private Residence, 488 Sumac Road, Highland Park, IL 60035
Joel walks his bicycle alongside Miles (Curtis Armstrong), who bestows his sage advice: "Every now and then say, 'What the fuck.' 'What the fuck' gives you freedom. Freedom brings opportunity. Opportunity makes your future." Please be respectful and do not loiter or disturb the residents.

3. THE AIRPORT
O'Hare International Airport, 10000 Bessie Coleman Drive, Chicago, IL 60666
Joel's parents say good-bye at the American Airlines ticketing area.

4. THE DINER
Shelton's Ravinia Grill, 481 Roger Williams Avenue, Highland Park, IL 60035
In this local diner (now closed), Joel and his friends discuss their plans for the future.

5. IMPRESSING THE GIRLS
445 Central Avenue, Highland Park, IL 60035
Joel drives the 1979 Porsche 928 west along Central Avenue, stopping to rev the engine in front of the girls standing under the marquee of the Highland Park movie theater.

6. MUSIC STORE AND RESTAURANT

1815 and 1813 St. Johns Avenue, Highland Park, IL 60035

"That was just bullshit," says Miles, as he and Joel walk between these two businesses. "I'm surprised you listened to me."

7. DRAKE HOTEL

140 East Walton Place, Chicago, IL 60611

Joel meets prostitute Lana (Rebecca De Mornay) in the Palm Court, a lavish restaurant in one of the Magnificent Mile's most luxurious hotels.

8. THE CHASE

North Michigan Avenue and East Oak Street, Chicago, IL 60611

Guido (Joe Pantoliano) chases Joel, Lana, and Miles in the Porsche north along North Michigan Avenue and onto East Lake Shore Drive.

9. BAHA'I HOUSE OF WORSHIP

100 Linden Avenue, Wilmette, IL 60091

Joel drives past this magnificent Baha'i temple, the first Baha'i house of worship in the Western Hemisphere. Designed by French Canadian architect Louis Bourgeois and completed in 1953, this Baha'i landmark was added to the National Register of Historic Places in 1978.

10. THE VIADUCT

Laurel Avenue and 1st Street, Highland Park, IL 60035

Joel drives his father's car east on Laurel Avenue, passes under the viaduct, and turns right on St. Johns Avenue.

11. THE MOVIE THEATER

445 Central Avenue, Highland Park, IL 60035

Joel drives east along Central Avenue, passes the movie theater, and turns left into the parking lot.

12. THE ALLEY

Norton's, 1905 Sheridan Road, Highland Park, IL 60035

Joel drives the Porsche west through the alley to the south of Norton's restaurant.

13. THE HIGH SCHOOL

Highland Park High School, 7700 North Lincoln Avenue, Skokie, IL 60077

The school was torn down, and Oakton Community College now stands in its place.

14. THE TRAIN STATION

Deerfield Metra Station, 860 Deerfield Road, Deerfield, IL 60015

Lana drives the Porsche to this station and waits on the platform for the next train.

15. THE PIER

Belmont Harbor Marina, 3600 North Recreation Drive, Chicago, IL 60613

The Porsche rolls onto the pier, which collapses into Lake Michigan.

16. THE PORSCHE SERVICE GARAGE

Bank of America, 1921 St. Johns Avenue, Highland Park, IL 60035

The Porsche building, where Joel takes the car to be repaired, was torn down and a colonial office building now stands in its place.

17. JOEL ON HIS BIKE

St. Johns Avenue and Central Avenue, Highland Park, IL 60035

Joel bicycles north on St. Johns Avenue and makes a right turn onto Central Avenue.

18. LANA'S APARTMENT

14 West Elm Street, Chicago, IL 60610

Joel takes a taxi west along Elm Street to this apartment building.

19. BANQUET ON A BUN

921 North Rush Street, Chicago, IL 60611

This diner was torn down and replaced by a parking garage.

20. DINNER

The Signature Room, John Hancock Center, 875 North Michigan Avenue, Chicago, IL 60611

Joel and Lana dine at this upscale restaurant on the 95th floor of the John Hancock Building.

The Untouchables

"Welcome to Chicago," says police officer Jim Malone (Sean Connery). "This town stinks like a whorehouse at low tide."

During Prohibition, Chicago boasted stunning architecture, grandiose opera houses, and elegant luxury hotels—and widespread corruption. Gangland kingpin Al Capone controlled the bootleg liquor markets, making him the richest man in Chicago and the unofficial mayor of the city. In 1929, the US Treasury Department assigned agent Eliot Ness the task of ridding Chicago of Capone, dubbed "Public Enemy No. 1" by the press. Ness formed a task force of incorruptible men, nicknamed "the Untouchables," to bring Capone to justice.

In 1957, Ness published his autobiography, *The Untouchables*, cowritten with Oscar Fraley. The bestselling novel sold more than a million copies and became the basis for the television series, starring Robert Stack as Ness. Based on both the book and the television series, director Brian de Palma shot the 1987 movie *The Untouchables* on location in Chicago, using Prohibition-era buildings to capture the opulence of the time period, juxtaposing heinous acts of violence against elegant buildings and impeccably tailored Armani suits.

"You wanna get Capone? Here's how you get him," says Malone. "He pulls a knife, you pull a gun. He sends one of yours to the hospital, you send one of his to the morgue. That's the Chicago way." (Sean Connery won the Academy Award for Best Supporting Actor.)

"*The Untouchables* is not a realistic recreation of Chicago during Prohibition," wrote movie critic Richard Schickel in *Time* magazine. "Instead, it goes to that place that all films aspiring to greatness must attain: the country of myth, where all the figures must be larger and more vivid than life."

1. THE CAFÉ
Houndstooth Saloon, 3369 North Clark Street, Chicago, IL 60657

With a bomb in a briefcase, racketeers blow up this café under the El.

2. ELIOT NESS'S HOUSE
Private Residence, 2030 West 22nd Place, Chicago, IL 60608

Outside this house, Frank Nitti (Billy Drago) threatens Eliot Ness (Kevin Costner) when he returns home for his daughter's birthday party. The Untouchables later run west along 22nd Place. Please be respectful and do not loiter or disturb the residents.

3. POLICE HEADQUARTERS

Rookery Building, 209 South LaSalle Street, Chicago, IL 60604

Eliot Ness works out of this Romanesque building completed in 1888. Frank Lloyd Wright redesigned the two-story lobby in 1905. Added to the National Register of Historic Places in 1970, the Rookery was designated a Chicago landmark in 1972. At the end of the movie, Ness walks south on LaSalle Street toward the Chicago Board of Trade Building.

4. POLICE HEADQUARTERS INTERIORS

Bilandic Building, 160 North LaSalle Street, Chicago, IL 60601

This building, constructed in 1920 and formerly known as the State of Illinois Building, was used for the interior shots of Chicago police headquarters, Ness's office, and various other offices and hallways.

5. LIQUOR RAID

917 West 19th Place, Chicago, IL 60608

During his first raid, Ness rides in a vehicle along the alley that runs from the north side of the street into the south side of the street. Ness fails to find any liquor in the crates marked with maple leafs, and since the movie was made, the buildings have been demolished.

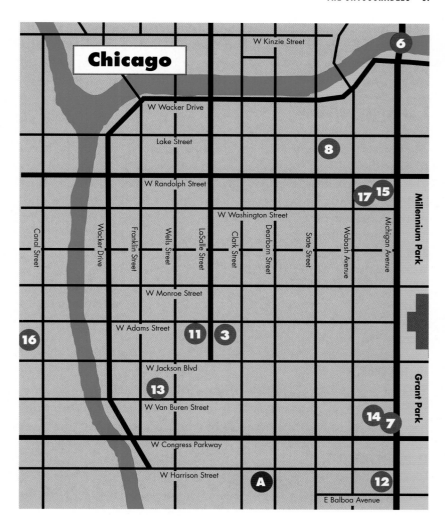

6. DUSABLE BRIDGE

Intersection of Michigan Avenue and East Upper Wacker Drive, Chicago, IL 60601

Ness walks down the round stairs to the lower pedestrian deck of this iconic bridge, where he meets police officer Jim Malone (Sean Connery).

7. THE LEXINGTON HOTEL EXTERIOR

Roosevelt University, 430 South Michigan Avenue, Chicago, IL 60605

The real Lexington Hotel, which Al Capone made his headquarters from 1928 to 1932, was demolished in 1995. The filmmakers used the exterior of the Auditorium Building, designed by architects Louis Sullivan and Dankmar Adler, opened in 1889, and made a part of Roosevelt University in 1947. Added to the National Register of Historic Places in 1970, the Auditorium Building was declared a National Historic Landmark in 1975.

8. AL CAPONE'S BEDROOM
Chicago Theatre, 175 North State Street, Chicago, IL 60601

The filmmakers designed Capone's Lexington Hotel suite in the upper foyer of the Chicago Theatre. Originally known as the Balaban and Katz Chicago Theatre, this lavish landmark theater opened in 1921 and was added to the National Register of Historic Places in 1979. For more information, visit www.thechicagotheatre.com.

9. MALONE'S APARTMENT
4600 South Calumet Avenue, Chicago, IL 60653

Although the address given for Malone's apartment is 1634 South Racine Avenue (at the corner of North Harrison Street), the filmmakers used a terraced house on South Calumet Avenue. Those houses have since been demolished, leaving an empty lot.

10. THE CHURCH
Our Lady of Sorrows Basilica, 3121 West Jackson Boulevard, Chicago, IL 60612

In this gorgeous Italian Renaissance–style basilica with a stunning barrel-vaulted ceiling, Malone explains "the Chicago way."

11. US POST OFFICE
City National Bank and Trust Company Building, 208 South LaSalle Street, Chicago, IL 60604

Ness and his men raid this pristine building across the street from the Rookery, with the Chicago Board of Trade Building in the distance.

12. THE BANQUET
Crystal Ballroom, Renaissance Blackstone Hotel, 636 South Michigan Avenue, Chicago, IL 60605

In the ballroom of this luxury hotel, Al Capone (Robert De Niro) gives his cronies a pep talk on teamwork before killing a gangster with a baseball bat. This 23-story architectural gem built in the Classic Revival Beaux Arts style opened in 1910 and has played host to presidents, foreign dignitaries, sports legends, and movie stars, including Harry Truman, Dwight Eisenhower, the Duke and Duchess of Windsor, and President John F. Kennedy. In 1920, Republican Party bosses held a secret meeting in suite 915 and nominated Warren G. Harding as the party's candidate for president. An AP reporter dubbed the suite a "smoke-filled room," originating the phrase.

SHOT ELSEWHERE

WATER UNDER THE BRIDGE

The filmmakers shot the scene where the Untouchables clash with whiskey runners at the Canadian border at the Hardy Bridge, which spans the Missouri River 14 miles southwest of Cascade, Montana. The rustic wooden cabin seen in the movie is long gone, and the Hardy Bridge was added to the National Register of Historic Places in 2010.

---

13. ALLEY BEHIND ELEVATOR SHOOTING
250 West Van Buren Street, Chicago, IL 60607

After the shooting in the elevator, Ness and Malone run down this alley. Later, in this alley, Malone confronts Police Chief Mike Dorsett (Richard Bradford). Only one building seen in the movie remains standing.

14. LEXINGTON HOTEL LOBBY
Roosevelt University, 430 South Michigan Avenue, Chicago, IL 60605

The foyer of Roosevelt University, with its grand staircase, became the lobby of the Lexington Hotel, where Ness confronts Capone.

15. OPERA HOUSE
Chicago Cultural Center, 78 East Washington Street, Chicago, IL 60602

On the Grand Staircase, made of white Italian Carrara marble decorated with glass mosaics, Al Capone tells the press, "Somebody messes with me, I'm gonna mess with him." On the third floor, where the staircase opens to Preston Bradley Hall with its magnificent translucent dome, 38 feet in diameter and made of Tiffany Favrile glass, Capone toasts the singer of the Italian opera *Pagliacci* by Ruggero Leoncavallo. Completed in 1897 as Chicago's first central public library, this stunning landmark building, home to two magnificent stained glass domes, offers hundreds of free music, dance, and theater events, films, lectures, art exhibitions, and family events. To plan your visit, see www.chicagoculturalcenter.org.

16. THE SHOOTOUT
Union Station, 210 South Canal Street, Chicago, IL 60606

This climactic shootout with the baby carriage in the Great Hall of this train station pays homage to the Odessa Steps sequence in the 1925 film *Battleship Potemkin*, directed by Sergei Eisenstein. Opened in 1925, Chicago Union Station is one of the Windy City's most iconic architectural gems, a combination of limestone Beaux Arts facades, Corinthian columns, and pristine marble floors. The magnificent Great Hall boasts a 300-foot-long barrel-vaulted skylight that soars 115 feet above the floor.

17. COURTHOUSE
Chicago Cultural Center, 82 East Randolph Street, Chicago, IL 60602

Entering the building from the north side on Randolph Street, the curving marble staircase leads to the Grand Army of the Republic Rotunda, with a 40-foot-diameter stained glass dome in the Renaissance style and Knoxville pink marble walls. In this room, Ness discovers the matchbook and chases Frank Nitti up to the roof of the building.

Other Feature Attractions _____

A. ELIOT NESS'S REAL HEADQUARTERS
600 South Dearborn Street, Chicago, IL 60605

Built in 1911, the 22-story Transportation Building housed the Bureau of Prohibition, an enforcement arm of the US Treasury Department. Eliot Ness and his Untouchables occupied offices on the third floor. Vacated by the 1970s, the building remains standing and has been converted into an upscale condominium development, with restaurants and shops on its ground floor.

INDIANA

Breaking Away

For decades, stonecutters cut limestone from the ground in Southern Indiana, leaving behind quarries—enormous holes in the ground that filled with water, creating local swimming holes. The privileged college students at Indiana University in Bloomington call the local townies "cutters," a nickname derived from the stonecutting trade. In the 1979 movie *Breaking Away*, cutter Dave Stoller (Dennis Christopher) yearns to become a professional bicycle racer and pretends to be an Italian exchange student in the hopes of winning the heart of a sorority girl at Indiana University.

Screenwriter Steve Tesich, born in Yugoslavia, moved to Bloomington at age 13, attended Indiana University, and was on the team that won the local Little 500 bicycle race in 1962. "In fact, there really was a character I knew who went around singing snatches of Neapolitan arias," Tesich told *People* magazine, "and he was definitely the inspiration for the film."

Director Peter Yates filmed the movie entirely on location in Bloomington. "*Breaking Away* cuts between a Bloomington campus of lavish college buildings and an abandoned quarry out in the woods," wrote film critic Xan Brooks in the *Guardian*. "It then shows us the link between the two. Without Bloomington, there would be no *Breaking Away*. But without the quarry, there would be no Bloomington. . . . Rooftop quarry is undeniably gorgeous, but it's more than just a backdrop. The place serves as the touchstone for the entire movie. Its presence adds grit, texture, and grandeur to what might otherwise have been a piece of likable, throwaway fluff."

From the film, we learn the stonecutters mined the quarry to create one of the most beautiful college campuses in America, where the upscale students deride the working-class townies whose parents mined the quarry to build the school. "I was damn proud of my work, and the buildings went up," says Dave's father (Paul Dooley). "When they were finished the damnedest thing happened. It was like the buildings was too good for us."

Nominated for four Oscars, including Best Picture, *Breaking Away* won an Academy Award for Best Original Screenplay.

1. ROOFTOP QUARRY
East Empire Mill Road, Bloomington, IN 47401

"Oh Lord, won't you bury me in the parking lot of the A&P"? Italian wannabe Dave Stoller (Dennis Christopher) and his working-class friends Cyril (Daniel Stern), Moocher (Jackie Earle Haley), and Mike (Dennis Quaid) swim in Rooftop Quarry. Diving from the 65-foot-tall cliffs into the quarry is extremely dangerous, and several people have died doing so. The quarry contains many underwater obstructions, including abandoned machinery, large slabs of rock, and unknown debris. Rooftop Quarry sits on private property owned by Indiana Limestone Company, trespassing is illegal, and the police frequently patrol the quarry and ticket violators. To get to Rooftop Quarry, go just beyond the entrance to Good Earth Compost at 650 East Empire Mill Road, and then walk the trail that veers off to the right.

2. NANCY'S HOUSE
Private Residence, 1300 South Lincoln Street, Bloomington, IN 47401

As Dave rides his Masi Gran Criterium bicycle north on South Lincoln Street, singing "Libiamo ne'lieti calici" from the opera *La Traviata* by Giuseppe Verdi, Nancy calls out to him. He continues riding north, passing East Driscoll Street. Please be respectful and do not loiter or disturb the residents.

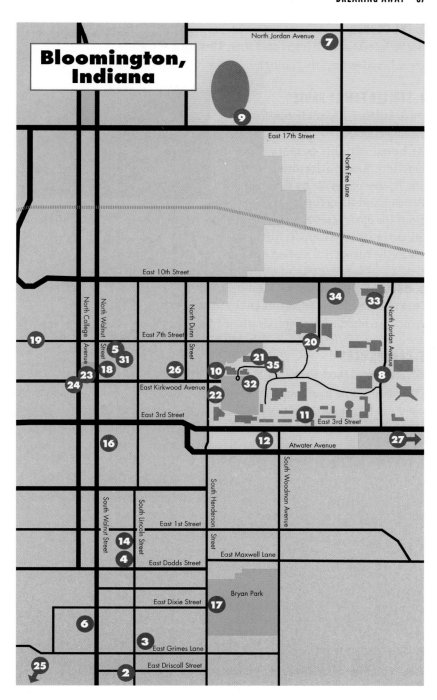

Bloomington, Indiana

3. THE CHURCH
Free Methodist Church, 1121 South Lincoln Street, Bloomington, IN 47401
Dave bicycles past this church.

4. STOLLER FAMILY HOUSE
Private Residence, 756 South Lincoln Street,
Bloomington, IN 47401

At home with his parents, Dave listens to "Largo al factotum" from *The Barber of Seville* by Gioachino Rossini and "Una furtiva lagrima" from *The Elixir of Love* by Gaetano Donizetti. Together, he and Cyril (Daniel Stern) practice "M'appari tutt' amor" from *Marta* by Friedrich von Flotow. Please be respectful and do not loiter or disturb the residents.

5. MOOCHER'S HOUSE
Butch's Grillacatessen and Eatzeria, 120 East 7th Street, Bloomington, IN 47408
A modern building now stands where Moocher (Jackie Earle Haley) resides.

6. CAMPUS CARS
1010 South Walnut Street, Bloomington, IN 47401
"No cash? Come in anyway," reads the sign at Ray Stoller's (Paul Dooley's) used car lot, now the site of several small buildings. At the end of the movie, Ray changes the name of the used car lot to Cutter Cars.

7. TENNIS COURTS
Intersection of North Fee Lane and North Jordan Avenue, Bloomington, IN 47408
The cutters drive by the Indiana University Tennis Center on the southwest corner of this intersection.

8. FRISBEE
Musical Arts Center, 101 North Jordan Avenue, Bloomington, IN 47408
The cutters run over a Frisbee with their car in front of Indiana University's most iconic outdoor statue, *Peau Rouge Indiana*, the last sculpture designed by Alexander Calder before his death in 1976.

9. FOOTBALL PRACTICE
Memorial Stadium, 701 East 17th Street, Bloomington, IN 47408
After sitting on a green slope to watch the Indiana University football team practice, the cutters walk east along 17th Street.

10. KATARINA
Franklin Hall, 601 East Kirkwood Avenue, Bloomington, IN 47408

While resting on the grass across from Franklin Hall and just inside Sample Gates, Dave sees the girl of his dreams (Robyn Douglass) emerge from the building and drop her notebook before she leaves on her blue Vespa scooter. Enraptured, he follows her along East Kirkwood Avenue to the beginning of "Saltarello: Presto" from Symphony no. 4 by Felix Mendelssohn.

11. GREENHOUSE
Jordan Hall Greenhouse, 1001 East 3rd Street, Bloomington, IN 47405

After heading south on South Hawthorne Drive, the dream girl heads west on East 3rd Street.

12. CHI DELTA DELTA SORORITY
Delta Delta Delta, 818 East 3rd Street, Bloomington, IN 47406

A bit south of the sorority house (the real-life Tri Delta), Dave returns the notebook to Katarina and later, accompanied by Cyril on guitar, serenades her with the song "M'appari tutt' amor" from the opera *Marta* by Friedrich von Flotow. Please be respectful and do not loiter or disturb the residents.

13. THE WOODS
West Gate Entrance Road, Brown County State Park, Nashville, IN 47448

While Dave rides his bicycle alone in the woods to "M'appari tutt' amor," his tire blows out.

14. THE MAIL MAN
Private Residence, 612 South Lincoln Street, Bloomington, IN 47401

In front of this house, Dave kisses the mailman to thank him for delivering a copy of *Sports Illustrated*. Please be respectful and do not loiter or disturb the residents.

15. THE CINZANO TRUCK
Highway 37, Pine Boulevard Entrance, Martinsville, IN 46151

Dave emerges from the Morgan Monroe State Forest, turns right to head north on Highway 37 toward Martinsville, and drafts behind the Cinzano semitrailer to the rest of "Saltarello: Presto" from Symphony no. 4 by Felix Mendelssohn.

16. CAMPUS STREET CAR WASH
331 South Walnut Street, Bloomington, IN 47401

"And don't forget to punch the clock, Shorty," says the owner of the carwash. The defunct carwash is now the site of Rhino's All Ages Music Club.

17. BRYAN PARK PLAYGROUND
South Henderson Street and East Dixie Street, Bloomington, IN 47401

Cyril jogs alongside Dave as he rides his bicycle.

18. PAGLIAI'S PIZZA RESTAURANT
Opie Taylor's, 110 North Walnut Street, Bloomington, IN 47404

The cutters hang out at this pizza joint.

19. THE CUTTERS TALKING
400 West 7th Street, Bloomington, IN 47404

The boys walk west on 7th Street alongside Johnson's Creamery and then cross the street, walking in front of Battery Xpress bicycle shop.

20. THE BLUE MERCEDES
Woodburn Hall, 1100 East 7th Street, Bloomington, IN 47405

Driving west along 7th Street, the cutters meet up with the blue Mercedes in front of Woodburn Hall.

21. THE FIGHT
Indiana Memorial Union, 900 East 7th Street, Bloomington, IN 47405

"Hi there, would you like to roll some balls?" The cutters seek a fight with the college boys at the student union and find them in the bowling alley, where Cyril gets his fingers stuck in a ball.

22. THE PRESIDENT'S OFFICE

Bryan Hall 200, 107 South Indiana Avenue, Bloomington, IN 47405

In this, the actual president's office, the genuine president of Indiana University, Dr. John W. Ryan, orders the boys to compete in the Little 500 bicycle race.

23. MONROE COUNTY COURTHOUSE

100 West Kirkwood Avenue, Bloomington, IN 47404

Moocher and Nancy go Dutch to buy a marriage license at this courthouse.

24. THE RED LIGHT

Intersection of South College Avenue and West Kirkwood Avenue, Bloomington, IN 47404

While bicycling south on College Avenue, Dave runs the red light at this intersection, cutting off his father, who is driving his car west on Kirkwood Avenue.

25. THE STONECUTTING FACTORY

2240 West Tapp Road, Bloomington, IN 47403

At the intersection of West Tapp Road and Kegg Road, a driveway leads to the remnants of the factory and an abandoned quarry.

26. RAY AND EVELYN

Nick's English Hut, 423 East Kirkwood Avenue, Bloomington, IN 47408

As Ray and Evelyn (Barbara Barrie) discuss their son's future, they pass Nick's English Hut Tavern and Baskin Robbins (now Panda Express), while Dave trains to "Allegro Vivace" of Symphony no. 4 by Felix Mendelssohn.

27. THE CINZANO BICYCLE RACE STARTING LINE

Intersection of East 3rd Street (Highway 46) and South Park Ridge Road, Bloomington, IN 47401

The race starts to the tune of the "Overture" to *The Barber of Seville* by Gioachino Rossini.

28. RIGHT TURN

Intersection of East 3rd Street and Knightridge Road, Bloomington, IN 47401

The racers make a quick right turn and follow Highway 446 south to the long causeway across Lake Monroe in Paynetown State Recreation Area.

29. THE RAILROAD TRACKS
Intersection of East State Road 58 and Elm Street, Heltonville, IN 47436

Heading south on Indiana 58, the racers cross the railroad tracks and nearly hit a dog.

30. THE CABIN RESTAURANT LOUNGE
4015 IN-446, Bloomington, IN 47401

As Dave catches up with the Italians, they pass the Cabin Restaurant, heading north on Knightbridge Road.

31. THE ALLEY
209 North Washington Street, Bloomington, IN 47408

Driving home, the boys drop off Moocher in the alley behind his house.

32. STONE PAVILION
Rose Well House, Dunn's Woods, Bloomington, IN 47405

In this stone pavilion (built from the old stone gates of the university), Dave confesses to Kathy that he's not Italian.

33. THE BENCH
Herman B. Wells Library, 1320 East 10th Street, Bloomington, IN 47407

While sitting on a bench outside the library, Dave and his father discuss the realities of being a cutter.

34. THE LITTLE 500 RACE
Indiana University Arboretum, East 10th Street and North Fee Lane, Bloomington, IN 47405

The arboretum stands where the track once was. During the parade lap around the stadium, we hear "Indiana, Our Indiana," the official fight song of Indiana University.

35. DIRECTIONS
Memorial Student Union, 900 East 7th Street, Bloomington, IN 47405

In front of this building, a French girl asks Dave for directions to the bursar's office.

Hoosiers

Inspired by the Milan High School basketball team that won the 1954 Indiana State Championship, the 1986 movie *Hoosiers* tells the fictitious story of newly hired basketball coach Norman Dale (Gene Hackman), who leads the Hickory Huskers—a team at a tiny Indiana high school—to victory at the state finals.

Determined to film *Hoosiers* in Indiana and to cast local basketball players as the Huskers, director David Anspaugh and screenwriter Angelo Pizzo (both natives of Indiana) initially chose to shoot the film in the small town of Waveland. Upon learning that construction was scheduled to begin in front of the school where they planned to film, they abandoned Waveland and sought a new location, ultimately deciding to patch together three different towns: New Richmond (for the fictional town of Hickory), Nineveh (for the school), and Knightstown (for the gym). The three towns are each within an hour's drive of Indianapolis but in three completely different directions.

"*Hoosiers* re-creates the organic nature of an actual community," observed film critic Paul Attanasio in the *Washington Post*. "You feel the basketball in relation to these people's lives, feel the people's relation to the land."

Los Angeles Times film critic Sheila Benson agreed. The filmmakers, she wrote, "have a great feel for all the facets of a small town like Hickory—its plainness, meanness, decency, and blank-faced solidity, as well as the almost orgiastic frenzy with which it supports its high school basketball players."

Considered by *Sports Illustrated* to be one of the best sports movies ever made, *Hoosiers* was selected in 2001 by the Library of Congress for preservation in the United States National Film Registry.

Says Coach Norman Dale: "If you put your effort and concentration into playing to your potential, to be the best that you can be, I don't care what the scoreboard says at the end of the game, in my book we're gonna be winners."

1. TERHUNE GRAIN CORN AND JAKE'S SERVICE STATION
Private Residence, 8400 North 1000 East, Sheridan, IN 46069

The granary no longer stands, but the building that housed the small service station remains. Please be respectful and do not loiter or disturb the residents.

2. BARN
Private Residence, 11649 Strawtown Road, Sheridan, IN 46069
Coach Norman Dale (Gene Hackman) drives past this white barn where two boys shoot hoops. Please be respectful and do not loiter or disturb the residents.

3. CHURCH
Concord Church, 5999 Pittsboro Road, Lebanon, IN 46052
Coach Dale stops at this intersection on his way to Hickory. An arsonist burned down the church in 1994 and was sentenced to life in prison.

4. DOWNTOWN HICKORY
Intersection of Wabash Street and Washington Street, New Richmond, IN 47967
Coach Dale drives south on County Road 400 West (Wabash Street), enters the town of Richmond, and turns east on Washington Street. This intersection stars as downtown Hickory.

5. HICKORY HIGH SCHOOL
US Post Office, 7544 South Nineveh Road, Nineveh, IN 46164
A target of arson in 1994, Nineveh Elementary School, used for the classroom scenes and the principal's office, was demolished in 2000. A modern US post office stands in its place. A plaque on a small brick post commemorates the school.

6. THE HICKORY HIGH SCHOOL GYM

The Hoosier Gym, 355 North Washington, Knightstown, IN 46148

Built in 1921, the Knightstown gym ceased being used in 1988, when the city closed the high school next door. A real estate developer turned the high school into apartments, and the town turned the gym into a community center. Used as the home gym of the Hickory Huskers for the film, the renamed Hoosier Gym offers tours of the locker room, hosts an annual Hoosiers Reunion All-Star Classic basketball game in June, and allows visitors to sit in the stands and shoot a basket from the spot where Jimmy made the game-winning toss as time expired. For more information, visit http://thehoosiergym.com.

7. NORMAN DALE'S HOUSE

Private Residence, 5200 North 400 West (north of West 500 North), Crawfordsville, IN 47933

The red house stills stands, but the barn and garage collapsed and sit in a heap. Please be respectful and do not loiter or disturb the residents.

8. ROOSTER'S BARBERSHOP

124 East Washington Street, New Richmond, IN 47967

In this barbershop, the men in the town convene to greet Coach Dale. The barbershop closed.

9. HICKORY CAFÉ

120 South Wabash Street, New Richmond, IN 47967

Coach Dale eats here and so can you. The café, open daily from 7 AM to 9 PM, displays photographs and memorabilia from the movie.

10. MYRA FLEENER'S HOUSE

Private Residence, 2084 South County Road 125 West, Danville, IN 46122

The 1847 house where Myra Fleener (Barbara Hershey) lives cannot be seen from the road, and the barn is long gone. Please be respectful and do not loiter or disturb the residents.

11. CEDAR KNOB GYM

St. Philip Neri Catholic School Gym, 545 Eastern Avenue, Indianapolis, IN 46201

In this gym, the Hickory Huskers play the Knights and a fight nearly breaks out. In 1994, vandals poured sulfuric acid on the original hardwood floor, which has been replaced with linoleum.

12. SHOOTER'S HOUSE

Private Residence, 3078 South County Road 101 East, Clayton, IN 46118

The "domicile" on the hillside where Coach Dales tells Shooter (Dennis Hopper), "You're embarrassing your son." Please be respectful and do not loiter or disturb the residents.

13. CHURCH TOWN MEETING

Elizaville Baptist Church, 5911 North Howard Street, Elizaville, IN 46052

"I apologize for nothing," says Coach Dale, before Jimmy Chitwood (Maris Valainis) announces that he'll start playing basketball again. "There's one other thing," says Jimmy. "I play, Coach stays. He goes, I go."

14. RED CHURCH

Southeast of New Richmond on West 750 North, New Richmond, IN 47967

The church where people are painting "Go Huskers" on the wall can be found along this dirt road.

15. SECTIONAL FINALS, DEER LICK, INDIANA

College Avenue Gym, South School Street and East College Avenue, Brownsburg, IN 46112

Demolished in 1990, the College Avenue Gym, where the Hickory Huskers play the Torhune Tigers, was torn down to make way for College Avenue Condominiums.

16. HOSPITAL

Eskenazi Health, 1001 West 10th Street, Indianapolis, IN 46202

This building originally housed Wishard Nursing Museum, used for the hospital where Shooter goes to dry out, in the museum on the second floor of the Bryce Building. When Wishard Memorial Hospital closed in 2013 and became part of the Eskenazi Health campus, the nursing museum was closed, and some of the props from the movie were moved to the Milan '54 Hoosiers Basketball Museum (see "Other Feature Attractions," below).

17. REGIONAL FINALS, JASPER, INDIANA

Memory Hall Senior Apartments & Community Center, 327 North Lebanon Street, Lebanon, IN 46052

Historic Memorial Gymnasium, where the Hickory Huskers play the Linton Wildcats, still exists as basketball courts inside this senior living community. In this gym, Ollie McLellan (Wade Schenck) shoots two foul shots.

18. STATE CHAMPIONSHIP

Hinkle Fieldhouse, 510 West 49th Street, Butler University, Indianapolis, IN 46208

Built in 1928 and originally named Butler Fieldhouse, this sports arena originally seated 15,000 people, which made it the largest basketball gym in the United States until 1950. Renamed Hinkle Fieldhouse in 1966 in honor of Tony Hinkle, who coached the Butler Bulldogs for 41 seasons, the fieldhouse was named to the National Register of Historic Places in 1983 and declared a National Historic Landmark in 1987.

19. AVON MOVIE THEATER

216 North Lebanon Street, Lebanon, IN 46052

This classic neon-lit movie theater, built in 1924, where the marquee reads "Closed for big game," burned down in 1999.

Other Feature Attractions

THE MILAN '54 HOOSIERS MUSEUM

201 West Carr Street, Milan, IN 47031

This museum houses the world's largest collection of *Hoosiers* movie props, including the uniforms worn by Jimmy Chitwood, Buddy, and Strap. You'll also see Myra Fleener's Betty Rose vintage coat and uniforms of the opposing teams (Cedar Knobs, Birdseye, Oolitic, South Bend Central, Decatur, and Terhune). To plan your visit, telephone (812) 654-2772 or visit http://milan54.org.

A League of Their Own

"There's no crying in baseball!" shouts Coach Jimmy Dugan (Tom Hanks) to the players on his all-female baseball team.

In 1943, in response to the disappearance of minor league baseball teams after players left to fight in World War II, chewing gum magnate and Chicago Cubs owner Philip K. Wrigley founded the All-American Girls Professional Baseball League (AAGPBL), which continued until 1954. Inducted into the Baseball Hall of Fame in Cooperstown, New York, in 1988, the AAGPBL became the subject of a documentary titled *A League of Their Own*. Inspired by the documentary, director Penny Marshall decided to make a movie about the Rockford Peaches, one of the four teams in the league's first season.

Filmed mostly around Evansville, Indiana, and Chicago, the 1992 movie stars Geena Davis, Lori Petty, Rosie O'Donnell, Megan Cavanaugh, and Madonna. Tom Hanks plays washed-up and boozing coach Jimmy Dugan. "Marshall shows her women characters in a tug-of-war between new images and old values," wrote film critic Roger Ebert in the *Chicago Sun-Times*, "and so her movie is about transition—about how it felt as a woman suddenly to have new roles and freedom."

"As shooting began, I felt more like a coach than a director," recalls Marshall in her autobiography. "The girls worked constantly on their throwing and catching, and took daily batting practice. . . . I also brought in a Slip 'N Slide so they could practice slides (and have fun at the same time)."

In 2012, the Library of Congress selected *A League of Their Own* for preservation in the United States National Film Registry.

SHOT ELSEWHERE

A WHOLE NEW BALL GAME

Dottie Hinson's (Geena Davis's) kids play basketball in the backyard of a private residence at 4222 Agnes Avenue, Studio City, CA 91604. Please be respectful and do not loiter or disturb the residents.

The Greyhound bus pulls up in front of Doubleday Field, a baseball stadium located at 1 Doubleday Court, Cooperstown, NY 13326, two blocks from the National Baseball Hall of Fame and Museum.

1. THE WALTER HARVEY MANSION
Cantigny Park, One South 151 Winfield Road, Wheaton, IL 60189
The estate of "candy bar king" Walter Harvey (Garry Marshall) was filmed at the former home of Robert R. McCormick, publisher of the *Chicago Tribune*. Built in 1896, this stately mansion, now called the McCormick Museum, opened to the public in 1958 and provides guided tours only. For more information, visit www.cantigny.org.

2. WILLIAMETTE OREGON SOLFBALL FIELD
St. Philip Field, 11300 Creamery Road, Mt. Vernon, IN 47620
While playing for Lukash Dairy at this softball field, Kit Hinson (Lori Petty) strikes out.

3. DOTTIE AND KIT'S FARM
Private Property, 1980 St. Philip Road, Evansville, IN 47712
Baseball scout Ernie Capadino (Jon Lovitz) finds Dottie and Kit milking cows on this "Oregon" farm, where the house seen in the movie is no more. Please be respectful and do not loiter or disturb the residents.

4. TRAIN DEPOTS
Illinois Railway Museum, 7000 Olson Road, Union, IL 60180
About 60 miles northwest of Chicago, the Illinois Railway Museum, the largest railroad museum in the United States, supplied period trains and the filmmakers used its depot as various stations. Explains Ernie Capadino: "See, how it works is—the train moves, not the station."

5. FT. COLLINS PROSPECT GYM
Ribeyre School Gymnasium, 433 Tavern Street, New Harmony, IN 47631
Inside this neoclassical building, Marla Hooch (Megan Cavanaugh) practices batting, breaking windows. "You know General Omar Bradley?" says Ernie. "Well, there's too strong a resemblance."

6. HARVEY FIELD
Wrigley Field, 1060 West Addison Street, Chicago, IL 60613
The girls try out at the massive baseball stadium owned by candy bar king Walter Harvey (Garry Marshall). Wrigley Field, named in honor of chewing gum magnate William Wrigley and home of the Chicago Cubs, also stars in *The Blues Brothers* and *Ferris Bueller's Day Off*. To plan your visit, see http://chicago.cubs.mlb.com/chc/ballpark.

7. CHARM AND BEAUTY SCHOOL

South Shore Cultural Center, 7059 South Shore Drive, Chicago, IL 60649

Inside this former country club with magnificent interiors, the Rockford Peaches learn to "sip, down, don't slurp." Founded in 1905 and built in a Mediterranean Revival style, South Shore Cultural Center sits on more than 65 acres of parkland and includes a theater, stables, nine-hole golf course, formal dining hall, a private beach, a nature sanctuary, a butterfly garden, and the Washburne Culinary Institute and its elegant restaurant, the Parrot Cage. Besides hosting cultural programs, the center offers a wide variety of classes. Barack and Michelle Obama held their wedding reception at this opulent facility, added to the National Register of Historic Places in 1975. For more information, visit www.chicagoparkdistrict.com.

8. ROCKFORD PEACHES STADIUM

League Stadium, 203 South Cherry Street, Huntingburg, IN 47542

This stadium, built in 1894, fell into a state of neglect until the filmmakers renovated it, as commemorated by a plaque. Now home of the Dubois County Bombers, the stadium still boasts the advertisements painted on the outfield fence for the movie. Coach Jimmy Dugan (Tom Hanks) urinates in the sink in the locker room. To arrange for a tour, telephone (812) 683-2211.

9. WILLIE'S SUDS BUCKET EXTERIOR

Hornville Tavern, 2607 West Baseline Road, Evansville, IN 47720

The filmmakers added an arched facade to the building, which they removed after shooting the movie.

10. WILLIE'S SUDS BUCKET INTERIOR

Fitzgerald's, 6615 West Roosevelt Road, Berwyn, IL 60402

The team sneaks out of their hotel to dance up a storm to the music of Doc's Rhythm Cats in this bar. The same backdrop created for the film graces the stage.

11. CHURCH

St. James Lutheran Church, 2101 North Fremont Street, Chicago, IL 60614

Inside this church, Mae Mordabito (Madonna) confesses, causing the priest to break out in a sweat. Later, Marla gets married here.

12. RACINE BELLS FIELD

Bosse Field, 1701 North Main Street, Evansville, IN 47711

Built in 1915 and home to the Evansville Otters, this stadium is the third-oldest ballpark still in use in the United States, after Boston's Fenway Park (1912) and the Chicago's Wrigley Field (1914). At this field, Jimmy and Dottie give conflicting signals to Marla Hooch, and the Peaches play for *Life* magazine.

13. THE BOARDING HOUSE

Private Residence, Soaper-Esser House, 612 North Main Street, Henderson, KY 42420

The Rockford Peaches stay in this large Queen Anne brick house, built by William Soaper between 1884 and 1887 (with bricks made on the property) and subsequently owned by Augustus Owsley Stanley, a former governor and US senator. The house is listed on the National Register of Historic Places. Please be respectful and do not loiter or disturb the residents.

14. NATIONAL BASEBALL HALL OF FAME AND MUSEUM

25 Main Street, Cooperstown, NY 13326

At this sentimental reunion, the alumni of the AAGPBL become the first women inducted into the Baseball Hall of Fame.

Rudy

Based on a true story, the 1993 movie *Rudy* tells the story of Daniel "Rudy" Ruettiger (Sean Astin), who yearns to play football at the University of Notre Dame but lacks the talent, size, grades, and money to live his dream. Through sheer persistence, grit, and determination, Rudy achieves his goal of getting into Notre Dame and playing for the Fighting Irish. Film critic Roger Ebert wrote, "In *Rudy*, Astin's performance is so self-effacing, so focused and low-key, that we lose sight of the underdog formula and begin to focus on this dogged kid who won't quit."

Reuttiger saw the 1986 movie *Hoosiers* and with the same determination that landed him on the football team, pursued the directing and writing team of David Anspaugh and Angelo Pizzo to bring his story to the screen. "The principal reason the film was ever made was Rudy's persistence," said Anspaugh. "He never left us alone, and his story kept sticking in our minds."

Securing permission to film on the Notre Dame campus provided a significant hurdle for Anspaugh and Pizzo. The university had previously granted permission for only one film, *Knute Rockne: All American*, to be shot on campus—in 1940—and had forever after adhered to a strict no-film policy. "We had to do it here," Anspaugh told *ND Today*, "or there was no movie."

Reuttiger provided university vice president Fr. William Beauchamp with a videotape copy of *Hoosiers* and a draft of the *Rudy* script. Touched by *Hoosiers* and convinced the script captured the spirit of Notre Dame, Beauchamp acquiesced.

In the movie, rated one of the 25 Best Sports Movies of all time by ESPN, Ruettiger appears in a cameo as a fan in the stands during the final football game.

1. FOOTBALL
Northwest corner of Front Street and 119th Street, Whiting, IN 46394

The boys play football in a field that is now a parking lot, and they run along a railroad track long since removed.

2. THE REUTTIGER RESIDENCE
1718 East 119th Street, Whiting, IN 46394

This clapboard house with three entrances is now gone.

3. JOLIET CATHOLIC HIGH SCHOOL
Claremont Academy Elementary School, 2300 West 64th Street, Chicago, IL 60636

St. Rita High School in Chicago stood in for Rudy's school in Joliet. St. Rita's has since moved to a new location, and a new building stands where the football field was.

4. THE STARTER HOUSE
Private Residence, 2209 South Scott Street, South Bend, IN 46613

Sherry (Lili Taylor) brings Rudy (Sean Astin) to look at this house. Please be respectful and do not loiter or disturb the residents.

5. THE BAR
Game Time, 1708 119th Street, Whiting, IN 46394

This bar where Rudy drinks with his friends has been demolished.

6. THE CHURCH
St. Casimir's Parish, 1308 Dunham Street, South Bend, IN 46619

Inside this redbrick church, built in 1924 with Romanesque architecture and Italianate chandeliers, Pete's funeral takes place.

7. THE GREYHOUND BUS STATION
409 South Walnut Street, South Bend, IN 46619

In front of this building, which has since been torn down, Rudy's father (Ned Beatty) tells Rudy, "Chasing a stupid dream causes you and everyone around you heartache."

8. THE GUARD GATE
Circle at the northern end of North Notre Dame Avenue, South Bend, IN 46556

Rudy speaks with the guard sitting at a gatehouse built by the filmmakers at the circle at the end of Notre Dame Avenue.

9. ST. JOSEPH'S LAKE
St. Joseph's Lake, South Bend, IN 46556

Walking along the north shore of St. Joseph's Lake, Rudy sees the Notre Dame administration building with its iconic cupola.

10. CORBY HALL
St. Mary's Drive, Notre Dame, IN 46556
Inside this campus building, Father Cavanaugh (Robert Prosky) asks Rudy, "Are you fully aware of the sacrifices you're going to have to make?"

11. THE MAIN QUAD
Main Quad, Notre Dame, IN 46556
From the main quad with its statue of Jesus, Rudy walks southeast to the football stadium.

12. NOTRE DAME STADIUM
Moose Krause Circle,
Notre Dame, IN 46556
Rudy gazes at the front of the stadium, enters, and walks into the center of the field. Since the movie was made, the stadium has been significantly renovated and expanded.

13. HOLY CROSS
Holy Cross Hall, Holy Cross Circle, South Bend, IN 46616
With help from Father Cavanaugh, Rudy enrolls at this Catholic liberal arts college.

14. CLASSROOM
O'Shaughnessy Hall, Room 118, south end of St. Joseph Drive, Notre Dame, IN 46556
Rudy takes classes in this room and meets D-Bob (Jon Favreau), who agrees to tutor him in exchange for his help dating women.

15. THE PRACTICE FIELD
113 Joyce Center, Notre Dame, IN 46556
Rudy shows up for practice at this field, east of Notre Dame Stadium.

16. THE ARCHWAY
Lyons Hall, Holy Cross Drive (near Dorr Road), Notre Dame, IN 46556
At this spot, Rudy tries to entice several girls to date D-Bob.

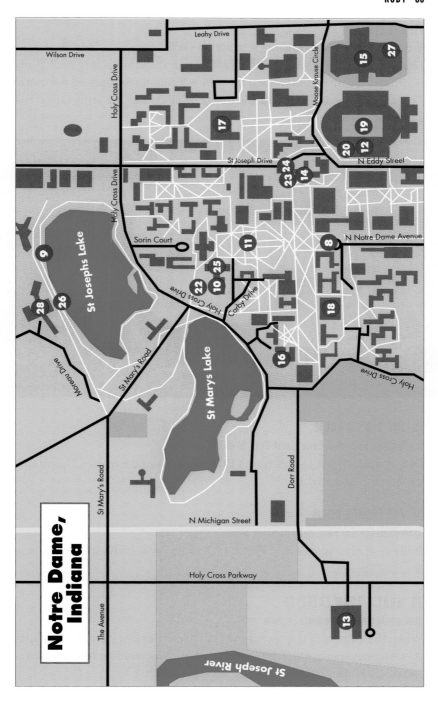

Notre Dame, Indiana

17. THE LIBRARY
Hesburgh Library, 221 Hesburgh Library, Notre Dame, IN 46556

Outside this library with its *World of Life* mural and reflecting pool, Rudy continues trying to find women for D-Bob. Students nicknamed the mural "Touchdown Jesus," because the image of Jesus has his arms raised the same way a referee signals a touchdown.

18. THE DINING ROOM
South Dining Hall, Notre Dame, South Bend, IN 46556

In this dining hall, D-Bob tutors Rudy, and a woman invites D-Bob to a dance on Friday night.

19. THE LOCKER ROOM
Notre Dame Football Field, Notre Dame, IN 46556

Rudy reads the plaque with Knute Rockne's speech about winning one for the Gipper.

20. RUDY'S ROOM EXTERIOR
Somewhere inside Notre Dame Stadium

When the university renovated and expanded the exterior of the stadium, it built a new perimeter, completely altering the window to the maintenance room where Rudy slept.

21. CORBY'S IRISH PUB

441 East Lasalle Avenue, South Bend, IN 46617

In this popular Notre Dame watering hole, Rudy confesses his non-student status to Mary (Greta Lind).

22. CANDLES

Grotto of Our Lady of Lourdes, Holy Cross Drive (and St. Mary's Road), Notre Dame, IN 46556

Rudy lights candles inside this replica of Our Lady of Lourdes Grotto in Lourdes, France, built one-seventh the size of the original in 1896 with boulders from nearby farms. The Grotto of Notre Dame, with its statue of the Virgin Mary, provides a spiritual oasis for Notre Dame students and alumni—most notably during football weekends and finals. Hundreds of students have proposed marriage here.

23. THE HOLY CROSS MAILROOM

O'Shaughnessy Hall, Room 118, south end of St. Joseph Drive, Notre Dame, IN 46556

Rudy checks Box 620 for an acceptance letter to Notre Dame. The mailroom no longer occupies this spot in the building.

24. WADDICK'S

O'Shaughnessy Hall, Main Hallway, south end of St. Joseph Drive, Notre Dame, IN 46556

In this 1950s-style café, Rudy and D-Bob sit in a booth together. A campus institution, Waddick's serves home-style soups, sandwiches, salads, yogurt, beverages, and coffee.

25. CHURCH
Basilica of the Sacred Heart, 1 Holy Cross Drive, Notre Dame, IN 46556

"In 35 years of religious studies, I've come up with only two hard, incontrovertible facts," Father Cavanaugh tells Rudy inside this basilica. "There is a God, and I'm not Him." Notre Dame president Reverend Theodore Hesburgh and Chief Financial Officer Reverend Edmund Joyce, dressed as priests, make cameo appearances in this scene. This magnificent, Gothic-inspired place of worship contains 19th-century French stained glass windows and beautiful artwork.

26. THE BENCH
Moreau Seminary, Moreau Drive, Notre Dame, IN 46556

Sitting on a bench by St. Joseph's Lake, Rudy reads his acceptance letter.

27. PARKING GARAGE
113 Joyce Center, Notre Dame, IN 46556

In this garage, Rudy learns that he made the football team.

28. RUDY'S DORM ROOM
Moreau Seminary, Moreau Drive, Notre Dame, IN 46556

From Rudy's dorm room, we see the Basilica of the Sacred Heart in the distance. From the front of the building, Rudy says good-bye to D-Bob and his pious girlfriend. Explains D-Bob: "I'm not allowed to say 'goddamn' no more." Please be respectful and do not loiter or disturb the residents.

IOWA

The Bridges of Madison County

Madison County, Iowa, is the home to six scenic covered bridges. Five of these landmarks are listed on the National Register of Historic Places.

Based on the bestselling novel *The Bridges of Madison County* by Robert James Waller, the 1995 movie tells the fictional story of a four-day love affair between Francesca Johnson (Meryl Streep), a lonely housewife from Italy, and *National Geographic* photographer Robert Kincaid (Clint Eastwood), who stumbles into her home to ask directions to one of the covered bridges he is on assignment to shoot.

Directed by Eastwood, the movie was filmed on location in Winterset, Iowa, the county seat of Madison County and the home of the actual bridges that serve as the backdrop for the romance.

"One of the sources of the movie's poignancy is that the flowering of the love will be forever deferred," wrote film critic Roger Ebert in the *Chicago Sun-Times*. "They will know they are right for each other, and not follow up on their knowledge."

The lone farmhouse embodies Francesca's emotional isolation, and the bridges seem to symbolize a romantic route for her escape. Ebert explained, "*The Bridges of Madison County* is about two people who find the promise of perfect personal happiness, and understand, with sadness and acceptance, that the most important things in life are not always about making yourself happy."

For her role in the film, Meryl Street was nominated for an Academy Award as Best Actress.

1. FRANCESCA'S FARMHOUSE
Private Residence, 3257 130th Street, Cumming, IA 50061

To make the movie, the filmmakers renovated and restored an abandoned farmhouse that had stood vacant for more than 35 years. When the movie was released, the owners of the property turned Francesca's house, built in 1870 by an Argentine sea captain and sitting on a 1,000-acre

farm, into a popular tourist attraction, open to the public for guided tours throughout the summer months, its exterior and interior preserved just as they appeared in the movie. Visitors could pose for photographs at the kitchen table and in the very bathtub used by Francesca (Meryl Streep)
and Robert (Clint Eastwood) in the film. Unfortunately, an arson fire damaged the house on October 6, 2003, prompting the owners to shut the house and cease offering tours. Please be respectful and do not loiter or disturb the residents.

2. THE ROSEMAN COVERED BRIDGE

Elderberry Avenue (south of Roseman Bridge Road), Winterset, IA 50273

Francesca says this bridge is two miles from her farmhouse. In reality, the bridge is roughly 28 miles from the house. Built in 1883, this 107-foot bridge that Robert seeks to find when he knocks on the door to Francesca's farmhouse is also the bridge to which Francesca pins a note inviting Robert to dinner and where her children scatter her ashes.

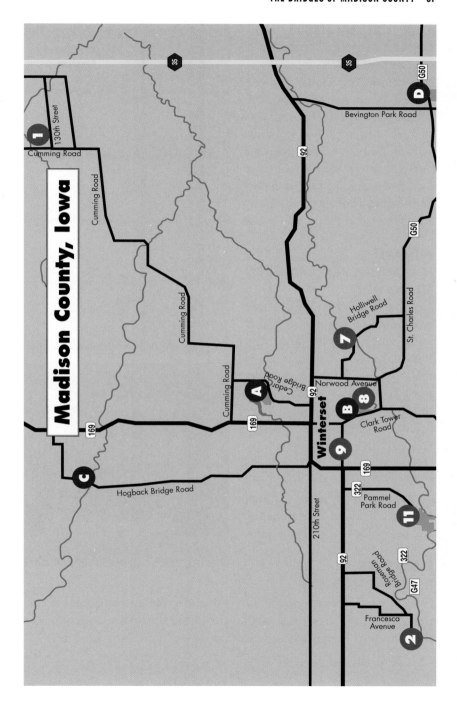

3. THE TEXACO GAS STATION

Intersection of John Wayne Drive and Green Street, Winterset, IA 50273

The filmmakers transformed a closed Conoco station on the southwest corner of this intersection into a 1965-era Texaco station, where Robert Kincaid uses a phone booth. After filming, local entrepreneurs turned the gas station into a gift shop, which was torn down in 2008.

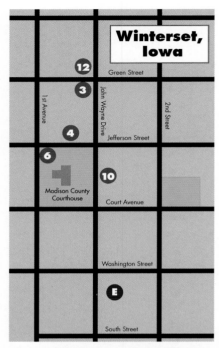

4. THE CAFÉ

The Northside Cafe, 61 West Jefferson Street, Winterset, IA 50273

In a booth at this family-style restaurant, author Robert Waller wrote portions of his novel, and Robert Kincaid drinks a cup of coffee at the counter and offers Lucy Redfield a seat. Rated the number-one restaurant in Winterset on Tripadvisor.com, the Northside Cafe, situated across the street from the Madison County Courthouse, is open from 11 AM to 8 PM Tuesday through Friday, 8:30 AM to 8 PM on Saturday, and 9 AM to 2 PM on Sunday.

5. DRESS SHOP

823 Main Street, Adel, IA 50003

Francesca walks west along Main Street and enters this store on the corner of South 9th Street, across the street from the ornate Dallas County District Court House, whose reflection we see in the store windows.

THE BRIDGES OF MADISON COUNTY 93

6. PHONE BOOTH

Intersection of West Jefferson Street and North 1st Avenue, Winterset, IA 50273

Although the phone booth no longer stands on the southeast corner of this intersection, from this spot Robert telephones Francesca with second thoughts about another rendezvous.

7. THE HOLLIWELL COVERED BRIDGE

Holliwell Bridge Road (near 225th Trail), Winterset, IA 50273

The longest covered bridge in Madison County, the 122-foot Holliwell Bridge, built in 1880 and spanning Middle River, is where Francesca and Robert go after visiting the town.

8. THE STONE BRIDGE

Winterset's City Park, Winterset, IA 50273

Francesca and Robert picnic together near this bridge, just south of the Cutler-Donahue covered bridge. Clark Tower, erected in 1926 as a monument to the county's first pioneer family, offers a handsome view of the Middle River valley.

9. THE BLUE NOTE LOUNGE EXTERIOR

Madison County Fairgrounds, 1204 West Summit Street, Winterset, IA 50273

The filmmakers dressed the outside of a tractor garage to create the exterior for the Blue Note Lounge.

10. THE BLUE NOTE LOUNGE INTERIOR

Pheasant Run Pub & Grill, 103 South John Wayne Drive, Winterset, IA 50273

A sign outside this tavern reads "Home of the Blue Note in the Movie." Francesca and Robert sat on the two bar stools with red covers standing in the corner. According to the movie credits, one of the members of the jazz band that performs in Blue Note is Kyle Eastwood, Clint's son.

11. THE RIVER CROSSING

Pammel State Park, Pammel Park Road, southwest of Winterset, IA 50273

Michael (Victor Slezak) and Carolyn (Annie Corley) sit by the Middle River Ford in this park to read and discuss their mother's diaries.

12. WINTERSET GENERAL STORE
Northwest corner of John Wayne Drive and Green Street, Winterset, IA 50273

The filmmakers dressed the M. Young & Co. Feed Store, which has since been demolished, as the Winterset General Store.

Other Feature Attractions _____

FOUR MORE BRIDGES OF MADISON COUNTY
Covered with inexpensive lumber to preserve the more costly flooring timbers, the original nineteen bridges of Madison County were named after the family that lived closest to each bridge. Today, only six of those bridges remain. For more information, visit www.madisoncounty.com.

A. CEDAR COVERED BRIDGE (1883)
Cedar Bridge Park, Nature Trail and Cedar Bridge Road, Winterset, IA 52073

Burned down by an arsonist in 2003 and reconstructed the following year, this bridge is the only covered bridge that allows vehicle traffic.

B. CUTLER-DONAHOE COVERED BRIDGE (1870)
Northwest corner of Winterset City Park, Winterset, IA 52073

This 79-foot-long bridge with a pitched roof originally crossed the North River near Bevington, but was relocated to Winterset City Park in 1970.

C. HOGBACK COVERED BRIDGE (1884)
Hogback Bridge Road, Winterset, IA 52073

This 97-foot-long covered bridge allowed vehicle traffic until 1993, when the county built a concrete bridge 200 feet south of it. Not named after a family, the Hogback Bridge may have been named after a nearby limestone ridge or the style of construction used to build its pitched roof.

D. IMES COVERED BRIDGE (1870)
East Main Street and Imes Bridge Road, St. Charles, IA 50240

The oldest surviving Madison County bridge, the 81-foot pitch-roofed bridge originally spanned the Middle River near Patterson. In 1887, the bridge was moved to cross Clinton Creek southwest of Hanley. The bridge was moved to its current location in 1977.

E. JOHN WAYNE BIRTHPLACE AND MUSEUM
205 John Wayne Drive, Winterset, IA 50273

Born in Winterset in 1907 as Marion Robert Morrison, actor John Wayne lived in this one-bedroom house that became a museum in 1982. The 6,100-square-foot museum displays letters, family photos, a life-size statue of the actor, the eye patch Rooster Cogburn wore in *True Grit*, and costumes, including a uniform from *The Green Berets*. For more information, visit www.johnwaynebirthplace.museum.

Children of the Corn

Based on the 1977 short story of the same name by horror novelist Stephen King, the 1984 movie *Children of Corn* tells the story of a Dr. Burt Stanton (Peter Horton) and his girlfriend, Vicky (Linda Hamilton), who, while driving to Seattle, happen upon the small corn town of Gaitlin, Nebraska, which has been overrun by macabre children who have used knives, hatchets, sickles, and cleavers to kill all the adults. Dictated by a demonic child preacher named Isaac (John Franklin) and his lieutenant Malachai (Courtney Gains), the cult of children worship a bloodthirsty deity they call "He Who Walks Behind the Rows" and sacrifice interloping adults ("outlanders") and any child who reaches puberty. *Children of the Corn* grossed more than $14 million and spawned eight sequels and a 2009 television remake.

"Especially effective is the film's physical look," wrote film critic Vincent Canby in the *New York Times*. "Shot in Iowa, which passes for Nebraska, the film is full of beautifully evocative, broad, flat, sun-baked landscapes, in which even cornfields are made to seem menacing." To create the fictional town of Gatlin, "the Nicest Little Town in Nebraska," the filmmakers shot in three small towns in Iowa—Whiting, Hornick, and Salix.

"If the thought even fleetingly crosses your mind that somebody should have reported all the missing adults, you're in the wrong movie," wrote film critic Roger Ebert in the *Chicago Sun-Times*. "This was apparently a town where none of the adults made or received long-distance calls, used charge cards, had out-of-town relatives, or knew anybody who would miss them. Maybe they deserved to die."

1. GRACE BAPTIST CHURCH OF GATLIN EXTERIOR
315 Tipton Street, Salix, IA 51052

The facade of the church is long gone, and Salix Fire & Rescue stands in its place.

2. HANSEN'S CAFE EXTERIOR
Variety Store, 623 Whittier Street, Whiting, IA 51063

Dad (David Cowen) stops here to use the pay phone, while his son Job (Robby Kiger) enjoys a strawberry shake.

3. HANSEN'S CAFÉ INTERIOR
The Wagon Masters Cafe, 317 Main Street, Hornick, IA 51026

The café where Malachai and his followers attack the adults burned down on Christmas Eve 2008 and only an empty lot remains.

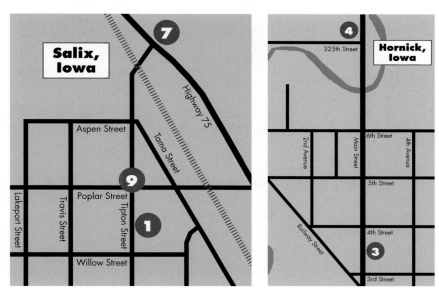

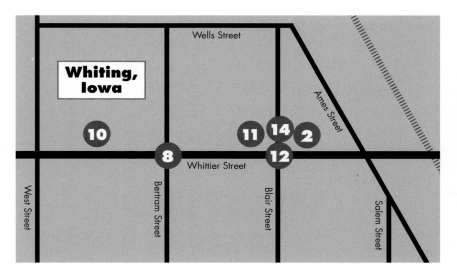

4. JOB AND SARAH'S HOUSE EXTERIOR

Private Residence, northwest corner of 325th Street and Grand Avenue, Hornick, IA 51026

Job and Sarah (Anne Marie McEvoy) hide in this house. The barn that stood behind the house is no more. The filmmakers built a faux cellar door on the east side of the house, which was removed after filming. Please be respectful and do not loiter or disturb the residents.

5. MOTEL EXTERIOR

Econo Lodge, 103 Sergeant Square, Sergeant Bluff, IA 51054

In this seedy motel with blue and vermillion doors, Dr. Burton Stanton (Peter Horton) celebrates his birthday with his girlfriend, Vicky (Linda Hamilton), who serenades him by singing "School Is Out" by Gary U.S. Bonds. Horton later played Professor Gary Shepherd on *thirtysomething* and Linda Hamilton later starred as Sarah Conner in the *Terminator* movies.

6. CHURCH INTERIOR

New Creation Ministries, 423 George Street, Sioux City, IA 51103

"Any religion without love and compassion is false," Burt tells the satanic children gathered inside this church.

7. GAS STATION

Highway 75 and Tipton Street, Salix, IA 51052

The service station run by Diehl (R. G. Armstrong) on the east side of Highway 75 was demolished.

8. ENTERING GAITLIN

Intersection of Whittier Street and Bertram Street, Whiting, IA 51063

"Looks like a swingin' place," says Burt, as he and Vicky drive west along Whittier Street, starting at Bertram Street. Burt later strolls along these deserted streets.

9. MORE GAITLIN
Intersection of Tipton Street and Poplar Street, Salix, IA 51502
Burt and Vicky continue exploring Gaitlin, driving south along scenic Tipton Street.

10. THE GARAGE
Whiting Garage, 443 Whittier Street, Whiting, IA 51063
Burt and Vicky drive past this abandoned garage, where two kids hide behind an oil drum.

11. TOWN HALL EXTERIOR
Sloan State Bank, 520 Whittier Street, Whiting, IA 51063
The filmmakers dressed up this bank building as the town hall.

12. THE FLAGPOLE
Intersection of Whittier Street and Blair Street, Whiting, IA 51063
The flagpole, with is yellow concrete base, sits in the middle of the street.

13. TOWN HALL INTERIOR
Mills-Shellhammer-Puetz & Associates, 117 Pierce Street, Sioux City, IA 51101
Burt finds the offices of this former train depot decorated with corn.

14. THE WAY TO THE BARN
Intersection of Whittier Street and Blair Street, Whiting, IA 51063
Job, Sarah, and Burt run east along Whittier Street, turn left to head north on Blair Street, run north between the grain towers at Ames Street, and turn west on Wells Street.

Field of Dreams

"If you build it, he will come," declares a mysterious voice.

Based on the 1982 novel *Shoeless Joe* by W. P. Kinsella, *Field of Dreams* tells the story of Iowa farmer Ray Kinsella (Kevin Costner), who hears a mysterious voice telling him to build a baseball field in his cornfield. When he does, the ghost of "Shoeless" Joe Jackson (Ray Liotta), an outfielder and star hitter with the Chicago White Sox who was banned from baseball for accepting bribes to intentionally lose the 1919 World Series, appears on the baseball diamond. "Is this heaven?" asks Shoeless Joe. "No," Ray replies, "it's Iowa."

In 1987, Sue Riedel, a local volunteer for the Iowa Film Office, scouted northeast Iowa for the perfect farming landscape for the 1989 movie version of the novel, which was set in Iowa City. A few miles northeast of Dyersville, she found a white, two-story clapboard farmhouse with a red barn and lush cornfields. She sent pictures of the farm to Universal Studios, and the filmmakers secured permission from the owners to make the movie on the farm and the adjacent property, plowing the cornfield to create a baseball field in a spot where views of the sunset would be unobstructed. The farmhouse and baseball field still exist, and people come from all over the world to visit.

"It was hot. It was dry. It was full of flies," recalled director Phil Alden Robinson in the *Des Moines Register*. To contend with that year's drought, the film crew dammed Hewitt Creek and irrigated the field to grow lush, green corn beyond the outfield. "To make the corn look as high as an elephant's thigh," recalled actor James Earl Jones, who played author Terence Mann in the film, "they had to dig trenches between the rows so that when Kevin Costner walked down the row of corn, it was over his head."

"This is the kind of movie Frank Capra might have directed, and James Stewart might have starred in—a movie about dreams," wrote film critic Roger Ebert in the *Chicago Sun-Times*. *Field of Dreams* was nominated for an Academy Award for Best Picture of the Year.

"Hey, Dad, you wanna have a catch?"

1. FIELD OF DREAMS MOVIE SITE
28995 Lansing Road, Dyersville, IA 52040

"It's okay, honey, I'm just talking to the cornfield," says Ray Kinsella (Kevin Costner), compelled to build a baseball field on his farmland. The baseball diamond still exists, and you can visit it. The filmmakers built the baseball field on two properties (one owned by Don Lansing, the other by Al and Rita Ameskamp), and after filming, the Ameskamps ploughed up their portion (left and center field) and returned to farming. But after an estimated 60,000 people visited the field within the first three years of the film's release, the owners restored the field for tourists. For a short time, the two families operated competing souvenir stands, but in 2007, Rita Ameskamp sold her portion of the field to the Lansings, who, in turn, sold the house and field in 2011 to Go the Distance Baseball LLC. Admission is free, and you can sit on the porch swing, sit on the bleachers, and play baseball on the actual Field of Dreams. For more information and to tour the field virtually, visit www.fodmoviesite.com

2. FARM SUPPLY STORE
Hendrick's Feed and Seed, 880 Central Avenue, Dubuque, IA 52001

While talking with fellow customers in this store, Ray denies hearing voices out in the field. "Noises," he insists.

3. THE SCHOOL
Drexler Elementary School, 405 3rd Avenue NE, Farley, IA 52046

The school building where Annie Kinsella (Amy Madigan) stands up against censorship at the PTA meeting was demolished and replaced with the modern Drexler Middle School and the Dubuque County Library buildings. In the novel *Shoeless Joe*, radical writer Terence Mann, author of *The Boat Rocker*, was J. D. Salinger, author of *The Catcher in the Rye*.

The filmmakers, fearing litigation from Salinger, changed the author to a fictional character.

4. LIBRARY INTERIOR
Charles C. Myers Library, University of Dubuque, Grace Street, Dubuque, IA 52001

In this library, Ray researches the reclusive Terence Mann.

5. LIBRARY EXTERIOR
Van Vliet Hall, University of Dubuque, 2105 Grace Street, Dubuque, IA 52001

Ray and Annie walk down the steps from this building and head west. Strangely, they then appear a block east and walk west across North Algona Street to their truck parked in front of Blades Hall.

6. HYMIE'S KOSHER BUTCHER
Central Avenue at 17th Street, Dubuque, IA, 52001

When Ray searches for Terence Mann (James Earl Jones), the filmmakers dressed up a few blocks of Dubuque's Central Avenue to masquerade as a Jewish section of Boston.

7. ROTH & ADLER CLEANSERS & TAILORS
Club Heat, 1706 Central Avenue, Dubuque, IA 52001

Outside this building, Ray hassles an elderly woman, who says, "I ain't gonna tell you nothing."

8. GAS STATION
Intersection of 3rd Street and Locust Street, Dubuque, IA 52001

On the southeast corner of this intersection, Ray tips a gas station mechanic who tells him, "First door that don't have a chicken in the window is his." The gas station was demolished and a parking lot now sits in its place.

9. TERENCE MANN'S APARTMENT
1735 Central Avenue, Dubuque, IA, 52001

The entrance to Terence Mann's apartment is the white door to the left of Jerry's Pawn & Jewelry. The interior of the apartment was filmed on a set built in a Dubuque warehouse.

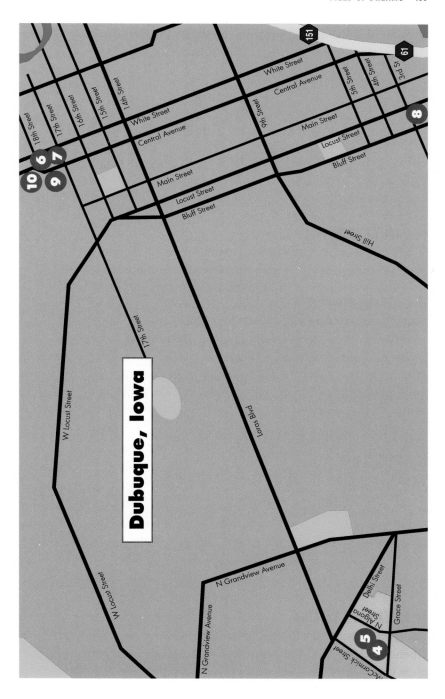

TAKE ME OUT TO THE BALLGAME

Ray brings author Terence Mann to Boston's Fenway Park, home of the Boston Red Sox since the stadium opened in 1912, to watch a baseball game. Both Ray and Terence see a message about Archibald "Moonlight" Graham (Burt Lancaster) on the scoreboard. Fenway Park was added to the National Register of Historic Places in 2012. To plan a visit, see http://boston.redsox .mlb.com/bos/ballpark/.

10. BANK OF BOSTON
Engine House Number 1, 20 West 18th Street, Dubuque, IA 52001

When Terence gets in the van, we see the Bank of Boston behind him.

11. CHISHOLM, MINNESOTA
Intersection of Main Street and Green Street, Galena, IL 61036

The quaint main street in the historic downtown district of Galena, roughly 12 miles southeast of Dubuque, doubles as Chisholm, Minnesota. Across the street sits the De Soto House, at one time the largest and most luxurious hotel west of the Mississippi. The phone booth no longer stands on the southeast corner. Terence instructs Ray to follow him east on Green Street.

12. BAR INTERIOR
Big Bill's Sandwich Shop, 301 North Main Street, Galena, IL 61036

Formerly the Logan House, this restaurant is home to the bar where Terence Mann interviews locals about Doc Graham.

13. MOTEL
Air Line Motel, 10784 Highway 61, Dubuque, IA 52003

Ray and Terence stay in this motel, supposedly in Chisholm, Minnesota.

14. PLAZA MOVIE THEATER
Country Crafts & Sports, 113 South Main Street, Galena, IL 61036

Opened in 1937, the Stanley Theatre, with its large, triangular neon marquee, closed in the late 1960s and remained shuttered until the filmmakers turned it into the Plaza for this movie.

15. NELSON'S BAKERY
Klein's Market Bakery, 118 South Main Street, Galena, IL 61036
In front of this bakery, Ray spots a car with a 1972 license plate.

16. DOC GRAHAM
101 South Main Street, Galena, IL 61036
On the northwest corner of South Main Street and Hill Street, Ray meets Dr. Graham. Together, they walk southwest along South Main Street.

17. WALKING IN THE MOONLIGHT
Intersection of South Bench Street and Green Street, Galena, IL 61036
From the bottom of Green Street, we see Ray and Doc Graham walking south along South Bench Street.

18. DOC GRAHAM'S OFFICE
Galena Chiropractic Center, 400 North Main Street, Galena, IL 61306
Ray and Doc Graham walk south along Meeker Street and turn left into this building.

19. THE HITCHHIKER
17030 US Highway 20 West, East Dubuque, IL 61025
Ray and Terence pick up a young Archie Graham and head west.

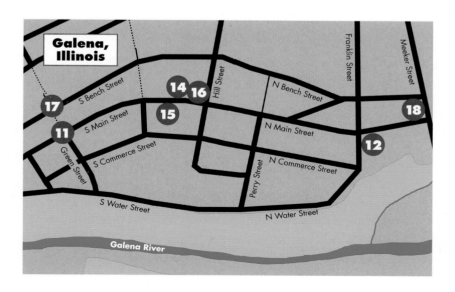

COMING ATTRACTIONS

THE GHOST PLAYERS

During the summer, a local baseball team called the Ghost Players, dressed in Chicago White Sox uniforms and composed of former semipro baseball players, play an interactive baseball game with visitors on Sunday afternoons on the Field of Dreams baseball field. The Ghost Players also play charity games against celebrity teams. For more information, visit www.ghostplayer.us.

COMING ATTRACTIONS

MAJOR LEAGUE

The three-day 25th anniversary celebration for *Field of Dreams*, held on Father's Day weekend in 2014, and attended by thousands of fans, featured Governor Terry Branstad, sportscaster Bob Costas, and actors Kevin Costner and Timothy Busfield. Events included celebrity softball games and musical performances from the Gin Blossoms, Joan Jett and the Blackhearts, and Costner's band, Modern West. Costner brought his wife and kids.

QUIET ON THE SET

THE MUSIC MAN

The 1962 movie *The Music Man*, starring Robert Preston and Shirley Jones, takes place in River City, Iowa, a fictional town based on Mason City, Iowa, the hometown of playwright Meredith Willson. Although the movie is set in Iowa, director Morton DaCosta filmed the movie on the Midwest Street backlot at the Warner Bros. Studio in Burbank, California.

However, Music Man Square in Mason City sits adjacent to Willson's boyhood home and contains a museum featuring costumes and other artifacts from the movie and the original Broadway play. For more information, visit www.themusicman square.org/

The Straight Story

In 1994, 73-year-old Alvin Straight, unable to drive a car due to his limited vision and lack of a driver's license, traveled on his John Deere lawn mower—from Laurens, Iowa, to Blue River, Wisconsin—to make peace with his dying 80-year-old brother, Henry. The 240-mile trip, at a top speed of 5 miles per hour, took Straight nearly six weeks and turned him into a folk hero.

Director David Lynch, whose movies include *Blue Velvet* and *The Elephant Man*, turned Straight's story into a movie starring 78-year-old actor Richard Farnsworth. Lynch filmed the 1999 movie starting in Laurens and continued his way across the state—in chronological order and on location along the actual route driven by the real Alvin Straight on his way to see his brother (renamed Lyle in the film). Along the way, Straight dispenses down-home wisdom to a runaway pregnant girl ("That bundle . . . that's family"), a group of young bicyclists ("The worst part of being old is rememberin' when you was young"), and a pair of bickering twin brothers who run an auto repair shop ("There's no one knows your life better than a brother that's near your age").

Wrote film critic Jonathan Crocker in the *Guardian*: "Filming the Midwest in its autumnal glory—wheat fields and sunsets, lightning and gentle rain—Lynch transforms a geriatric road trip into a gentle American parable that's quietly awestruck by life itself."

"Anger, vanity, you mix that together with liquor, you've got two brothers that haven't spoken in ten years," Alvin tells a priest. "Ah, whatever it was that made me and Lyle so mad don't matter anymore. I want to make peace, I want to sit with him, look up at the stars—like we used to do, so long ago."

1. THE LAURENS WATER TOWER

Intersection of Ralston Street and Alley Street, Laurens, IA 50554

We see a shot of the city's hallmark water tower, standing in the heart of "the Busiest Little Town in Iowa."

2. DOWNTOWN LAURENS

Intersection of West Main Street and North 3rd Street, Laurens, IA 50554

A tractor heads north on 3rd Street, and we see the Laurens water tower in the background.

3. ALVIN'S HOUSE
120 West Section Line Road, Laurens, IA 50554

"Listen to that old grain elevator," says Alvin Straight (Richard Farnsworth). The house, where he lives with his daughter, Rose (Sissy Spacek), was demolished and the property is now an empty lot. Dorothy's house remains standing next door to the east.

4. THE RESERVATION
117 North 3rd Street, Laurens, IA 50554

The downtown bar from which Bud (Joseph A. Carpenter) emerges, looking for Alvin.

5. ACE HARDWARE STORE
Fit Exercise Center, 110 South 3rd Street, Laurens, Iowa 50554

In this store, Alvin buys the grabber for "grabbin'."

6. ALVIN LEAVES TOWN
South 3rd Street, Laurens, IA 50554

Determined to see his brother, Lyle, Alvin drives his Rehds lawn mower south on North 3rd Street, passing the intersection of West Main Street.

7. JOHN DEERE DEALERSHIP
Lauren's Equipment, 12140 440th Street, Laurens, IA 50554

At this dealership, Alvin buys "a good machine" for $325.

8. THE GROTTO OF REDEMPTION

300 North Broadway Avenue, West Bend, IA 50597

In 1912, German American priest Paul Dobberstein began building the Grotto of the Redemption, and after his death in 1954, others continued the work. The site contains nine separate grottoes depicting different moments in the life of Jesus.

9. SOUTH 63, EAST 18

Intersection of North Line Avenue and West Milwaukee Street, New Hampton, IA 50659

Alvin heads south in the rain, encountering trucks and traffic.

10. BURNING BARN

Intersection of US 18 and Lakeview Drive, Clermont, IA 52135

At this intersection, Alvin, heading west, burns out his transmission. "You don't have brakes on that trailer, do ya?" asks Danny Reardon (John Cava).

11. THE REARDON HOUSE

Intersection of US 18 and Pine Street, Clermont, IA 52135

Alvin bivouacs in the yard and meets the bickering twin brothers. "There's no one knows your life better than a brother that's near your age. He knows who you are and what you are better than anyone on earth. My brother and I said some unforgivable things the last time we met, but, I'm trying to put that behind me . . . and this trip is a hard swallow of my pride. I just hope I'm not too late . . . a brother's a brother."

12. THE TRUCK RIDE

Intersection of Mill Street and Water Street, Clermont, IA 52135

Starting at Water Street, Verlyn Heller (Wiley Harker) drives Alvin northeast along Mill Street in his pickup truck.

13. LEAVING CLERMONT
Intersection of Mill Street and Clay Street, Clermont, IA 52135
Alvin drives his lawn mower north through Clermont.

14. THE BRIDGE
Black Hawk Bridge, Lansing, IA 52151
Alvin crosses the Mississippi River, heading southwest.

15. CEMETERY
Mount Zion Cemetery, County Road W (at Circle Drive), Mount Zion, WI 53805
Although the movie indicates the cemetery sits on a bluff above the Mississippi River, Alvin camps in a cemetery in Mount Zion (approximately 30 miles east of Iowa), where he has a heart-to-heart talk with a priest. "Well sir, I say amen to that," says the priest.

16. MT. ZION PUB
43499 County Road West, Boscobel, WI 53805
"I haven't had a drink in a lotta years, but now I'm gonna have me a cold beer," says Alvin.

17. COUNTY ROAD W
County Road W, Mount Zion, WI 53805
Alvin drives east along this road until his tractor putters to a halt.

18. LYLE STRAIGHT'S HOUSE
Remington Hill Road, Blue River, WI 53518
From the front porch, Alvin and Lyle look at the stars together. As for the location of the house, the bartender at the Mt. Zion Pub says, "Take W on down to Weed Road and then onto Remington Road. On your right will be Lyle's place."

Other Feature Attractions ─────────────────────────

THE STRAIGHT STORY TRACTOR
254 Mill Street, Clermont, IA 52135
See the 1966 John Deere lawn tractor used in the movie, complete with a small set of antlers, on display in the window of this small brown building. Seeing this replica helps you better appreciate the difficulty of Alvin Straight's extraordinary pilgrimage.

KANSAS

In Cold Blood

On a farmstead in Holcomb, Kansas, Herb Clutter built a two-story farm-house in 1948 for his family of six. On the night of November 14, 1959, two felons—Perry Smith and Richard Hickock—released on parole from Lansing Penitentiary, broke into the Clutters' home to rob the family. While in prison, Hickock had heard a rumor that Clutter kept $10,000 in a safe in his house. Clutter had no safe, nor did he keep any cash in his home. Enraged, Smith and Hickock killed Clutter, his wife, Bonnie, their daughter, Nancy, and son, Kenyon.

First published as a four-part serial in the *New Yorker* in 1965, Truman Capote's nonfiction novel *In Cold Blood* chronicles the crime and became a bestseller in 1966.

Adapting the book into the 1967 movie, director Richard Brooks shot the film in the actual locations where the crime occurred. Some citizens of Holcomb played themselves in the film.

"To the degree that *In Cold Blood* is an accurate, sensitive record of actual events, it succeeds overpoweringly," wrote film critic Roger Ebert in the *Chicago Sun-Times*. Others accused both Brooks and Capote of prof-iting from the misfortune of the innocent victims and stirring up maca-bre fascination with the tragic murders. In the *Lawrence Journal-World*, reporter Van Jensen says many citizens of Holcomb "want to stem the tide of visitors, the questions and interest in Holcomb's darkest chapter." He notes that *In Cold Blood* "fuels the lingering pain so many in Holcomb and Garden City feel."

The movie was nominated for four Academy Awards, and in 2008, the Library of Congress selected the film for preservation in the United States National Film Registry.

1. THE HICKOCK FAMILY HOME
207th Street and Spoon Creek Road, Edgerton, KS 66021
Richard Hickock (Scott Wilson) uses the outhouse.

2. TRAIN STATION HOLCOMB
Main Street, Holcomb, KS 67851
The sign and the small wooden train station are gone. Later in the movie, Smith (Robert Blake) and Hickock drive south along Main Street, racing a westbound train across the tracks.

3. RIVER VALLEY FARM
Private Residence, Oak Avenue, Holcomb, KS 67851
From the intersection of Old US 50 and North Main Street, drive south on Main Street, make a right onto Oak Avenue, and stop when you get to South West Street. Oak Street turns into a private, tree-lined dirt road that leads to the former Clutter family house. If you make a right turn onto South West Street and look to your left, you can see the house across the fields. Obey the "No Trespassing" signs posted on the lane to the former Clutter house. Please be respectful and do not loiter or disturb the residents.

4. BUS STATION
Union Bus Terminal, 942 McGee Street, Kansas City, MO 64106
Smith arrives at this bus terminal with his guitar and uses a payphone. The Pickwick Plaza complex, a former hotel and bus station, became an apartment complex.

5. EDGERTON
East Nelson Street and East 5th Avenue, Edgerton, KS 66021
Hickock drives west along East Nelson Street and crosses the railroad tracks.

6. RAY'S GAS STATION
5854 East Morgan Street, Edgerton, KS 66021
Hickock drives past this service station.

7. HOTEL OLATHE
Intersection of West Santa Fe Street and North Cherry Street, Olathe, KS 66061
The hotel, which stood on the northwest corner of this intersection, is long gone, along with all the buildings seen in the movie.

8. I-70 BRIDGE
I-70 Bridge over the Kansas River, Kansas City, MO 66118
Hickock and Smith drive across this bridge into Kansas and head south on I-70.

9. EMPORIA CITY LIMIT

Intersection of US 50 and North Peyton Street, Emporia, KS 66801

Hickock and Smith drive west along US 50.

10. HARDWARE STORE

Junque Drawer Emporium, 624 Commercial Street, Emporia, KS 66801

After Smith buys rope and Hickock steals a packet of razor blades, the two criminals drive the car north on Commercial Street. The building that housed the hardware store has been renovated.

11. PAWNEE ROCK

US 56 South and Centre Street, Pawnee Rock, KS 67567

Heading southwest on US 56, Hickock and Smith pass Santa Fe Mercantile.

12. HARTMAN'S CAFÉ

El Rancho Cafe, 305 North Main Street, Holcomb, KS 67851

Citizens of Holcomb dine and gossip is this down-home café, now a Mexican restaurant.

13. COURTHOUSE

Finney County Courthouse, 425 North 8th Street, Garden City, KS 67846

The investigators and police operate from this courthouse, where Hickock and Smith are put on trial for the murders.

14. GARDEN CITY CO-OP EQUITY GRANARY
Amtrak Station, 105 North 7th Street, Garden City, KS 67846

A hearse and police cars drive west alongside the train station and head south on US 83.

15. HOLCOMB POST OFFICE
137 North Main Street, Holcomb, KS 67846

The original building was destroyed and a modern building put in its place, which was used as the post office until a new one was built on the north side of town.

16. ELKO CAMERA STORE
719 Minnesota Avenue, Kansas City, KS 66101

The killers buy a movie camera at this store.

17. BRIDGE
Central Avenue Viaduct Bridge, Kansas City, KS 66118

The killers drive west over this two-level truss bridge built in 1918 and rebuilt in 1984.

18. THE RIVER
Arkansas River, River Road, Holcomb, KS 67851

Just south of Oak Avenue and the corner of Main Street, the police search the river for evidence.

19. PUBLIC LEVEE TERMINAL
1301 Fairfax Trafficway, Kansas City, KS 66115

After switching license plates by the railroad tracks, the killers head south on Fairfax Trafficway.

Other Feature Attractions

VALLEY VIEW CEMETERY
2901 North 3rd Street, Garden City, KS 67846

The four murdered members of the Clutter family lie in this cemetery, and nearby is the grave of Kansas Bureau of Investigation agent Alvin Dewey Jr., chief investigator of the killings.

Paper Moon

"I want my $200!"

Adapted from the bestselling novel *Addie Pray* by Joe David Brown, the 1973 movie *Paper Moon* follows swindler Moses "Moze" Pray (Ryan O'Neal) and precocious orphan Addie Loggins (O'Neal's real-life daughter Tatum) who, during the Great Depression, deliver embossed bibles to grieving widows. They claim each deceased husband ordered the good book but had yet to pay for it in full.

Although the novel takes place in the American South, director Peter Bogdanovich, persuaded by his then wife Polly Platt, moved the setting of *Paper Moon* to Kansas, whose flat and bare vistas conveyed the starkness of the Depression.

In 1964, Bogdanovich and Platt had driven from New York to California, and the vastness of the flat farmland across the Midwest made a lasting impression on them. "It was to the Midwest and to Hays in Kansas that they would return to shoot *Paper Moon*," wrote Andrew Yule in *Picture Shows: The Life and Films of Peter Bogdanovich*, "for not only was it a perfect setting for the film, but interior props such as furniture and exterior props like automobiles and farm implements were plentiful. None of them could have been duplicated in Hollywood with much authenticity."

Ten-year-old Tatum O'Neal won the Academy Award for Best Supporting Actress, becoming the youngest Oscar winner in history.

1. CEMETERY

Nickel Cemetery, Avenue E and Country Road 160, McCracken, KS 67556

Moze (Ryan O'Neal) shows up just in time for the funeral.

2. MAIN STREET

301 Main Street, McCracken, KS 67556

Moze and Addie (Tatum O'Neal) drive south on Main Street, from Locust Avenue to Maple Avenue. Most of the buildings are no longer standing. The filmmakers dressed the furniture store as the Dream Theater, showing the 1935 Will Rogers movie *Steamboat 'Round the Bend*.

3. SOUKUP GRAIN COMPANY

Avenue E, between Old US 40 and 26th Street, Wilson, KS 67490

Moze drives east on the dirt road alongside the granary, parking in front of the office to talk with Mr. Robertson (Noble Willingham).

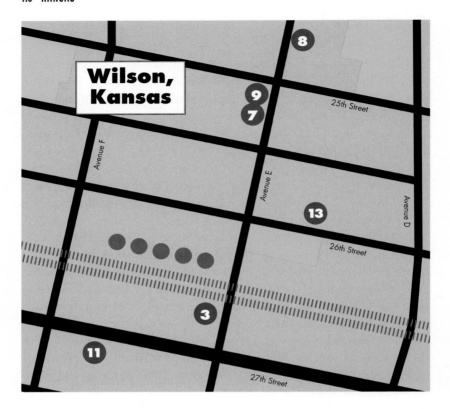

4. GAS STATION
Southeast corner of Main Street and East Maple Avenue, McCracken, KS 67556
The gas station, owned by Schuler and Dome Proprietors, has long since been demolished.

5. RAILWAY DEPOT
2nd Street, between Chicago Street and Clifford Street, Gorham, KS 67640
The train station where Moze sends a telegraph with "love, affection, and $20 cash" is gone, but the granary across from the station looks exactly the same as it does in the movie.

6. THE RESTAURANT
Main Street, between Maple Avenue and Beech Avenue, McCracken, KS 67556
"You want a Nehi and a Coney Island?" asks Moze. The restaurant, which stood on the east side of the street, across from the Dream Theatre, has been demolished. "I want my $200," insists Addie.

7. BARBER SHOP
2508 Avenue E, Wilson, KS 67490

"I ain't a boy!" insists Addie. She and Moze leave the barbershop, walk north along Avenue E, cross 25th Street, and cross the street to the General Merchandise store.

8. GENERAL MERCHANDISE EXTERIOR
Somer Hardware Co., 2411 Avenue E, Wilson, KS 67490

In this store, Moze buys a new dress for Addie.

9. GENERAL MERCHANDISE INTERIOR
Schermerhorn & Lang, 2504 Avenue E, Wilson, KS 67490

Addie cries for the $20 bill she got from her Aunt Helen in Wichita. The scene was shot inside this store. You can see the hardware store that provided the exterior out the window.

10. THE CARNIVAL
Rush County Fairgrounds, Main Street, LaCrosse, KS 67548

While Moze sees the Harem Slave for the umpteenth time, Addie gets her photo taken at the paper moon photo booth.

11. TRAVEL INN
Made from Scratch, 527 27th Street, Wilson, KS 67490

"This little baby has to go winky-tinky all the time," says Miss Trixie Delight (Madeline Kahn). Moze drives east on 27th Street and pulls into a gas station and diner that was torn down and is now occupied by a restaurant.

12. WHITE CLOUD HOTEL
Ozz & Ends Stuff Store, 130 Market Street, Gorham, KS 67640

Addie and Imogene (P. J. Johnson) sit on the steps of this building, and Moze and Miss Trixie drive west along Market Street, stopping across the street in front of the post office, now Wrangler Trading Post.

13. EXCHANGE HOTEL
Midland Railroad Hotel & Restaurant, 414 26th Street, Wilson, KS 67490

Built in 1899, this three-story limestone building with 28 elegant rooms was once considered one of the finest hotels in the Midwest. The hotel, where Addie and Imogene conspire against Miss Trixie, closed in 1978. Nearly 20 years later, the Wilson Foundation purchased and renovated the historic hotel, which reopened in 2003. A year earlier it became listed on the National Register of Historic Places. Still photographs from *Paper Moon* adorn the wall where the stairway leads up to the second floor.

14. THE MCCRACKEN HOTEL
Southwest corner of Main Street and Maple Avenue, McCracken, KS 67556

Moze makes a deal to sell crates of Three Feathers Whiskey to a bootlegger operating from this hotel, built in 1909. Once considered the finest hotel between Kansas City and Denver, the McCracken Hotel was demolished in 1988.

15. DONIPHAN COUNTY SHERIFF'S DEPT.
115 Main Street, White Cloud, KS 66094

When Moze and Addie flee the sheriff's office, they drive northeast on Main Street, and then make a left on Kansas 7, heading northwest along the Missouri River, then make a U-turn and head southeast.

16. BRIDGE
US 159 Bridge, Rulo, NE 68431

This truss bridge crossing the Missouri River from Rulo, Nebraska, to Holt County, Missouri, was demolished in 2014 after a new bridge was built just south of it. Built in 1939 by the Works Progress Administration and Kansas City Bridge Company, the original bridge was added to the National Register of Historic Places in 1993.

17. HOTEL ST. JO
Empty lot, 301 South 5th Street, St. Joseph, MO 64501

Addie sings "Let's Have Another Cup of Coffee" by Irving Berlin. After sitting empty for many years, the St. Charles Hotel on the southeast corner of 5th Street and Charles Street was torn down in 2010.

18. RUNNING
American Electric Company, 302 3rd Street, St. Joseph, MO 64501

Moze runs west along Jules Street.

19. ALLEY
240 Jules Street, St. Joseph, MO 64501

Moze runs along the railroad track in the alley on the north side of Jules Street and then jumps the railing onto another railroad track. The alley remains to this day, but the railroad tracks are gone.

20. EMPIRE TRUST COMPANY
The Missouri Valley Trust Building, 402 Felix Street, St. Joseph, MO 64501

Addie waits for Moze under the elaborate arched doorway of this building, constructed in 1859 to house the St. Joseph branch of the Bank of the State of Missouri.

21. THE ROAD
King Hill, Codell Avenue (north of Mendota Road), Plainville, KS 67663

Park at the top of the hill to admire the view where Moze and Addie drive off into the horizon. Unfortunately, a power line now juts across the road, and two trees now stand on opposite sides of the road.

Other Feature Attractions

THE MCCRACKEN HISTORICAL MUSEUM
200 Main Street, McCracken, KS 67556

Located in the former city jail, this museum displays numerous items on the history of McCracken and the filming of *Paper Moon*.

Picnic

The 1955 film adaptation of the Pulitzer Prize–winning Broadway play by Kansas native William Inge, *Picnic* tells the story of 24 hours in the life of a small Kansas town. Handsome drifter Hal Carter (William Holden) hops off a freight train in a small Kansas town during the Labor Day celebration to look up his old college roommate Alan (Cliff Robertson) in the hope of landing a job. At the town's picnic celebration, Hal ends up stealing Alan's fiancée Madge (Kim Novak), flirting with her underage sister (Susan Strasberg), and intoxicating a spinster schoolteacher (Rosalind Russell), upending the town's genteel manners.

The movie takes place in fictional Salinson, Kansas—a hybrid of the actual Kansas towns of Salina and Hutchinson. Director Joshua Logan, who won a Tony Award for directing the play, achieved the film's small-town authenticity by filming in several Kansas locales. "It's gotta look like Kansas," he reportedly yelled to his cast and crew, "and it will if I have to kill every last one of ya!" Hailstorms and tornado warnings interrupted filming almost daily, and the cast and crew constantly complained of being "half-consumed" by insects.

To curtail the play's frank sexual content, the studio forced William Holden, who spends much of the film topless, to shave his chest, and the filmmakers cut any insinuation that Hal and Madge sleep together after the picnic.

Picnic earned an estimated $6.3 million, garnered two Academy Awards, and turned Kim Novak into a star. It provides a richly detailed Norman Rockwell portrait of a typical Labor Day picnic in the Midwest in the 1950s.

1. THE TRAIN TRACKS
275 East Iron Avenue, Salina, KS 67401

Hal Carter (William Holden) arrives in Kansas after bumming a ride on a freight train, washes in the waterfall in the Smoky Hill River, and walks north along the train tracks. The grain tower painted "Salina Seed Co." burned down.

2. MRS. POTT'S HOUSE
Private Residence, 207 South Nickerson Street (Highway 96), Nickerson, KS 67561

Hal strolls west along the alley behind this house and into the backyard of Mrs. Potts (Verna Felton). Please be respectful and do not loiter or disturb the residents.

3. THE OWENS FAMILY HOUSE

Private Residence, 211 South Nickerson Street (Highway 96), Nickerson, KS 67561

Next door to Mrs. Potts lives the Owens family: Flo (Betty Field), Madge (Kim Novak), and Millie (Susan Strasberg), and schoolteacher Rosemary Sydney (Rosalind Russell). The house no longer has a porch railing or a porch swing. Please be respectful and do not loiter or disturb the residents.

4. THE BENSON MANSION

Private Residence, 456 East Country Club Road, Salina, KS 67401

At this estate facing the Salina Country Club golf course, Hal meets Alan Benson (Cliff Robertson) and his father (Raymond Bailey). Later, when Hal attempts to return Alan's car, he winds up fleeing from the police. The interiors of the home were filmed on a soundstage in Hollywood. Please be respectful and do not loiter or disturb the residents.

5. GRANARY

Cargill Grain, 309 North Halstead Street, Hutchinson, KS 67501

At this towering granary owned by the Benson family, Hal and Alan ride a grain elevator to the top of the building for a sweeping panoramic view of Hutchinson.

6. THE LAKE

Sterling Park, Sterling, KS 67579

At the local swimming hole, Hal jumps off the diving board, Alan kisses Madge under a tree, and the couples change clothes in the bathhouse. The wooden dock is no longer there, and the park now includes a municipal swimming pool.

7. DRIVING TO THE PICNIC

Crescent Boulevard, Hutchinson, KS 67502

Howard Bevans (Arthur O'Connell) and Rosemary Sydney drive to the picnic along this hidden street so they can each take a sip of whiskey.

8. RIVERSIDE PARK

Main Street and K-89, Halstead, KS 67056

The annual Labor Day picnic and the sensuous "Moonglow" dance with Hal and Marge take place at this park where a pedestrian suspension bridge spans the Little Arkansas River. The picnic games are played in the ballpark across the suspension bridge. The spot where the Owens party picnics is now a pile of rocks. The filmmakers built a bandstand and dance floor, a set of stairs, and a second dock across the river to accommodate the swan boat and the arrival of the Queen of Neewollah and her acceptance speech. A plaque at the entrance to Riverside Park reads, "The 1955 movie *Picnic* was filmed here."

9. THE TRAIN TRACKS
275 East Iron Avenue, Salina, KS 67401

Hal drives Madge back to this spot, where he goes down to the Smoky Hill River to wash beneath the waterfall. The couple shares their first kiss, embracing as the train passes by. Later, Hal, running from the police, hides under the waterfall and tumbles into the river.

10. RENO COMMUNITY HIGH SCHOOL
Nickerson High, 305 South Nickerson Street, Nickerson, KS 67561

As Howard drives, Rosemary Sydney waves good-bye to the school where she taught, located directly across the street from the Owenses' house.

11. TRAIN TRACKS
Intersection of West Avenue G and South Peabody Street, Nickerson, KS 67561

After running up the alley from the Owenses' house, Hal hops a freight train headed northwest to get a job as a bellboy in Tulsa, Oklahoma. The train tracks that ran along what is now West Avenue G have been removed and replaced with an asphalt road.

MICHIGAN

Anatomy of a Murder

In 1952, Army lieutenant Coleman Peterson walked into the Lumberjack Tavern in Big Bay, Michigan, and fired six shots into the owner, bartender Maurice "Mike" Chenoweth. Peterson committed the murder after his wife, Charlotte Anne, came home crying and beaten, insisting that Chenoweth had raped her. At the trial, defense attorney John Voelker argued that an "irresistible impulse" had possessed Peterson, and the jury found Peterson not guilty by reason of temporary insanity.

In 1956, Voelker, using the pen name Robert Traver, published a fictional novel titled *Anatomy of a Murder*, whose plot mirrored the Peterson case. When the novel became a bestseller, director Otto Preminger decided to film the movie version almost entirely on location in Michigan's Upper Peninsula. "Our presence created great excitement in those little towns," recalled Preminger in his autobiography. "The special train carrying cast, crew, and equipment arrived at six-thirty on a March day, but half the population was at the station to greet us."

Over the next few months, actors Jimmy Stewart, Lee Remick, Eve Arden, George C. Scott, and Ben Gazzara attended a ski tournament at Suicide Hill and dined in local restaurants. Duke Ellington, who wrote part of the movie score at the piano in the lounge in Ishpeming's Mather Inn, accepted an invitation to perform at the annual spring dinner-dance of the Delta Sigma Nu Sorority at Northern Michigan University.

Offended by the graphic discussion of sex and rape during the trial in the film (and the use of such salacious words as *contraceptive*, *sexual climax*, and *panties*), Chicago mayor Richard J. Daley banned the movie—until Preminger filed a motion in federal court in Illinois and the judge overturned the mayor's decision. *Anatomy of a Murder* became one of the biggest box office hits of 1959, winning seven Oscar nominations.

1. CLIFFS SHAFT MINE MUSEUM

501 West Euclid Street, Ishpeming, MI 49849

Paul Biegler (Jimmy Stewart) drives south along Lake Shore Drive and makes a left turn, heading east along West Euclid Street, passing the Cliff Shafts Mine Museum on his right.

The Cliffs Shaft Mine Museum, listed on the National Register of Historic Places in 1992, celebrates the history of the Marquette Iron Range, features displays on the history of mining, exhibits more than 500 minerals, and offers a guided tour of the tunnels that the miners walked to the base of the C-Shaft. See old underground iron ore cars, visit the blacksmith shop, and stand inside the 30-ton shovel bucket. Open June through September, Tuesdays through Saturdays, 10 AM to 4 PM, for a nominal admission fee. For more information, visit www.michigan.org/property/cliffs-shaft-mine-museum/.

2. PENINSULA BANK

100 South Main Street, Ishpeming, MI 49849

Paul Biegler drives east along Cleveland Avenue, passing this bank on his right.

3. J. C. PENNEY COMPANY

Intersection of South Main Street and Cleveland Avenue, Ishpeming, MI, 49849

Biegler makes a left turn on Main Street, heading north, passing the J. C. Penney on the southeast corner of the intersection.

4. THE BAR

Jack's Tee Pee Bar, 108 South Main Street, Ishpeming, MI 49849

Biegler makes a right turn on Bank Street, passing a bar on the northeast corner, where Parnell McCarthy (Arthur O'Connell) is having one last drink for the road.

5. PAUL BIEGLER'S HOUSE

205 West Barnum Street, Ishpeming, MI 49849

Heading north on Pine Street, Biegler turns left on West Barnum Street, and parks in front of his house, where he lives with his law books.

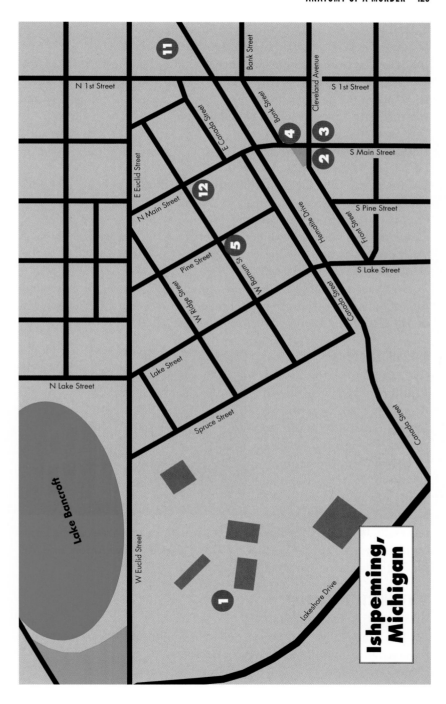

Ishpeming, Michigan

6. THE JAIL
Department of Human Services, 234 West Baraga Avenue, Marquette, MI 49855

In the driveway on the right side of this building, Paul meets Laura Manion (Lee Remick) and her dog Muff. Inside he visits Frederick Manion (Ben Gazzara). The stone building seen in the movie was demolished and replaced with a modern office building.

7. MARQUETTE COUNTY COURTHOUSE
234 West Baraga Avenue, Marquette, MI 49855

Biegler meets with officials in this stately courthouse, built in 1904, with views of the city and Lake Superior. The trial takes place on the second floor in the courtroom. In the movie, Joseph N. Welch played the role of Judge Weaver. Welch, the chief counsel for the US Army during the televised Un-American Activities hearings, asked Senator Joseph McCarthy, "Have you no sense of decency, sir?"

A display in the lobby features photographs of courtroom scenes being filmed and a section devoted to John Voelker. The courthouse was listed on the National Register of Historic Places in 1978.

8. THUNDER BAY INN
400 Bensinger Street, Big Bay, MI 49808

Biegler drives north on Bensinger Street, passing St. Mary's Catholic Church, to this lakeside inn, once owned by Henry Ford. The filmmakers built the annex on the south side of the inn for the bar where Manion killed Barney Quill. In real life, the murder took place down the street at the Lumberjack Tavern. Paul has lunch with Maida Rutledge (Eve Arden) and Mr. McCarthy in the hotel restaurant.

9. MT. SHASTA RESTAURANT
1915 US Highway 41, Michigamme, MI 49861

Pie-Eye (Duke Ellington) plays a piano duet with Paul Biegler while customers dance. Ellington wrote the movie score.

10. LAURA'S TRAILER
Perkins Park Campground, County Road 550, Big Bay, MI 49808

Biegler visits Laura in the actual trailer where the Petersons lived. In the movie, the name Peterson can be seen on the trailer door.

11. ISHPEMING TRAIN STATION
Bell Forest Products, 200 Hematite Drive, Ishpeming, MI 49849

The Ishpeming Railway Depot, which stood at this address and where Mr. McCarthy greets Dr. Smith (Orson Bean), was relocated away from downtown. The railroad tracks were removed, and the station was torn down. The train that pulls into the station in the movie was Chicago & North Western Railway's Iron Country Express, an overnight train to and from Chicago.

12. ISHPEMING CARNEGIE LIBRARY
317 North Main Street, Ishpeming, MI 49849

In this library where Paul Biegler does his legal research, John Voelker did his legal research.

Other Feature Attractions

THE LUMBERJACK TAVERN
202 Bensinger Street, Big Bay, MI 49808

In this tavern, Peterson killed Chenoweth, inadvertently inspiring Voelker to pen the novel and Preminger to make the movie. The rustic tavern advertises the movie logo on the front of the  building and keeps another movie logo adhered to the floor on the spot where Chenoweth died. The tavern occasionally stages reenactments of the murder, and tourists frequently ask to have their photographs taken while lying on the spot. Display cases feature photographs, scrapbooks, newspaper clippings, and the coroner's slab. The tavern, which advertises itself as "Murder Free since 1952," sells "Home of *Anatomy of a Murder*" shot glasses.

MATHER INN
107 East Canda Street, Ishpeming, MI 49849

Upon arriving in Ishpeming, the cast met with the press at a noon cocktail reception and lunched with then–Michigan governor G. Mennen Williams. They stayed here during the filming of the movie in Ishpeming, and Duke Ellington, who won a Grammy for the movie soundtrack, composed some of the music at the piano in the pub. At night, Jimmy Stewart and Otto Preminger frequently joined him at the piano.

CONGRESS LOUNGE AND PIZZA
106 Main Street, Ishpeming, MI 49849

In this pizza restaurant, photographs of the movie cast cover the walls.

LANDMARK INN
230 North Front Street, Marquette, MI 49855

This elegantly restored hotel, known in 1959 as the Northland Hotel, housed the cast and crew during the filming of the courtroom scenes.

GLOBE PRINTING
200 West Division Street, Ishpeming, MI 49849

In 1959, this building housed the Roosevelt Supper Club, where the cast of the movie frequently dined. All of the cast members autographed a downstairs wall one night, and Globe Printings has dutifully maintained the wall.

THE MICHIGAMME MUSEUM
110 West Main Street, Michigamme, MI 49861

The museum features a John Voelker display, photos from the filming, and life-size replicas of the stars.

THE MARQUETTE COUNTY HISTORICAL SOCIETY MUSEUM
145 West Spring Street, Marquette, MI 49855

The museum holds John Voelker's scrapbooks.

NORTHERN MICHIGAN UNIVERSITY
Lydia M. Olson Library, 1401 Presque Isle Avenue, Marquette, MI 49855

The university archives hold many of Voelker's personal papers and other curious artifacts.

8 Mile

8 Mile Road, running east and west along the northern city limit of Detroit, creates a dividing line between the city to the south and more affluent suburbs to the north. The predominately lower-middle-class, African American neighborhood was home to controversial rapper Eminem during his formative years.

In the semibiographical 2002 movie *8 Mile*, filmed in the 8 Mile area, Eminem stars as a young white rapper named Jimmy "B-Rabbit" Smith Jr., determined to launch his career as a freestyle rap singer. The movie, filmed entirely on location, captures the gritty world of the impoverished lifestyle of a white trash kid living in a trailer park, working in a dead-end factory job, and striving to make a name for himself in Detroit's black hip-hop scene.

"One of a handful of films made in Detroit, *8 Mile* doesn't feature the Motown renaissance that Mayor Coleman A. Young dreamed of in the 1970s," wrote film critic Elvis Mitchell in the *New York Times*. "Instead it's the beaten-down city."

The movie, a squalid fusion of *Purple Rain* and *Rocky*, grossed more than $242 million worldwide, and Eminem won the Academy Award for Best Original Song for "Lose Yourself."

1. SHELTER BACKSTAGE
1120 Griswold Street, Detroit, MI 48226

The filmmakers used an abandoned Rite Aid store to create the backstage area of the Shelter, the club where B-Rabbit (Eminem) competes in several rap battles.

2. SHELTER INTERIOR
240 Chene Street, Detroit, MI 48207

The filmmakers re-created the Shelter, where Eminem started his rap career, in this warehouse. The real Shelter is located in the basement beneath St. Andrew's Hall (see "Other Feature Attractions," page 132).

3. SHELTER EXTERIOR
Downtown Louie's Lounge, 30 Clifford Street, Detroit, MI 48226

The filmmakers dressed up this building, now a restaurant, to provide the exterior of the club.

4. 8 MILE ROAD MOBILE COURT
A&L Mobile Home Park, 20785 Schultes Avenue, Warren, MI 48091

In this trailer park, Rabbit moves back in with his erratic and negligent mother (Kim Basinger) after splitting up with his girlfriend.

5. BUS STOP
Northwest corner of 8 Mile Road and Schultes Avenue, Warren, MI 48091

On this corner, Rabbit catches the bus to work, jotting down lyrics, inspired by the views of inner-city blight.

6. 19TH HOLE PENTHOUSE GOLF CLUB
Intersection of Garfield and Chene, Detroit, MI 48207

This abandoned club on the southwest corner of this intersection was demolished in 2007.

7. STAMPING PLANT
New Center Stamping Plant, 950 East Milwaukee Street, Detroit, MI 48211

Rabbit works as a press punch operator, making "crash parts."

8. COW HEAD
Abandoned ice cream shop, 13099 Mack Avenue, Detroit, MI 48215

Rabbit and his posse, Three One Third (named after the area code 313), use a paintball gun to shoot this giant cow head.

9. WHITE SUN CHOP SUEY
14521 East Jefferson Avenue, Detroit, MI 48215

As Rabbit and his crew drive west along Jefferson Avenue, they pass this iconic sign painted on a brick wall, which has since deteriorated, and shoot a paintball pellet at the adjacent liquor store.

10. JEFFERSON GROCERIES
14515 East Jefferson Avenue, Detroit, MI 48215
The grocery store was demolished and the site is now an empty lot.

11. HIDING FROM THE POLICE
14201 East Jefferson Avenue, Detroit, MI 48215
Driving west on East Jefferson Avenue, Rabbit makes a right turn on Newport Street, coming to a stop next to this building.

12. PARKING GARAGE
Michigan Building, 200 Bagley Street, Detroit, MI 48226
Three One Third face off against rival rappers the Free World in this parking garage with an ornate ceiling. Built in 1926, the extravagant 4,038-seat Michigan Theatre, designed in the French Renaissance style, became a movie theater in the 1940s, a nightclub in 1972, a concert venue in 1973, and closed for good in 1976. The following year, the owners gutted the building, leaving the ceiling intact, and built a three-level parking garage inside it.

13. CHIN TIKI CLUB
2121 Cass Street, Detroit, MI 48201
Rabbit and his crew hang out at this club, popular in the 1950s and '60s. The filmmakers revived this former Polynesian restaurant, vacant for nearly twenty years. It has since been demolished.

14. BURNING HOUSE
122 Beresford Street, Highland Park, MI 48203
On this empty lot stood the abandoned house that Rabbit and his friends set on fire.

15. EMPTY LOT
Intersection of Grand River Avenue and Quincy Street, Detroit, MI 48204
While driving west along Grand River Avenue through Petosky-Otsego, Rabbit spots Free World at this intersection. He makes a U-turn, parks his car in front of Cheddar Cadillac Body Service at 8461 Grand River Avenue, walks diagonally across the intersection to the empty lot in front of Leon's Repair Shop at 8505 Quincy Street, and picks a fight with the rival rappers. Cheddar Bob (Evan Jones) winds up shooting himself in the leg.

16. HOSPITAL
Intersection of Gratiot Avenue and McDougall Street, Detroit, MI 48207
As the crew drives wounded Cheddar Bob to the hospital, Rabbit yells, "Take Gratiot to McDougall!"

17. CHEDDAR BOB'S HOUSE
1250 McClellan Street, English Village, MI 48214
To check up on Cheddar Bob after the accident, Rabbit walks between the houses to go around back and enter through the back door.

18. INTERMEZZO
Detroit Seafood Market, 1435 Randolph Street, Detroit, MI 48226
At this restaurant, Rabbit's girlfriend Alex (Brittany Murphy) waits tables.

19. WJLB RADIO STATION
Penobscot Building, 645 Griswold Street, Detroit, MI 48226
Rabbit take the elevator to the 28th floor of the landmark 1928 art deco Penobscot Building to meet with Wink Harris (Eugene Byrd).

20. JANEANE'S APARTMENT
711 West Alexandrine Street, Detroit, MI 48201
The Plaza Liquor Shoppe across the street on 3rd Avenue has been demolished. Rabbit parks on West Alexandrine Street and stares through the apartment window.

Other Feature Attractions

EMINEM'S CHILDHOOD HOME
19946 Dresden Street, Detroit, MI 48205
The house where Eminem grew up, featured on the cover of Eminem's 2000 *Marshall Mathers* album and its sequel, was demolished by the State of Michigan in 2013.

THE SHELTER
St. Andrew's Hall, 431 East Congress Street, Detroit, MI 48226
Eminem got his start as a rap artist in this music venue in the basement of St. Andrews Hall, the former meeting place for the St. Andrew's Society of Detroit.

MINNESOTA

Fargo

Struggling car salesman Jerry Lundegaard (William H. Macy) hires two criminals—Gaear Grimsrud (Peter Stormare) and Carl Showalter (Steve Buscemi)—to kidnap his wife, Jean (Kristin Rudrüd), and ransom her for $80,000 from his wealthy father-in-law, Wade Gustafson (Harve Presnell). During the kidnapping, the criminals shoot a state trooper and two witnesses, prompting pregnant Minnesota police chief Marge Gunderson (Frances McDormand) to investigate the roadside killings.

Inspired by the 1986 murder of Helle Crafts, a Danish flight attendant killed by her husband, who disposed of her body through a wood chipper, brothers Joel and Ethan Coen used elements from other Minnesota cases to create their macabre story. The Coen brothers originally planned to shoot *Fargo* around Brainerd, Minnesota, but a mild winter forced the filmmakers to move production further north toward North Dakota for snow scenes. Despite its title, none of the 1996 movie was filmed in Fargo, North Dakota.

Fargo was nominated for five Academy Awards. Frances McDormand won the Academy Award for Best Actress, and Joel and Ethan Coen won the Academy Award for Best Original Screenplay. In 2006, the Library of Congress selected *Fargo* for preservation in the United States National Film Registry, doncha know.

1. THE KING OF CLUBS
Parking Lot, 957 Central Avenue NE, Minneapolis, MN 55413

The bar where car salesman Jerry Lundegaard (William H. Macy) meets with Carl Showalter (Steve Buscemi) and Gaear Grimsrud (Peter Stormare) to arrange the kidnapping of his wife has been demolished and replaced by a parking lot for an apartment building.

2. THE LUNDEGAARD HOUSE EXTERIOR
Private Residence, 6358 Edgemont North Circle, Minneapolis, MN 55428

Jerry and Jean (Kristin Rudrüd) live in this suburban home. Please be respectful and do not loiter or disturb the residents.

3. GUSTAFSON MOTORS
Best Buy Corporate Campus, 7601 Penn Avenue South, Richfield, MN 55423

The car dealership where Jerry works as a salesman for his father-in-law, Wade Gustafson (Harve Presnell), was Wally McCarthy Oldsmobile, now the location of corporate headquarters of Best Buy.

4. WELCOME TO BRAINERD STATUE OF PAUL BUNYAN
Pembina County Highway 1, four miles west of Bathgate, ND 58216

The filmmakers built a statue of Paul Bunyan, the legendary giant lumberjack accompanied by Babe the Blue Ox, specifically for the movie and planted it on this spot. After filming, the production team removed the faux statue.

5. BLUE OX
Stockmen's Truck Stop, 501 Farwell Avenue, South St. Paul, MN 55075

In a motel room at this popular truck stop, the two kidnappers engage two prostitutes and watch *The Tonight Show*.

6. ENTERING MINNEAPOLIS
MN-65 at East 15th Street overpass, Minneapolis, MN 55404

As the killers drive north along MN-65, Carl tries to engage Gaear in conversation. "'No.' That's the first thing you've said in the last four hours. That's a . . . that's a fountain of conversation, man. That's a geyser."

7. EMBER'S RESTAURANT
7527 Wayzata Boulevard, St. Louis Park, MN 55426

This restaurant overlooking Interstate 394, where Jerry and Wade discuss how to pay the ransom for Jean, was demolished and is now the parking lot of DaVita Dialysis.

8. THE CABIN
Square Lake, May Township, MN 55082

The yellow cabin where the kidnappers hold Jean and use a woodchipper was sold and relocated.

9. BRAINERD POLICE STATION
Edina Police Station, 4801 West 50th Street, Edina, MN 55424

The police station, completely renovated, no longer looks the way it did in the movie.

10. LAKESIDE CLUB
10 Old Wildwood Road, Mahtomedi, MN 55115

Marge interviews the two prostitutes about their clients at this family-owned steak restaurant.

11. THE RADISSON HOTEL
35 South Seventh Street, Minneapolis, MN 55402

Marge stays at this hotel and meets her old friend Mike Yanagita (Steve Park) in the hotel bar. "You were such a super lady."

12. AIRPORT PARKING LOT
Minneapolis–St. Paul International Airport, Minneapolis, MN 55450

Carl steals a license plate from a car on the roof of the short-term parking garage, stopping to argue over the $4 parking fee.

13. CARLTON CELEBRITY ROOM
Chanhassen Dinner Theatre, 501 West 78th Street, Chanhassen, MN 55317

Carl brings a prostitute to the Carlton Celebrity Room to see José Feliciano perform. The popular dinner theater, located at 8350 24th Avenue South in Bloomington, Minnesota, closed in 1986, and was demolished to make way for a highway interchange. The filmmakers staged this scene at the Chanhassen Dinner Theatre.

14. RADISSON HOTEL ROOF
Minneapolis Club Parking Garage, 261 South 8th Street, Minneapolis, MN 55402

Wade Gustafson brings the ransom money to the roof of this parking garage and confronts Carl.

15. MR. MOHRA'S HOUSE
Private Residence, southwest corner of 3rd Street South and Bryan Avenue, Hallock, MN 56728

Beneath a grain elevator, Mr. Mohra (Bain Boehlke) tells Officer Olson (Cliff Rakerd) about an odd customer he had at the bar. Please be respectful and do not loiter or disturb the residents.

16. MOTEL OUTSIDE OF BISMARCK, NORTH DAKOTA
Hitching Post Motel, 23855 Forest Boulevard North, Forest Lake, MN 55025

In room 7 of this motel, the police apprehend Jerry.

Other Feature Attractions

FARGO-MOORHEAD VISITORS CENTER
2001 44th Street South, Fargo, ND 58103

Although none of the movie *Fargo* was filmed in Fargo, at the visitors' center you can visit the actual woodchipper used in the movie, pose for a photograph with a replica of the woodchipper and a fake leg, and see copies of the script and memorabilia from the film. For more information, visit www.fargomoorhead.org.

Grumpy Old Men

MAX GOLDMAN: G'morning, dickhead.

JOHN GUSTAFSON: Hello, moron.

In the 1993 movie *Grumpy Old Men*, divorcé John Gustafson (Jack Lemmon) and widower Max Goldman (Walter Matthau) have been feuding next-door neighbors for fifty years, but their hostile relationship escalates to new heights when shapely and vivacious widow Ariel Truax (Ann-Margret) moves into the house across the street.

"The two are neighbors in Wabasha, Minnesota," explained film critic Ty Burr in *Entertainment Weekly*, "a wintry burg where a man can pass the whole day without saying much more than 'I need a six-pack of Schmidt and a can of bait,' and where the arrival of a new neighbor is an earth-shattering development."

Screenwriter Mark Steven Johnson, a native of Hastings, Minnesota, based the screenplay for *Grumpy Old Men* on characters he met while visiting his grandfather, an avid fisherman who lived in Wabasha and frequented Slippery's, a local bait shop and tavern. Johnson modeled many of the characters after patrons of Slippery's. He modeled free-spirited Ariel Truax after Vivian Fusillo, a beloved theater professor at Winona State University.

Director Donald Petrie chose to shoot the film in Faribault, Rockford, and St. Paul, Minnesota, to capture the essence of a small Minnesota town. He shot most of the interior scenes on a soundstage at Paisley Park Studios, owned by Prince, in Chanhassen, Minnesota.

Film critic Roger Ebert in the *Chicago Sun-Times* wrote, "Matthau and Lemmon are fun to see together, if for no other reason than just for the essence of their beings."

1. THE FROZEN LAKE

Lake Rebecca Park Reserve, 9831 Rebecca Park Trail, Rockford, MN 55373

Composed of gently rolling Big Woods landscapes and numerous wetland areas, Lake Rebecca Park Reserve is a haven for wildlife and part of the Three Rivers Park District Trumpeter Swan restoration program. The filmmakers modeled the Muskie-Ville ice-fishing shanty village on the lake after the winter villages that spring up on Mille Lac Lake, approximately 100 miles north of Minneapolis.

2. THE WABASHA RAILROAD DEPOT

Depot Bar and Grille, 311 Heritage Place, Faribault, MN 55021

With the old Milwaukee Road train depot in Wabasha gone, the filmmakers dressed the Rock Island depot in Faribault as the Wabasha depot. The depot was listed on the National Register of Historic Places in 1982.

3. DOWNTOWN WABASHA

2nd Street NW and 1st Avenue NE, Faribault, MN 55021

Looking west on 2nd Street, we see the Coca-Cola sign on the wall of the building at 24 2nd Street NE.

4. CHURCH

Chisago Lake Evangelical Lutheran Church, 1 Summit Avenue, Center City, MN 55012

John and Ariel get married in this church, built by Swedish Lutherans in 1889.

5. JOHN GUSTAFSON'S HOUSE

Private Residence, 1133 Hyacinth Avenue East, St. Paul, MN 55106

Here John Gustafson (Jack Lemmon) lives with his father, Pops (Burgess Meredith). Please be respectful and do not loiter or disturb the residents.

6. MAX GOLDMAN'S HOUSE

Private Residence, 1137 Hyacinth Avenue East, St. Paul, MN 55106

In the house right next door to John Gustafson lives Max Goldman (Walter Matthau). Please be respectful and do not loiter or disturb the residents.

7. ARIEL TRUAX'S HOUSE

Private Residence, 1122 Hyacinth Avenue East, St. Paul, MN 55106

On the corner of Hyacinth Avenue and Frank Street, across the street from the Goldman house, sits the home of Ariel Truax (Ann-Margret). Ariel drives her snowmobile up the hill to her home and installs a sauna on the east side of the house. Please be respectful and do not loiter or disturb the residents.

8. CHUCK'S BAIT SHOP EXTERIOR
Lake Rebecca Park Reserve, 9831 Rebecca Park Trail, Rockford, MN 55373

At the end of Foxglove Street North sits Chuck's Bait Shop, where John Gustafson and Max Goldman habitually crash into the trashcans. The filmmakers modeled this shop after Slippery's, a local bait shop and tavern (see "Other Feature Attractions," page 140).

9. DRUG STORE
Pawn Minnesota, 230 Central Avenue North, Faribault, MN 55021

John walks across Central Avenue and into this store, then the Poirier Pharmacy with a soda fountain, where Max says, "When I had my ulcers, I was farting razor blades."

10. SNOWMOBILING AND SNOW ANGELS
Memorial Park, Skyline Drive, Red Wing, MN 55066

John and Ariel ride a snowmobile through the field at the top of the bluff and then make snow angels. "There she is," announces John from the lookout point at the northwest end of Skyline Drive. "Wabasha!" Dedicated to soldiers and sailors from all wars, Memorial Park is specially dedicated to the sailors who lost their lives when the USS *Maine* exploded in Cuba, sparking the Spanish-American War.

11. SLIPPERY'S BAR INTERIOR
Half Time Rec Bar, 1013 Front Avenue, St. Paul, MN 55103

Although the real Slippery's is located in Wabasha (see "Other Feature Attractions," below), the filmmakers shot the interior Slippery's scenes at this Irish bar in St. Paul.

12. HOSPITAL
Cerenity Care Center, 724 19th Avenue North, South St. Paul, MN 55075

John recovers from his heart attack at Divine Redeemer Memorial Hospital in South St. Paul, which closed in 1994. This building now operates as a nursing home.

Other Feature Attractions

SLIPPERY'S BAR AND GRILL
10 Church Avenue, Wabasha, MN 55981

The genuine Slippery's bar and grill plays *Grumpy Old Men* and *Grumpier Old Men* on a loop daily, features a display of movie memorabilia, and sponsors the annual Grumpy Old Men Festival. The Ice Shanty sits in Slippery's Gift Shop. For more information, visit www.slipperys.com.

WABASHA-KELLOGG TOURIST INFORMATION OFFICE
137 Main Street West, Wabasha, MN 55981

This tourist office provides free Historic Walking Tour maps of Wabasha and features a fireplace from one of the *Grumpy Old Men* sets.

COMING ATTRACTIONS

GRUMPY OLD MEN FESTIVAL

On the last Saturday of February each year, Wabasha celebrates the Grumpy Old Men Festival, featuring ice fishing, the Grumpy Plunge (into an ice hole), winter baseball, ice-bike racing, a pet show, and minnow races. For more information, visit www.wabashamn.org/grumpyoldmenfest/events/.

The Mighty Ducks

When cutthroat lawyer Gordon Bombay (Emilio Estevez) gets arrested for drunk driving and is charged with reckless endangerment, the judge sentences him to coach a hockey team of troubled kids. Gordon gradually abandons his win-at-any-cost attitude, rekindles his own love of hockey, and adopts an it's-how-you-play-the-game philosophy. "You may make it, you may not," he says. "But that doesn't matter, Charlie. What matters is that we're here."

Director Stephen Herek shot the 1992 Disney movie *The Mighty Ducks* entirely on location in the Minneapolis area to showcase the city and its hockey lovers. "*The Mighty Ducks* is the kind of movie that might have been written by a computer program," wrote film critic Roger Ebert in the *Chicago Sun-Times*. In the *Washington Post*, film critic Rita Kempley said screenwriter Steven Brill "constructed the screenplay much as one would put together some of those particleboard bookcases from Ikea."

"The duck is one of the most noble, agile, and intelligent creatures in the animal kingdom," says Gordon, telling his Pee Wee team why they've been renamed the Ducks. "Have you guys ever seen a flock of ducks flying in perfect formation? It's beautiful. Pretty awesome the way they all stick together. Ducks never say die. Ever seen a duck fight? No way. Why? Because the other animals are afraid. They know that if they mess with one duck, they gotta deal with the whole flock. I'm proud to be a Duck, and I'd be proud to fly with any one of you. So how about it? Who's a Duck?"

The Mighty Ducks grossed more than $50 million in the United States, inspiring two sequels and an animated television series. In 1993, the Walt Disney Company formed an Anaheim-based pro hockey team called the Anaheim Ducks.

1. COURTROOM
Stearns County Courthouse, 725 Courthouse Square, St. Cloud, MN 56303

In the courtroom, Gordon Bombay (Emilio Estevez) wins a case, which he discusses afterward on the stairs in the lobby. The filmmakers added small, black circles resembling hockey pucks near the ceiling architecture, which remain in place to this day.

2. DUCKWORTH'S OFFICE
IDS Center, 80 8th Street, Minneapolis, MN 55402

Gordon works in this office, where his boss, Mr. Ducksworth (Josef Sommer), insists that he take a leave of absence to perform 500 hours of community service, coaching a kid's hockey team.

3. DUMPSTER
Drexel Apartments, 1009 Park Avenue, Minneapolis, MN 55404

In the alley behind this apartment building, Peter (J. D. Daniels) finds a purse in the dumpster and feeds a can of chili to Petey. Later, Gordon discovers Fulton Reed (Elden Henson) in this same alley.

4. BILLIARDS SNOOKER
717 South 10th Street, Minneapolis, MN 55404

In front of this pool hall, now empty, the dog "scores" and the boys plant the purse in the middle of the street. The red car drives west along 10th Street, and the boys run east, passing Band Box Diner and crossing the parking lot of Little Judge's Liquors on 14th Street (now North Central University Bookstore).

5. MEETING DISTRICT 5
Peavey Field Park, 730 East 22nd Street, Minneapolis, MN 55404

Gordon instructs his chauffeur to "drive out on the ice" to meet the District 5 Pee Wee hockey team. "Hey, I'll decide who sucks around here," insists Gordon.

6. DISTRICT 5 VERSUS HAWKS
Parade Ice Garden, 600 Kenwood Parkway, Minneapolis, MN 55403

Built in 1973 on the edge of downtown Minneapolis near the popular Walker Art Center/Minneapolis Sculpture Garden, this indoor ice rink is named for the military parades practiced here when a National Guard building occupied the site. Today the Parade Ice Garden is home to youth hockey leagues and high school teams.

7. HANS'S SPORT SHOP
Theodore Wirth Chalet, 1301 Theodore Wirth Parkway, Golden Valley, MN 55422

This quaint Swiss-style chalet, with an ambiance of a rustic lodge in the midst of the largest park in the Minneapolis park system, is open to the public and includes a bar and grill. Hans (Joss Ackland) urges Gordon to "Teach them to fly" and gives him a new pair of skates.

8. NICOLLET MALL SKYWAY
North of 7th Street South, Minneapolis, MN 55403

The team teaches Fulton Reed to skate by rollerblading through the Skyway, east from Minneapolis City Center.

9. GAVIIDAE COMMONS
651 Nicollet Mall, Minneapolis, MN 55403

The team skates through this shopping mall, where Fulton accidentally skates down a staircase and knocks a woman into a fountain.

10. COOK MEMORIAL ARENA
Coon Rapids Ice Arena, 11091 Mississippi Boulevard NW, Coon Rapids, MN 55433

The Ducks play their first official game at this arena, which was demolished in 2011 and replaced with Coon Rapids Ice Arena, a few blocks east.

11. MICKEY'S DINING CAR
36 West 7th Street, St. Paul, MN 55102

Charlie's (Joshua Jackson's) mom (Heidi Kling) works at this family-owned and operated art-deco diner, opened in the 1939 and operating 24 hours a day, 365 days a year ever since. Mickey's Diner was placed on the National Register of Historic Places in 1983. For more information, visit www.mickeysdiningcar.com.

12. THE NORTH STARS GAME

Met Center, American Boulevard East and Thunderbird Road, Bloomington, Minnesota 55420

Gordon takes the team to a professional hockey game at this 15,000-seat indoor arena best known as the home of the Minnesota North Stars, where they meet NHL players Mike Modano and Basil McRae. The Met Center, demolished in 1994, is now a parking lot.

13. ICE SCULPTURES

Rice Park, 109 West 4th Street, St. Paul, MN 55102

Gordon and Charlie's mom walk together amid ice sculptures in front of Landmark Center at the St. Paul Winter Carnival, an annual event begun in 1886. The pink granite Landmark Center, completed in 1902, is adorned by turrets, gables, dormers, and cylindrical corner towers. It was placed on the National Register of Historic Places in 1978.

14. CHAMPIONSHIP GAME

New Hope Ice Arena, 4949 Louisiana Avenue North, New Hope, MN 55428

At this ice arena, the Ducks play the final championship game against the Hawks.

15. GREYHOUND BUS STATION

Ramsey County Juvenile and Family Justice Center, 25 7th Street West, St. Paul, MN 55102

The bus terminal on the corner, where the Ducks say good-bye to Gordon, has been demolished. The bus heads off into the sunset, traveling west along 7th Street West.

Purple Rain

Dearly beloved, we are gathered here today . . . to introduce the world to rising young rock star Prince, who burst upon the music scene wearing black eyeliner, ruffled shirts, and purple military coats.

Directed by William Blinn, *Purple Rain* tells the story of an ambitious and talented rocker named the Kid (Prince) in Minneapolis, his romance with aspiring singer Apollonia (Apollonia Kotero), gratuitous rides on his purple motorcycle, his rivalry with singer Morris (Morris Day) and the band Apollonia 6, and internecine squabbles with the members of his band the Revolution. Although the plot fails miserably, Prince's energetic performances, captivating stage presence, syncopated dance moves, extraordinary guitar work, and astounding vocals propel this movie and firmly establish the musician as a star.

Unfortunately, misogyny and violence against women taints the film. The Kid's abusive relationship with Apollonia stems from witnessing his father routinely beat his mother. Only after his father commits suicide does the Kid attempt to overcome his misogynistic programming—by playing a song written by his female bandmates Lisa Coleman and Wendy Melvoin, whose songwriting talents he previously dismissed.

Purple Rain, wrote *New York Times* film critic Vincent Canby, "demonstrates the skills of the recording industry far more effectively than it does those of movie making. Though its women characters are supposed to be strong and independent, they are suckers for the men who knock them around with brutal regularity."

Purple Rain opened in theaters on July 27, 1984—just one month after the release of the titular album. The movie ranked number one in its first week, the album spent 24 consecutive weeks at number one on the *Billboard* albums chart, and four singles from the album ("When Doves Cry," "Let's Go Crazy," "Purple Rain," and "I Would Die 4 U") became US Top 10 singles. Prince won an Academy Award for Best Original Song Score for *Purple Rain*.

1. FIRST AVENUE & 7TH STREET ENTRY
701 First Avenue North, Minneapolis, MN 55403

In 1970, the abandoned Greyhound bus depot was converted into a music club, attracting legendary musicians, including B.B. King, Coldplay, Moby, Nirvana, Radiohead, Ray Charles, Run-D.M.C., the Beastie Boys, Tina Turner, and U2. The live version of the song "Purple Rain" was recorded here on August 3, 1983, during a benefit concert for the Minnesota Dance Theatre. First Avenue features events in its Mainroom Tuesday through Saturday nights. For more information and show times, visit http://first-avenue.com.

SHOT ELSEWHERE

LOS ANGELES

The Huntington Hotel, where Apollonia (Apollonia Kotero) lives, is located at 752 South Main Street, Los Angeles, CA 90014.

Wearing his gold jacket with tiger-skin lapels, Morris (Morris Day) darts down the stairs of his apartment building and into a waiting yellow taxi at 738 South Mariposa Avenue, Los Angeles, CA 90005.

2. THE FIRST AVENUE BACKSTAGE

The Orpheum Theatre, 910 Hennepin Avenue, Minneapolis, MN 55403

The backstage scenes of the green rooms and labyrinth basement in First Avenue were actually shot at the nearby Orpheum Theatre. To see these areas, take the Historic Theatre Tour offered by the Hennepin Theatre Trust. For more information, visit http://hennepintheatretrust.org /events.

3. THE KID'S HOUSE

Private Residence, 3400 South Snelling Avenue, Minneapolis, MN 55406

The house where "the Kid" (Prince) lives with the "freak show"—his mother (Olga Karlatos) and abusive father (Clarence Brown III). Please be respectful and do not loiter or disturb the residents.

4. THE DUMPSTER

18 North 7th Street, Minneapolis, MN 55402

Morris and Jerome (Jerome Benton) walk southwest on 1st Avenue and then turn left on 7th Street, and Jerome tosses Sue (Susan Moonsie) into the dumpster in the alley. "Such nastiness." The area has been renovated and the alley is gone.

5. LORRAINE'S

Crystal Court of the IDS Center, 80 South 8th Street, Minneapolis, MN 55402

Apollonia and the Kid visit the Skyway level of the glass-enclosed Crystal Court in the IDS Center in central downtown Minneapolis.

As Apollonia window shops for wedding dresses, the Kid asks for the jewelry from around her boot.

Other Feature Attractions

PAISLEY PARK STUDIOS
7801 Audubon Road, Chanhassen, MN 55317

Twenty miles from downtown Minneapolis stands the residence, record-ing studio, film production studio, soundstage, costume department, nightclub, and concert hall where Prince lived, worked, and died. The 65,000-square-foot compound looks like a white industrial warehouse, which Prince frequently illuminated with a purple hue.

The customized 1981 Honda CM400A Hondamatic that the Kid rode in *Purple Rain* sits near the front desk of Prince's executive office. The motorcycle was painted black for the 1990 movie *Graffiti Bridge*. A *Purple Rain* stunt bike sits inside a recording studio. Paisley Park is closed to the public.

6. BIKE RIDE
Henderson Station Road, Henderson, MN 56044

The Kid and Apollonia ride south from Salisbury Hill Road along Route 51, which turns into Route 34, to 290th Street.

7. RAILROAD TRESTLE AND LAKE SCENES
Minnesota River, Henderson, MN 56044

The Kid brings Apollonia to this "lake," where the elbow of the Minnesota River runs parallel to Chatfield Drive, approximately one mile north of the intersection with Highway 19. "You have to purify yourself in the waters of Lake Minnetonka," says the Kid. Apollonia strips down to her leather panties and jumps in the water. "That ain't Lake Minnetonka," says the Kid.

SHOT ELSEWHERE

THE TASTE EXTERIOR

The producers used a California location, 656 South Main Street, Los Angeles, CA 90014, as the exterior of the legendary Minne-apolis venue Taste Show Lounge (now defunct).

8. THE TASTE INTERIOR
Riddle Room, 507 East Hennepin Avenue, Minneapolis, MN 55414

Apollonia 6 performs not in the legendary Minneapolis nightclub Taste Show Lounge (originally located at 14 North Fifth Street and now defunct), but in the Union Bar, which closed and is now home to a "room escape" venue.

COMING ATTRACTIONS

RELIVE *PURPLE RAIN*

Morris Day and the Time continue to tour and perform. For more information, visit www.morrisdayandthetime.com.

MOVIE MAGIC

THE MUSIC OF PURPLE RAIN

The songs featured in the movie include:
- "Let's Go Crazy"—Prince and the Revolution
- "Jungle Love"—Morris Day and the Time
- "Take Me with U"—Prince and Apollonia Kotero
- "Modernaire"—Dez Dickerson
- "The Beautiful Ones"—Prince
- "God (Love Theme from Purple Rain)"—Prince
- "When Doves Cry"—Prince
- "Father's Song"—Prince
- "Computer Blue"—Prince
- "Darling Nikki"—Prince
- "Sex Shooter"—Apollonia Kotero, Brenda Bennett, and Susan Moonsie
- "The Bird"—Morris Day and the Time
- "Purple Rain"—Prince and the Revolution
- "I Would Die 4 U"—Prince and the Revolution
- "Baby I'm a Star"—Prince and the Revolution

A Simple Plan

In the 1998 movie *A Simple Plan*, adapted from the 1993 novel of the same name by Scott B. Smith, feed-store accountant Hank Mitchell (Bill Paxton), his half-witted brother Jacob (Billy Bob Thornton), and shiftless friend Lou Chambers (Brent Briscoe) accidentally discover in the snowy woods a crashed airplane containing a duffel bag with $4.4 million in $100 bills. The trio decides to keep the money hidden until they're absolutely sure no one will come looking for it, unleashing a torrent of unfortunate events.

Filmed in the small town of Delano, Minnesota, the threesome must feign ignorance in the midst of a tight-knit community. "The smallness of the community intensifies the paranoia," said director Sam Raimi. "The characters know the people they're deceiving. They walk by their houses, see them on the street. The policeman is a close friend of the brothers, and they must lie to him. Unlike a large city, there is no place to hide."

"It's hard to be a criminal and disappear in a town of 6,000 people," concurred Thornton. "Your neighbors are going to find out."

"The setting was Minnesota in the wintertime, so already that calls for a landscape of white skies and snow and bare trees," said director of photography Alar Kivilo. "But that also seemed appropriate for the psychological underpinnings of the story—the fight between right and wrong, the moral dilemma."

An unforeseen lack of snow in Delano forced the filmmakers to shoot most of the exterior scenes in Ashland, Wisconsin, most notably the road and woods near where the three characters find the crashed airplane. The filmmakers shot interiors on sets in St. Paul, Minnesota.

Film critic Owen Gleiberman wrote in *Entertainment Weekly*, "If you're going to stumble onto $4 million, there are few places to do it that are spookier, or more cinematic, than the site of a crashed propeller plane buried in the snowy serenity of a Midwestern wilderness." *A Simple Plan* was nominated for two Academy Awards.

1. GREAT RIVER REGIONAL LIBRARY
160 Railroad Avenue East, Delano, MN 55328

Sarah Mitchell (Bridget Fonda) works at this library, where she researches the plane crash.

2. DELANO FEED AND GRAIN MILL
119 Bridge Avenue East, Delano, MN 55328

"Are you mean to tell me that there were five weeks last month?" When Hank (Bill Paxton) leaves work, he walks west along the south side of Bridge Avenue.

3. HANK MITCHELL HOUSE EXTERIOR
Private Residence, 229 3rd Street South, Delano, MN 55328

Hank and Sarah Mitchell live in this quaint house in the shadow of the Delano Catholic Community Church. The filmmakers built the interiors on a soundstage. Please be respectful and do not loiter or disturb the residents.

4. PLANE CRASH
Lakehead Road and Henrickson Road, Saxon, WI 54559

In the woods, Lou Chambers (Brent Briscoe) throws a snowball in the nature preserve, revealing a crashed airplane filled with birds and a duffel bag full of money. The filmmakers shot the interior of the crashed plane on a soundstage.

5. JACOB'S APARTMENT
Private Residence, 137 Bridge Avenue E, Delano, MN 55328

Jacob (Billy Bob Thornton) lives in an apartment above Delano Floral and Gifts, accessible by a creaky wooden staircase behind the building. Please be respectful and do not loiter or disturb the residents.

6. BRIDGE OVER ANDERS CREEK
Bad River Bridge, Reimer Road, just north of Marengo River Road, Marengo, WI 54855

To cover up the murder of Dwight Stephanson (Tom Carey), Hank and Jacob stage a snowmobile accident from this bridge.

7. HOSPITAL
Memorial Medical Center, 1615 Maple Lane, Ashland, WI 54806

Jacob brings his childhood teddy bear as a baby gift, and Sarah convinces Hank to buy a tape recorder.

8. TOWN TAVERN

Private Residence, 144 North River Street, Delano, MN 55328

The owners of this pub converted the first floor into a living space connected to the apartments upstairs. The filmmakers transformed the first floor back into a bar for the movie. Please be respectful and do not loiter or disturb the residents.

9. POLICE STATION

136 Bridge Avenue East, Delano, MN 55328

On the east side of this building is the arched entrance to the Wright County Annex, where Carl Jenkins (Chelcie Ross) interrogates Hank.

MISSOURI

Escape from New York

In the 1981 movie *Escape from New York*, which takes place in 1997, the United States government has converted Manhattan into a maximum-security prison, by surrounding the island with a 50-foot-high containment wall, sealing off all tunnels, and mining all waterways and bridges. When Air Force One crashes on the island, Police Commissioner Bob Hauk (Lee Van Cleef) offers convicted criminal and Special Forces veteran Snake Plissken (Kurt Russell) the opportunity to rescue the president (Donald Pleasance) within 24 hours in exchange for his freedom.

Although the movie takes place in Manhattan, director John Carpenter filmed his dystopian action movie primarily in St. Louis, Missouri, transforming burned-out sections of the city into a hellish version of Manhattan using matte paintings.

"St. Louis—unbelievable!" Carpenter told the *Hollywood Reporter*. "We went there because, well, there were certain sequences we just couldn't do in New York; they would have tied up the whole city too much. And St. Louis, due to a major fire they had there in 1977, now has just the right amount of emptiness in the downtown area. Also the right architecture. So much of the city looks vacant and dead; perfect for our needs since we couldn't use anything looking new or fresh."

Escape from New York grossed $25.2 million in 1981 and inspired the sequel *Escape from L.A.*

> ### SHOT ELSEWHERE
>
> #### THE SECURITY WALL
>
> The containment wall around Manhattan is actually the Concrete Bridge at the Sepulveda Dam in Encino, California, built by the US Army Corps of Engineers in 1941 to withhold winter flood waters along the Los Angeles River. The flood-control basin doubles as a wildlife refuge and recreation area. Director John Carpenter

turned the flood-control basin into Central Park, using matte paintings of background buildings by James Cameron, who later directed *Titanic*. In California, he cleverly used the Art Center College of Design in Pasadena (for the interiors of the Liberty Island Security Control Center), California Institute of the Arts in Valencia (for the World Trade Center lobby), and Century Plaza Towers in Century City (for the exterior entrance of the World Trade Center).

1. THE HELICOPTER LANDS
Parking lot, St. Charles Street, between 16th and 17th Streets, St. Louis, MO 63103
The helicopter lands in this parking lot.

2. AIR FORCE ONE CRASH SITE
North 21st Street, between St. Charles Street and Olive Street, St. Louis, MO 63103
The plane crashes in the empty lot on the northeast corner of North 21st Street and Locust Street. Snake Plissken (Kurt Russell) walks north along 21st Street, then east along Locust Street.

3. BROADWAY THEATER
Fox Theatre, 527 North Grand Boulevard, St. Louis, MO 63103
Snake uses his tracking device to follows the president's signal to a dilapidated "Broadway" theater. This former movie palace, opened in 1929,

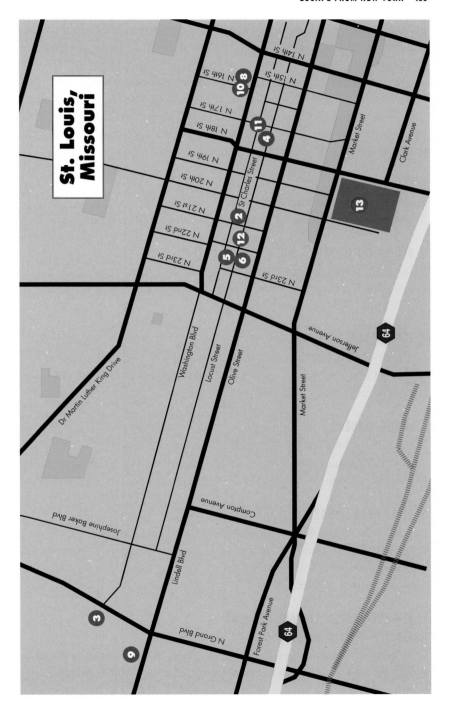

closed in 1978, fell into disrepair, and was restored in 1982. Snake walks north through Strauss Park and crosses North Grand Boulevard to enter the theater.

Director John Carpenter filmed the interior scenes of this derelict theater, where Snake discovers Cabbie (Ernest Borgnine) watching a musical revue, inside the abandoned Wiltern Theatre in Los Angeles (3790 Wilshire Boulevard). Carpenter makes a cameo appearance playing the violin in the pit orchestra.

4. ESCAPE POD
St. Charles Street, between 17th and 18th Streets, St. Louis, MO 63103
Snake walks west along St. Charles Street to find the red pod.

5. BEHIND CHOCK FULL O' NUTS
St. Charles Street, between 22nd and 23rd Streets, St. Louis, MO 63103
On the south side of St. Charles Street sits the alley behind the abandoned Chock Full o' Nuts.

6. THE MOLOTOV COCKTAIL
Alley to west of 2221 Locust Street, St. Louis, MO 63103
Snake gets into the taxi, Cabbie hurls a Molotov cocktail at the alley, and they drive east along Locust Street.

7. BRIDGE GIRDERS
MacArthur Bridge, Risley Street, St. Louis, MO 63102
Cabbie drives past the massive bridge girders on the south side of the MacArthur Bridge in Chouteau's Landing, a commercial district in the city.

8. ALLEY NEAR LIBRARY
North 16th Street, between Washington Avenue and Lucas Avenue, St. Louis, MO 63103
Cabbie parks on the southeast corner of this intersection. These buildings in the Washington Avenue Historic District date from the late 19th century to the early 1920s.

9. NEW YORK PUBLIC LIBRARY EXTERIOR
The New Masonic Temple, 3681 Lindell Boulevard, St. Louis, MO 63108
Cabbie brings Snake to see Brain (Harry Dean Stanton) at the New York Public Library, in reality a Masonic temple built in 1926. This majestic building houses the former office of Senator Harry S. Truman (who

served as Freemason grand master). Before flying solo to Paris in 1927 aboard the *Spirit of St. Louis*, aviator Charles Lindbergh was initiated and participated as a mason at this temple. Ernest Borgnine was a mason and also attended meetings here.

The filmmakers shot the interior of the lobby at Doheny Library at the University of Southern California in Los Angeles, and the interior of the stacks, where a donkey powers an oil derrick, in the Hoose Library of Philosophy, similarly at USC.

10. THE DUKE'S CAR

Intersection of Lucas Avenue and North 16th Street, St. Louis, MO 63103

At this intersection, the Duke's (Isaac Hayes's) car, with chandeliers above the headlights, comes into view, heading east along Lucas Avenue.

11. STATION WAGON

Intersection of North 17th Street and St. Charles Street, St. Louis, MO 63103

The station wagon heads west on St. Charles Street and makes a right turn on 17th Street, heading north.

12. BROADWAY

2201 Locust Street, St. Louis, MO 63103

"What's wrong with Broadway?" asks Snake. Inmates attack and chase after the station wagon as it heads east along Locust Street from North 23rd Street to North 21st Street.

13. RAILWAY SHEDS

St. Louis Union Station, 1820 Market Street, St. Louis, MO 63103

When the movie was filmed, St. Louis Union Station, opened in 1894 and once the world's largest and busiest train station, had fallen into disrepair and been deserted. The filmmakers used this abandoned railway shed as the location where the Duke holds the president captive in a rail carriage. Since then, Union Station has been renovated into an extravagant shopping and entertainment complex. The area where the Duke shoots target practice at the president was demolished and transformed into an entry. The boxing ring fight was staged in the station's then dilapidated barrel-vaulted Grand Hall, now a passageway near the DoubleTree Hotel. The stained glass window seen in the background during the boxing scene continues to grace the front entry into the Grand Hall.

14. 69TH STREET BRIDGE ENTRANCE
Martin Luther King Bridge, 700 North Front Street, St. Louis, MO 63102
Renovated in the 1980s, the tunnel through which the Duke drives on the north side of the Martin Luther King Bridge no longer exists.

15. THE 69TH STREET BRIDGE
Chain of Rocks Bridge, St. Louis, MO 63137

When Cabbie drives Snake, Brain, Maggie (Adrienne Barbeau), and the president to the 69th Street Bridge to cross the East River, they actually drive over the Chain of Rocks Bridge, which connects St. Louis with Chouteau Island on the Mississippi River. Closed to heavy traffic in 1970 and abandoned, the Chain of Rocks Bridge was renovated at a cost of $4 million and reopened in 1999 to pedestrians and bicycle traffic.

Gone Girl

Adapted by author Gillian Flynn from her bestselling novel, the 2014 movie *Gone Girl* tells the story of Nick Dunne (Ben Affleck), who returns home on his fifth wedding anniversary to discover his wife, Amy (Rosamund Pike), missing and apparently kidnapped during a burglary. The police soon suspect Nick of murdering his wife.

Set in fictitious North Carthage, Missouri, *Gone Girl* was filmed primarily in Cape Girardeau. Flynn, who grew up in Kansas City, Missouri, created North Carthage from her memory of similar towns in Missouri. "I remember when [director David Fincher] sent me photos of Cape Girardeau, and there was that great length of street heading down to the river," Flynn told the *Southeast Missourian*. "It looked absolutely what I had pictured in my mind. It was perfect when I saw it. I hadn't been to Cape Girardeau in a number of years, but it was the exact type of location I had in mind. I wanted the river to be a big character, and the corner bar just looked perfect. I felt everything about it was straight out of my brain."

Flynn felt dumbfounded seeing a place she had imagined come to life. "I was free to be on the set as much as I wanted," she told the *Kansas City Star*. "Of course, the script was locked in by then. I was there purely as a tourist to the 3-D version of my own brain. . . . It was really fun to visit this thing that had been kicking around my head for a year. To have a drink with David Fincher at The Bar [operated by the fictional Nick and his twin sister], that was pretty mind-blowing."

"*Gone Girl* has the impact of a body-slam, hitting home in every scary, suspenseful, seductive particular," wrote film critic Peter Travers in *Rolling Stone*. "It's a movie inferno with combustible performances."

1. THE MISSISSIPPI RIVER
Riverfront Park, Broadway Street and North Water Street, Cape Girardeau, MO 63701

From Riverfront Park, accessible through a floodgate in the wall, the camera looks north along the Mississippi River. From this spot, you can watch the mighty river flow by and see big riverboats and vintage steamboats, like the *Delta Queen*.

2. COCA-COLA SIGN
Port Cape Girardeau Restaurant and Lounge, 19 North Water Street, Cape Girardeau, MO 63701

We see the vintage Coca-Cola advertisement painted on the north side of this brick building.

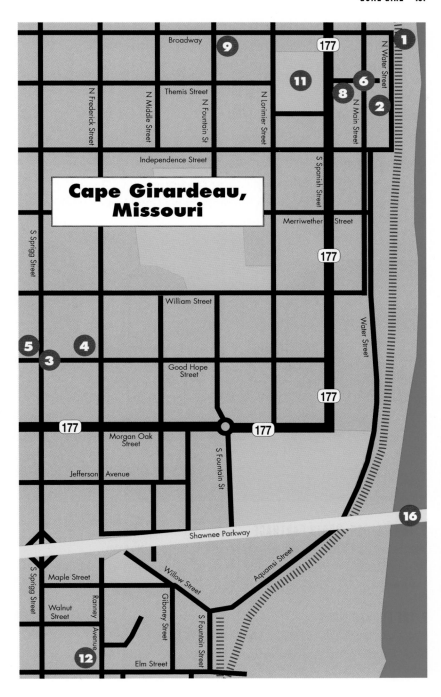

Cape Girardeau, Missouri

3. DOWNTOWN NORTH CARTHARAGE
Intersection of Good Hope Street and South Sprigg Street, Cape Girardeau, MO 63703

We look west along Good Hope Street.

4. MEYER SUPPLY CO.
608 Good Hope Street, Cape Girardeau, MO 63703

We see a quick shot of this store.

5. ART DECO DOOR
Baisch & Skinner Wholesale, 241 South Sprigg Street, Cape Girardeau, MO 63703

On the south side of this brick building, facing Good Hope Street, we see this beautiful door.

6. TOWN CLOCK, NORTH CARTHAGE
Intersection of North Main Street and Themis Street, Cape Girardeau, MO 63701

We see the town clock of downtown Cape Girardeau in the middle of the intersection, looking south along Main Street.

7. THE DUNNES' HOME
Private Residence, 3014 Keystone Drive, Cape Girardeau, MO 63701

Nick Dunne (Ben Affleck) returns home on his fifth wedding anniversary to the Amazing Amy (Rosamund Pike) to discover that his wife has disappeared under suspicious circumstances. The house, just west of Cape Woods Conservation Area, sits across the street from Walt's (Pete Housman's) brick house. The interiors were filmed on a soundstage. Please be respectful and do not loiter or disturb the residents.

8. THE BAR
The Bar, 117 Themis Street, Cape Girardeau, MO 63107

Nick drives north along North Spanish Street to the Bar, where Nick and his sister, Margo (Carrie Coon), play the Game of Life at the bar. The Bar did not exist until the filmmakers transformed a closed café into the fictional bar for the movie. A local company converted the fake bar into a real one, retaining some of the set dressings and the Bar logo painted on the outside wall. Unaffiliated with the movie or 20th Century Fox, the Bar attracts residents eager to share their experiences about the filming of the movie and tourists interested in visiting the movie locations.

9. NORTH CARTHAGE POLICE DEPARTMENT
Old Federal Building, 339 Broadway, Cape Girardeau, MO 63701

Detective Rhonda Boney (Kim Dickens) questions Nick in the city's old federal building, dedicated in 1967, shuttered in 2010, and converted into an office building.

FAR GONE

The filmmakers shot most of the scenes that take place in New York City in Los Angeles. The bookstore where Nick and Amy make love while searching for books by Jane Austen is the Last Bookstore (453 South Spring Street). The Chinese restaurant where Amy says "We're so cute, I wanna punch us in the face" is Beso Hollywood (6350 Hollywood Boulevard), owned and operated by *Desperate Housewives* star Eva Longoria and celebrity chef Todd English. And Nick and Amy move out of a brownstone on New York City Street on the Universal Studios backlot in Universal City.

Nick does indeed get out of a taxi at Park Avenue and East 52nd Street in Manhattan to meet with Tanner Bolt (Tyler Perry), but the meeting takes place in Los Angeles inside the lobby of Gas Company Tower (555 West 5th Street).

10. MARGO'S HOUSE

Private Residence, 2404 Albert Rasche Drive, Cape Girardeau, MO 63701

When his home turns into a crime scene overrun by the press, Nick stays with his sister and later discovers an unexpected stash of gifts in the woodshed in the backyard. Please be respectful and do not loiter or disturb the residents.

11. THE COMMON PLEAS COURTHOUSE

44 North Lorimier Street, Cape Girardeau, MO 63701

Built in 1854, the courthouse stands on one of the highest points in Cape Girardeau, across the street from the Bar. At this courthouse, the American Indian council held meetings, Civil War prisoners were locked in the dungeon, and slave auctions took place on the steps. It was added to the National Register of Historic Places in 2010. On the west side of the grounds stand three memorials: a statue of a Union soldier sitting atop a fountain, a second fountain made from Georgia silver gray marble as a Civil War memorial, and a Vietnam War memorial. At the gazebo on the north side of the courthouse, Nick addresses a crowd during a candlelight vigil. The gazebo, opened in 1922, serves as a music venue on most Friday evenings during the summer.

12. NICK'S FATHER'S HOUSE
Private Residence, 831 Ranney Avenue, Cape Girardeau, MO 63703
Nick's father (Leonard Kelly-Young) lives in this house with a view of the Bill Emerson Memorial Bridge. Please be respectful and do not loiter or disturb the residents.

13. DRURY HOTELS NORTH CARTHAGE
Drury Lodge, 104 South Vantage Drive, Cape Girardeau, MO 63701
Amy's parents (David Clennon and Lisa Banes) use this hotel as the command center for the search for their daughter.

14. THE SEARCH
Thebes Boat Ramp, Second Street, Thebes, IL 62990
From the beach on the east side of the Mississippi River, you can see the Thebes Bridge, a truss railroad bridge opened in 1905.

15. WOODS
Intersection of Edgewood Road and William Street, Cape Girardeau, MO 63703
On this hill west of Edgewood Road, a search party looks for Amy.

16. BILL EMERSON MEMORIAL BRIDGE
Shawnee Parkway at the Mississippi River, Cape Girardeau, MO 63703
Amy Dunne leaves town by driving east across this cable-stayed bridge, opened in 2003 and named after an eight-term Missouri congressman.

17. MISSOURI OZARKS CAMPGROUND
Giant City State Park Lodge, 460 Giant City Lodge Road, Makanda, IL 62958
This Southern Illinois landmark served as a Missouri Ozarks campground. Amy checks in and uses the computer at the rustic stone lodge (built by the Civilian Conservation Corps in 1939), stays in Cabin 22, and enjoys the outdoor pool.

SHOT ELSEWHERE

DESI COLLINGS'S MANSION
Although Amy's wealthy, obsessed ex-boyfriend, Desi Collings (Neil Patrick Harris) is supposed to live in St. Louis, Missouri,

the mansion seen in the movie sits in Los Angeles (104 Fremont Place) and also served as the home of silent star George Valentin (Jean Dujardin) in the 2011 movie *The Artist*.

18. RESTAURANT
Sands Pancake House, 1448 North Kingshighway Street, Cape Girardeau, MO 63701

At a table in this restaurant, Bolt, Nick, and Margo discuss their strategy to find Amy.

19. MINIATURE GOLF COURSE
Arena Golf, 2901 Hawthorne Road, Cape Girardeau, MO 63701

Amy, Greta (Lola Kirke), and Jeff (Boyd Holbrook) play miniature golf at this 18-hole Putt-Putt golf course.

20. MOTEL PARKING LOT
Budget Inn Motel and Restaurant, 1448 North Kingshighway Street, Cape Girardeau, MO 63701

In the parking lot of this low-budget motel, Amy sleeps in her car and gets woken by a security guard.

21. GAS STATION
Rhodes 101, 546 South Sprigg Street, Cape Girardeau, MO 63703

Amy uses the pay phone on the north side of the gas station.

22. THE GATEWAY ARCH
100 Washington Avenue, St. Louis, MO 63102

From the Gateway Arch, we see the Old Courthouse.

MOVIE MAGIC

GONE BUT NOT FORGOTTEN
To download a free PDF of the *Gone Girl* Driving Tour, provided by the Cape Girardeau Convention & Visitors Bureau, visit www.visitcape.com/gonegirl

Up in the Air

Adapted from the 2001 novel by Walter Kirn, the 2009 movie *Up in the Air* follows the travels of corporate downsizer Ryan Bingham (George Clooney), who crisscrosses the country firing employees from companies too cowardly to do their own dirty work. The self-proclaimed "career transition" counselor also gives motivational speeches titled "What's in Your Backpack?"—ballyhooing the benefits of minimizing material possessions and personal relationships while simultaneously starting an affair with a fellow frequent flier named Alex (Vera Farmiga). When new hire Natalie Keener (Anna Kendrick) advocates cutting costs by switching to videoconferencing to conduct the layoffs, Bingham begrudgingly takes her along on his face-to-face firings to show her how to terminate employees effectively and humanely.

Director Jason Reitman shot the film on 80 different sets at 50 locations throughout the St. Louis area. "There's an immediate and ingratiating novelty to the fact that so much of Jason Reitman's *Up in the Air* unfolds in cubicles and conference rooms in nondescript office buildings in Wichita, Kansas City, and other outposts of the great American in-between," wrote movie critic Scott Foundas in *Film Comment*.

"I was location scouting and constantly confronted by these abandoned buildings," Reitman said on the NPR radio show *Fresh Air* with Terry Gross. "One of the big reasons we shot in St. Louis is it has so many offices available to shoot in because all these companies have ceased to exist."

The filmmakers also placed classified ads in St. Louis and Detroit newspapers seeking recently fired individuals whom Reitman could interview on camera for the film. The director shot interviews with 60 people who shared their raw feelings about getting fired, and clips from 20 of these genuine testimonials appear in the finished movie.

"It's funny," Reitman told the *Washington Post*, "if you had asked me before this movie, what's the hardest part about losing your job, I would have said loss of income. But that would rarely come up. What people would always say is, 'I don't know what I'm supposed to do.' That's such an interesting statement and everyone said it: 'I don't know what I'm supposed to do.'"

1. AIRPORTS
Lambert–St. Louis International Airport, 10701 Lambert International Boulevard, St. Louis, MO 63145

Concourse C and concourse D played the part of several airports across America. Ryan Bingham (George Clooney) shops for shirts in the Brooks Brothers Store, across from the CNBC News Store, near Gate C8. The filmmakers built the enormous flight information board seen at the end of the movie.

2. THE BAR
The Washington Avenue Bistro, 827 Washington Ave, St. Louis, MO 63101

Ryan Bingham and Alex Goran (Vera Farmiga) meet here and compare frequent flier cards.

3. MORNING SHOT WITH SPRINKLERS
Hilton St. Louis Airport, 10330 Natural Bridge Road, St. Louis, MO 63134

Ryan checks into this hotel and dines in the World's Away restaurant. The hotel lobby has since been renovated.

4. INDOOR SWIMMING POOL
Hilton St. Louis at the Ballpark, 1 South Broadway, St. Louis, MO 63102

Ryan goes for a swim in the indoor swimming pool, gets his shoes shined, and speaks at the Goalquest XX conference.

5. UNION PACIFIC'S HOME PLATE
Intersection of Cumming Street and North 10th Street, Omaha, NE 68102

At the southwest corner of this intersection, we see the Omaha gates and the Union Pacific Railroad display—near the starting point of the transcontinental railroad.

6. PIONEER COURAGE PARK
1601 Dodge Street, Omaha, NE 68102

This park sits across the street from the First National Bank and Double-Tree by Hilton Omaha Downtown.

7. RYAN'S APARTMENT
Mansion House, 300 North 4th Street, St. Louis, MO 63102

Ryan lives in apartment 407, supposedly in Omaha, with a menu from an Omaha pizza restaurant on the refrigerator door.

8. CTC OFFICES AND OTHER COMPANIES
The GenAmerica Building, 700 Market Street, St. Louis, MO 63101

In the conference room, Natalie Keener (Anna Kendrick) urges the company to start firing people through videoconferencing, and in Craig Gregory's (Jason Bateman's) office, Craig tells Ryan to mentor Natalie. In this office building Ryan also fires a slew of employees and encourages Bob (J. K. Simmons) to pursue a career in French cooking. You can see the Gateway Arch outside the window. A conference room in this building also serves as a conference room in Wichita where Natalie fires people.

9. OMAHA AIRPORT
Eppley Airfield, 4501 Abbott Drive, Omaha, NE 68110

At the south end of the main terminal, Ryan forces Natalie to repack her suitcase more efficiently.

10. WICHITA OFFICE BUILDING EXTERIOR
1 Bank of America Plaza, 800 Market Street, St. Louis, MO 63101

On the northeast corner of Walnut Street and 8th Street, this building sits directly across the street from the GenAmerica Building.

SHOT ELSEWHERE

ON CLOUD NINE

In Miami, Florida, the Hilton courtesy shuttle heads west along MacArthur Causeway (east of Fountain Street). Natalie breaks down in the lobby of the Hilton Miami Airport (5101 Blue Lagoon Drive), where the threesome crashes the Alpha Tech party. Ryan and Alex sail on a yacht in Biscayne Bay.

11. CHALET HOTEL IN MILWAUKEE, WISCONSIN
The Cheshire Inn, 6300 Clayton Road, St. Louis, MO 63117

Ryan and Alex stay in this Bavarian hotel and attend his sister's rehearsal dinner in the Fox & Hounds Tavern.

12. ASHTON HIGH SCHOOL

Affton High School, 8309 MacKenzie Road, St. Louis, MO 63123

Ryan and Alex break into the high school through a window in room 40. The filmmakers filled the trophy case with trophies and shot a scene of Ryan and Alex sitting on the bleachers in the gym and sharing a kiss on the steps near the entrance to the weight room.

13. SHEPHERD PINES LUTHERAN CHURCH OF WAUPACA

Maplewood United Methodist Church, 7409 Flora Avenue, Maplewood, MO 63143

Ryan gives his sister's fiancé (Danny McBride) a pep talk in the nursery, the couple gets married in the church, and the reception takes place in the basement.

14. ALEX'S HOUSE IN CHICAGO

2340 Whittemore Place, St. Louis, MO 63104

In the Lafayette Square neighborhood, Ryan shows up at Alex's door only to discover her true relationship status.

NEBRASKA

Boys Town

In 1917, a 31-year-old Irish priest, Father Edward J. Flanagan, opened a home for troubled and neglected boys in Omaha, Nebraska, eventually buying a 160-acre tract of land complete with barns and a large house, which soon became known as the Village of Boys Town. By the 1930s, hundreds of boys lived at Boys Town, electing their own mayor from among their own ranks, making their own laws, and growing their own food. In 1936, the State of Nebraska declared the community an official village.

Metro-Goldwyn-Mayer offered Boys Town a $5,000 donation to make a movie about the home. At first, Father Flanagan rejected the offer, but he agreed after seeing a draft of the script that conveyed the true mission of the home.

"There isn't any such thing in the world as a bad boy," says Father Flanagan (Spencer Tracy) in the inspiring 1938 biopic based on the true story of the founding of Boys Town and filmed on location on the actual campus, using actual Boys Town boys as extras. Aside from being one of the first movies filmed on location in Omaha, *Boys Town* was also one of the first movies ever filmed at the original location of the movie's subject.

Before filming began, Tracy spent a week with Father Flanagan, studying his mannerisms and the way he interacted with the boys. During production, Tracy and his costar Mickey Rooney also spent time playing with the boys of Boys Town.

For the world premiere of *Boys Town*, held in Omaha, Nebraska, an estimated crowd of 30,000 people lined the streets and crowded the train station to greet the arrival of the Hollywood stars. *Boys Town* became one of the most successful films of 1938, and Spencer Tracy won the Academy Award for Best Actor, which he gave to the real Father Flanagan.

The actual Boys Town, located at West Dodge Road at 137th Street in Omaha, is open to visitors. There is no entrance fee to the campus, and all sites are free, including the museums. At the visitor's center, you can get a map of the campus and a self-guided tour on CD, visit the gift shop, and dine at the cafe. For more information, telephone (800) 625-1400 or visit www.boystown.org.

1. FATHER FLANAGAN HISTORIC HOUSE
Grodinsky Circle, Boys Town, NE 68010

At this former residence of the Boys Town founder, constructed in 1927, Father Flanagan (Spencer Tracy) gets on the bus and promises to give Pee-Wee (Bobs Watson) candy. Restored and decorated to look as it did in 1929, the house contains many of Father Flanagan's personal possessions, including a desk made for him by the boys and consisting of more than 250,000 inlaid pieces of wood from 25 different varieties of trees.

2. FATHER FLANAGAN'S OFFICE
Monsignor Wegner Middle School, Norton Drive, Boys Town, NE 68010

On the north side of the gym, a two-story attachment to the building housed Father Flanagan's office, but that attachment has since been demolished to make room for Monsignor Wegner Middle School.

3. OMAHA UNION STATION
801 South 10th Street, Omaha, NE 68108

"You probably got that big schnoz sticking it into somebody else's business," says Whitey (Mickey Rooney).

4. BIRCH DRIVE
Grodinsky Circle, Boys Town, NE 68010
Slabs of pavement lined with birch trees run north from the Father Flanagan Historic House to West Dodge Road.

5. HOMELESS BOY STATUE
Parking lot, intersection of Mother Theresa Lane and Oddo Road, Boys Town, NE 68010
This statue of a boy with his arms outstretched heavenward disintegrated and once stood roughly in the middle of the parking lot on the southwest corner of this intersection.

6. POST OFFICE
Witcofski Building, 14100 Mother Theresa Lane, Boys Town, NE 68010
"Well, what do you know about that?" says Whitey, upon learning that Boys Town has its own post office. The old post office now houses accounting offices, and the stone engraved with the words *Post Office* now graces the new post office at 139 South 144th Street.

7. BASEBALL FIELD
Intersection of Norton Drive and Walsh Drive, Boys Town, NE 68010
The baseball field seen in the movie stood south of this intersection and Monsignor Wegner Middle School, and is now the site of cottages where the boys and girls of Boys Town currently reside.

8. OLD MAIN DORMITORY
Monsignor Wegner Middle School, Norton Drive, Boys Town, NE 68010
Also known as the Omaha Building, this four-story brick building seen in the movie housed the dormitory, classrooms, a dining hall, laundry room, library, infirmary, and chapel. The building, which stood just south of the Father Flanagan Historic House, was demolished to make room for the Monsignor Wegner Middle School.

9. DINING HALL
Hall of History, 14057 Flanagan Boulevard, Boys Town, NE 68010
Built by Father Flanagan in 1939, the dining hall where the boys say grace before their meals is now a museum with displays that tell the story of Boys Town, complete with artifacts, photos and memorabilia from the film, and the Best Actor Oscar presented to Spencer Tracy for his portrayal of Father Flanagan in the movie.

10. THE GYM AND AUDITORIUM
Monsignor Wegner Middle School, Norton Drive, Boys Town, NE 68010

In the movie, the choir sings and the boys hold their election for town mayor inside this gymnasium, located on the southeast corner of the middle school.

11. PEE-WEE HIT AND RUN
Service Road, between Oddo Road and Norton Drive, Boys Town, NE 68010

On the service road to the west of the Hall of History, Pee-Wee gets hit by a car.

Other Feature Attractions _____

FATHER FLANAGAN'S TOMB
Dowd Chapel, 13943 Dowd Drive, Boys Town, NE 68010

"All boys need to learn how to pray," said Father Flanagan. "How they pray is up to them." Dowd Chapel, the church built in the style of 15th-century Gothic design, contains Father Flanagan's tomb. Visitors and Boys Town residents attend Mass here throughout the year.

CHURCH AT 19TH AND DODGE
St. Mary Magdalene Church, 109 South 19th Street, Omaha, NE 68103

The exterior and interiors of the church seen in the movie do not match those of the actual church that sits at the address given by Joe Marsh (Edward Norris) in the film. The church features stained glass windows and a beautiful vaulted ceiling.

Election

"What's the difference between morals and ethics anyway? Anybody?"

In the satiric 1999 movie *Election*, based on the novel by Tom Perrotta, dedicated high school teacher Jim McAllister (Matthew Broderick), irked by ruthlessly ambitious overachiever Tracy Flick (Reese Witherspoon), attempts to sabotage her campaign for school president.

Although the novel takes place at a high school in Winwood, New Jersey, director Alexander Payne filmed the movie on location in his hometown of Omaha, Nebraska.

Why Omaha? "You don't ask Woody Allen or Spike Lee why they want to shoot in New York, or Paul Thomas Anderson or Quentin Tarantino why they want to shoot in L.A., or Claude Lelouch why he wants to shoot in Paris," Payne told the *New Yorker*. "I happen to be from here and, like many writers and filmmakers, at least earlier in your career, you want to explore the mystery of the place you're from—those early buttons, how it haunts you."

Payne wanted to film in a typically drab high school with cinder-block walls, and Papillion–La Vista High School in an Omaha suburb agreed to let him shoot the movie during school days and use students and teachers as extras.

Urged by Payne, Reese Witherspoon spent two weeks attending class at the high school and hanging out with the teenagers "pretending to be a transfer student," she said. "It was really interesting because I was escorted by a girl very much like my character—president of the student council, captain of the volleyball team and head cheerleader—a total overachiever. The experience helped me to get back in the mind-set of teenagers and empathize with their problems."

Payne told the *Huffington Post*: "Barack Obama has told me twice that it's his favorite political film."

1. GEORGE WASHINGTON CARVER HIGH

Papillion–La Vista High School, 402 East Centennial Road, Papillion, Omaha, NE 68046

We see the sprinkler watering the football field on the west side of the school, and Jim McAllister (Matthew Broderick) jogs around the football field on the northwest side of the school. He weaves through the fence on the southeast end of the running track and walks up the pathway on the north side of the school building, passing the tennis courts, and showers in the men's locker room. In the movie, we see the teachers' workroom, faculty lounge, hallways, classrooms, gym, auditorium, principal's office, and parking lot. Jim McAllister teaches in room 301.

2. GODFATHER'S PIZZA
7920 South 84th Street, La Vista, NE 68128
At this pizza restaurant, the editors of the yearbook celebrate after meeting a deadline, and teacher Dave Novotny (Mark Harelik) begins an affair with Tracy Flick (Reese Witherspoon).

3. DUMPSTER
Alegent Creighton Clinic, 5002 Underwood Avenue, Omaha, NE 68132
Jim throws Tracy's signatures in the dumpster behind this building.

4. THE MCALLISTERS' HOUSE
5011 Cass Street, Omaha, NE 68132
In this modest house, Jim and his wife, Diane (Molly Hagan), try to conceive a baby.

5. PAUL METZLER'S HOUSE
1562 South 187th Circle, West Omaha, NE 68130
At this beautiful home overlooking Shadow Ridge Country Club, Paul Metzler (Chris Klein) interrupts his sister Tammy (Jessica Campbell) "experimenting" with her friend Lisa Flanagan (Frankie Ingrassia).

6. OPPD NORTH OMAHA POWER STATION
7475 John J Pershing Drive, North Omaha, NE 68112
"Sometimes when I'm sad, I sit and watch the power station," says Tammy Metzler, who later witnesses Tracy throwing campaign posters in a nearby dumpster. "They say if you lie between two of the main wires, your body just evaporates. You become a gas. I wonder what that would feel like."

7. LINDA NOVOTNY'S HOUSE
683 Parkwood Lane, Omaha, NE 68132
Dave Novotny's estranged wife, Linda (Delaney Driscoll), asks Jim to stop by "to help her out with a little plumbing problem."

8. YOUNKERS
Oak View Mall, 3201 South 144th Street, Omaha, NE 68144
Jim and Linda visit the makeup counter in this department store in the Oak View Mall.

9. AMERICAN FAMILY INN
Rodeway Inn, 1110 Fort Crook Road South, Bellevue, NE 68005
"So what do you think?" Jim asks Linda, as they drive past this motel. "Should we get a room?" Later, Jim prepares "suite 246."

10. SOCCER GAME
Memorial Park, 6005 Underwood Avenue, Omaha, NE 68132
Tammy rides her bicycle around Robert H. Storz Drive in Memorial Park and stops to watch the girls of Immaculate Heart Catholic School play soccer in the field below at the Brownell-Talbot School.

11. WALGREENS
344 North Saddle Creek Road, Omaha, NE 68131
In this drug store, Jim buys flowers, chocolates, and champagne for his rendezvous with Linda.

12. ZOO AND AQUARIUM
Omaha's Henry Doorly Zoo and Aquarium, 3701 South 10th Street, Omaha, NE 68107

Lisa and Jennifer (Kaitlin Ferrell) visit the penguins and monkeys at this zoo, consistently ranked one of the best zoos in the United States and nationally renowned for its leadership in animal conservation. The zoo features the world's largest nocturnal exhibit, America's largest indoor rainforest, and the world's largest indoor desert. For more information, visit www.omahazoo.com.

13. PEDESTRIAN BRIDGE
Gene Leahy Mall, 1203 Farnam Street, Omaha, NE 68102

Lisa and Jennifer frolic across this bridge spanning the lagoon in this ten-acre park in the heart of downtown Omaha.

SHOT ELSEWHERE

TALK OF THE TOWN

"What's the difference between igneous and sedimentary anyway?" In Manhattan, Jim McAllister works as a docent at the American Museum of Natural History on Central Park West and 79th Street and bides his time gazing at the Statue of Liberty from a bench in Battery Park.

Then, after visiting the Lincoln Memorial in Washington, DC, Jim catches a final glimpse of Tracy leaving the Hay-Adams Hotel (800 16th Street NW) with a senator in a limousine.

Nebraska

Senior citizen Woody Grant (Bruce Dern), convinced that a letter from Mega-Sweepstakes Marketing guarantees him a $1 million prize, decides to leave his home in Billings, Montana, to collect his fortune in Lincoln, Nebraska. His forlorn son, David (Will Forte), agrees to drive his alcoholic father to Lincoln, and as they make the 750-mile journey together, stopping to visit Woody's kin in the fictitious town of Hawthorne, Nebraska, the aging father and dutiful son reconnect.

Director Alexander Payne, who grew up in Omaha, drove some 20,000 miles to scout locations for the movie. "I needed to find a town big enough to house the crew, around which were smaller towns that we could use to piece together the mythical town of Hawthorne, Nebraska," Payne told *Condé Nast Traveler*. "By the time official pre-production started, I had found Norfolk, Nebraska—Johnny Carson's hometown, a town of about 25,000 people—which had a real smorgasbord of small towns orbiting it that I could use." Payne used Plainview, located about 20 miles northwest of Norfolk, as the fictitious town of Hawthorne, capturing the ambiance of a vibrant dullsville.

"I wanted a town with a population between eleven hundred and sixteen hundred, but not a county seat, which often have the town squares," Payne told the *New Yorker*. "A town square would have added a little pizzazz I didn't want. I didn't want the buildings to be two-story with ornate façades, like you see a lot—especially in Iowa but in Nebraska, too. I didn't want it to be as solidly nineteenth-century as a town like Hooper, where we filmed a little, which is very picturesque but more of a period piece. I wanted a layering of old and new."

1. WOODY'S ESCAPE
L. P. Anderson Tire Co., 3741 Montana Avenue, Billings, MT 59101

Woody walks south along Montana Avenue alongside the railroad tracks, across the street from the tire shop.

2. BILLINGS CITY LIMITS
South 27th Street (above Nall Avenue), Billings, MT 59101

The sheriff intercepts Woody, walking east past the city limit sign, at this spot, near the entrance to the interstate highway.

3. WOODY'S HOUSE
Private Residence, 405 Cedar Avenue, Laurel, MT 59044
Woody's son, David (Will Forte), drives him home to his wife, Kate (June Squibb). "I never knew the son of a bitch even wanted to be a millionaire," says Kate. "He should have thought about that years ago and worked for it." Please be respectful and do not loiter or disturb the residents.

4. MID-CITY SUPERSTORE
Aaron's, 17 New York Street, Rapid City, SD 57701
David works in this audio store, selling stereo equipment.

5. GREYHOUND BUS STATION
The Pub Station, 2502 1st Avenue North, Billings, NE 59101
David drives west on 1st Avenue to the art deco Trailways Bus Station, where he finds Woody walking along the sidewalk.

6. LAKE STOP GASOLINE AND ELBOW ROOM LOUNGE
9 Lake De Smet Road, Buffalo, WY 82834
David drives his father in the Subaru southeast along I-90 and stops for gas, where Woody disappears into the bar to quench his thirst. "Beer ain't drinkin'," he explains. The filmmakers added the mounted heads on the walls of the bar.

7. BIKERS
Interstate-90 (1 mile south of Stagestop Road), Summerset, SD 57718
While David and Woody drive northwest on this highway, a group of bikers pass by them.

8. JUNCTION TO MT. RUSHMORE
Interstate 90, 1 mile west of Exit 57 to Interstate-190, Rapid City, SD 57702
David suggests they stop off to see Mount Rushmore. "It's just a bunch of rocks," says Woody.

9. MOUNT RUSHMORE NATIONAL MEMORIAL
13000 SD-244, Keystone, SD 57751
"It doesn't look finished to me," says Woody, observing the sculptures of four presidents carved into the granite face of Mount Rushmore. "Washington's the only one with any clothes, and they're just kind of roughed in. Lincoln doesn't even have an ear."

Sculpted by Danish American Gutzon Borglum and his son, Lincoln Borglum, Mount Rushmore features the heads of George Washington, Thomas Jefferson, Theodore Roosevelt, and Abraham Lincoln. The carving began in 1927 and finished in 1941. To plan your visit, see www.nps.gov /moru/index.htm.

10. STARDUST MOTEL
520 East North Street. Rapid City, SD 57701

Woody and David stay overnight in this two-star motel, and so can you.

11. EMERGENCY ROOM
Faith Regional Health Services, 2700 West Norfolk Avenue, Norfolk, NE 68701

Woody gets treated in the intensive care unit, and later, when he collapses outside Blinker Tavern (see #18), David drives him to this hospital.

"I won a million dollars," says Woody.

"Congratulations," replies the doctor, "that'll just about pay for a day in the hospital."

12. RAILROAD TRACKS
Intersection of North 5th Street and Braasch Avenue, Norfolk, NE 68701

Near this junction, David and his father search for Woody's dentures. "They're not my teeth," says Woody.

13. ENTERING HAWTHORNE
South West Street, just south of Front Street, Plainview, NE 68769

David and Woody drive north on South West Street and make a right turn on West Locust Avenue, heading east into downtown Plainview.

14. RAY'S HOUSE

112 North Plum Street, Plainview, NE 68769

They drive south on Plum Street to the home of Woody's brother, Ray (Rance Howard), his wife, Martha (Mary Louise Wilson), and their two unemployed sons.

15. DOWNTOWN HAWTHORNE

Intersection of Main Street and West Locust Avenue, Plainview, NE 68769

From this intersection, Woody and David walk west along West Locust Street to explore the town.

16. OK AUTO SERVICE

Northeast corner of West Locust Avenue and South West Street, Plainview, NE 68769

"You're using the wrong wrench," Woody tells a mechanic at the garage he once owned.

17. SODBUSTER SALOON

110 North Main Street, Hooper, NE 68031

"Have a drink with your old man," urges Woody. "Be somebody!" While drinking with David, Woody explains why he drinks a lot. "You'd drink too if you were married to your mother."

18. BLINKER TAVERN EXTERIOR

Fat's Lounge, 409 West Locust Avenue, Plainview, NE 68769

Woody and David walk across the street to another bar, where they meet Ed Pegram (Stacy Keach).

19. BLINKER TAVERN INTERIOR

Sodbuster Saloon, 110 North Main Street, Hooper, NE 68031

The interior of the Blinker Tavern, where Woody announces he's a millionaire, is located 70 miles away from Plainview.

20. HAWTHORNE BUS STOP

Intersection of West Locust Avenue and Maple Street, Plainview, NE 68769

On the northeast corner of this intersection, across the street from the Sodbuster Saloon, Woody and David sit on a bench to wait for Kate to arrive on a bus.

21. CEMETERY

West Cedar Valley Cemetery, NE-14 (and 841st Road), Elgin, NE 68636

Kate gives David a blunt rundown of his family history. "I liked Rose but my God she was a slut."

22. THE HAWTHORNE REPUBLICAN

Plainview News Office, 508 West Locust Avenue, Plainview, NE 68769

The filmmakers changed the signs on *Plainview News* office to the *Hawthorne Republican*, where David talks with Pat Nege (Angela McEwan).

23. BACK ROAD STEAKHOUSE

108 South West Street, Plainview, NE 68769

At this karaoke restaurant with a soup-and-salad bar, Woody insists on ordering meatloaf.

24. THE GRANTS' HOUSE
867th Road and 539th Avenue, Plainview, NE 68769

Just north of this intersection on the west side of the avenue, the Grant family visits the house Woody built. "Just a bunch of old wood and some weeds," says Woody.

25. ESCAPING THE HOSPITAL
West Norfolk Avenue and 29th Street, Norfolk, NE 68701

David picks up his AWOL father, walking west along Norfolk Avenue.

26. ENTERING LINCOLN
Salt Creek Bridge, West O Street, Lincoln, NE 68508

David drives the Subaru east across the bridge and then through the intersection at 13th Street.

27. CORNHUSKER MARKETING AND PROMOTIONS, 11522 WEST COTNER STREET
Eclipse, 3400 Madison Avenue, Lincoln, NE 68504

In this office, Woody hands in his letter and discovers he doesn't have one of the winning numbers. "I can give you a free gift," says the receptionist. "Would you like a hat or a seat cushion?"

28. AUTO R&D SALES
B & D Auto Sales, 2040 O Street, Lincoln, NE 68510

At this dealership, David trades in his Subaru for a truck.

OHIO

The Avengers

When the evil Loki (Tom Hiddleston) steals a pulsating energy cube to open an intergalactic portal to attack Earth with flying leviathan-like machines, Nick Fury (Samuel L. Jackson), who runs S.H.I.E.L.D. (Strategic Hazard Intervention Espionage Logistics Directorate) from a massive helicarrier, calls upon the Avengers—Iron Man, Captain America, Thor, Black Widow, Hawkeye, and the Hulk—to drop their personal differences and team up to save the Earth from destruction.

While bringing together a band of diverse superheroes risks creating an incomprehensible muddle, writer/director Joss Whedon decided to treat this flick like a *Dirty Dozen* war movie, creating a riveting action epic. "He sees the Avengers as the ultimate dysfunctional family," observed film critic Peter Travers in *Rolling Stone*. "Their powers have estranged them from the normal world. As a result, they're lonely, cranky, emotional fuck-ups, which the actors have a ball playing."

Although the movie supposedly takes place in New York City, the filmmakers shot most of the street scenes in Cleveland, Ohio, and interiors on sets built in Albuquerque, New Mexico. And while the action sequences and special effects are certainly stunning, the best moments in this film are the banter between the characters. *New York Times* film critic A. O. Scott sums it up best: "This movie revels in the individuality of its mighty, mythical characters, pinpointing insecurities that are amplified by superhuman power and catching sparks that fly when big, rough-edged egos (and alter egos) collide."

"It's good to meet you, Dr. Banner," says Tony Stark (Robert Downey Jr.). "Your work on anti-electron collisions is unparalleled. And I'm a huge fan of the way you lose control and turn into an enormous green rage monster."

1. S.H.I.E.L.D. FACILITY INTERIOR

NASA Plum Brook Station, 6100 Columbus Avenue, Sandusky, OH 44870

The 122-foot-tall aluminum vacuum chamber of NASA's Space Power Facility, a remote test facility for the NASA Glenn Research Center in Cleveland, Ohio, served as the inside of the S.H.I.E.L.D. facility. Located on 6,400 acres, Plum Brook is home to three world-class test facilities. In addition to the Space Power Facility, the research center also houses the Spacecraft Propulsion Research Facility (for testing launch vehicles and rocket engines under simulated high-altitude conditions) and the Cryogenic Components Laboratory (for testing materials at very low temperatures by using liquid hydrogen, oxygen, and nitrogen). Plum Brook is closed to the public but has offered free open houses in the past.

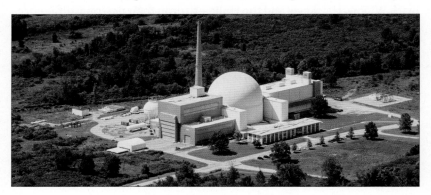

SHOT ELSEWHERE

SHIELD YOURSELF

The filmmakers shot the exterior of the S.H.I.E.L.D. facility in Albuquerque, New Mexico, at Atrisco Heritage Academy High School (10800 Dennis Chavez Boulevard SW), enhancing the school with high-tech decor and adding a helicopter landing pad. The underground passages through which Loki (Tom Hiddleston) escapes with the hypercube were filmed in the 150-mile maze of abandoned limestone tunnels burrowed 300 feet beneath the ground at Creekside Mushrooms Farm in Worthington, Pennsylvania (1 Moonlight Drive). The world's largest single-site mushroom growing facility, Creekside Mushrooms is the only underground mushroom farm in the United States.

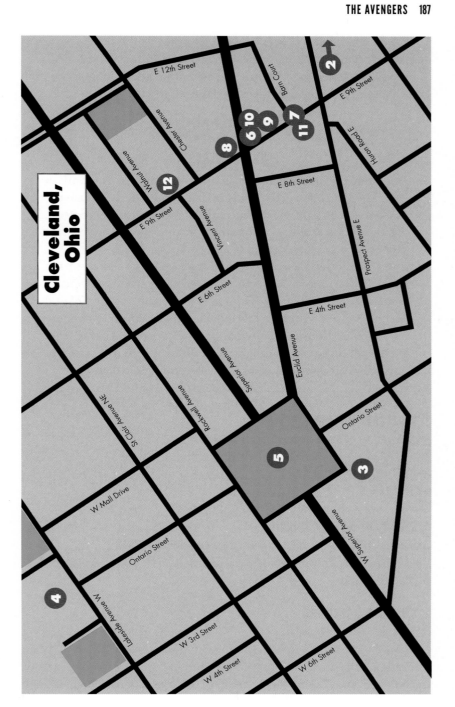

2. RUSSIAN WAREHOUSE

Abandoned warehouse, southeast corner of Ashland Road and Cedar Avenue, Cleveland, OH 44103

The Russians interrogate Natasha Romanoff (Scarlett Johansson), tied to a chair, until she receives an important phone call.

SHOT ELSEWHERE

UNSUNG HEROES

The filmmakers dressed the abandoned Albuquerque Rail Yards in New Mexico, constructed between 1915 and 1925, to create the backstreets of Calcutta, India, and the warehouse where Bruce Banner (Mark Ruffalo) crashes through the roof and encounters a nonchalant security guard (Harry Dean Stanton).

In Manhattan, Tony Stark (Robert Downey Jr.) operates from Stark Tower, his headquarters towering over Grand Central Station and the Chrysler Building through the magic of digital technology, replacing the MetLife Building at 200 Park Avenue.

To create the tarmac scenes on the helicarrier, the filmmakers built a set on an old landing strip at Albuquerque International Airport in New Mexico and added everything else digitally.

---

3. STUTTGART MUSEUM EXTERIOR

Tower City Center, 50 Public Square, Cleveland, OH 44113

The museum benefit takes place inside the 52-story Terminal Tower, opened in 1928 and added to the National Register of Historic Places in 1976.

4. STUTTGART MUSEUM INTERIOR

Probate Court of Cuyahoga County, 1 Lakeside Avenue West, Cleveland, OH 44113

Loki (Tom Hiddleston) crashes the party, steals a man's eye, and then proceeds outside.

5. STUTTGART, GERMANY

Public Square, Cleveland, OH 44113

Loki orders the crowd to kneel to him in Public Square, where Captain America (Chris Evans) and Iron Man fight Loki. In the esplanade stands the Soldiers' and Sailors' Monument, a Civil War memorial dedicated on July 4, 1894, and consisting of a 125-foot-tall column above a Memorial

Room containing four bronze relief sculptures. For more information, visit www.soldiersandsailors.com.

6. HIPSTERS

Cleveland Trust Company Building, 900 Euclid Avenue, Cleveland, OH 44115

Iron Man nearly crashes onto the sidewalk just outside this former bank, barely missing a group of young hipsters. The building was added to the National Register of Historic Places in 1973.

SHOT ELSEWHERE

PARK AVENUE VIADUCT

Loki opens a portal above Stark Tower to let the Chitauri descend on the city and do battle on the viaduct above Park Avenue in front of Grand Central Station at 42nd Street. The filmmakers built a replica of the viaduct surrounded by green screen inside a train station in Albuquerque so that shots of Grand Central Station could be added later.

---

7. NEW YORKERS FLEE

East 9th Street, between Euclid Avenue and Prospect Avenue East, Cleveland, OH 44115

The filmmakers dressed two blocks on East 9th Street as a street in Manhattan, and when the letter *K* falls from Stark Tower, innocent bystanders flee, running north on East 9th Street from Prospect Avenue East.

8. POLICE CARS AND ABANDONED TAXIS

The 925 Building, 925 Euclid Avenue, Cleveland, OH 44115

Police cars head west on Euclid Avenue, make left turns, heading south on East 9th Street, in front of this high-rise office building, formerly known as the Huntington Building, originally the Union Trust Building. This building, completed in 1924, contains one of the world's largest bank lobbies, which features massive marble Corinthian columns, barrel-vaulted ceilings, and stunning murals by Jules Guérin.

9. GRAND CENTRAL-42 STREET STATION
Metropolitan at the 9, 2017 East 9th Street, Cleveland, OH 44115

The southern corner of this 29-story upscale hotel, set in the converted Cleveland Trust Tower, became the subway station entrance. Built in 1971 by architect Marcel Breuer after his plan to build a similar skyscraper atop the real Grand Central Terminal in Manhattan fell through, the Cleveland Trust Tower now contains elegant bedrooms, suites, conference rooms, restaurants, and a rooftop cocktail lounge.

10. BANK INTERIOR
Cleveland Trust Company Building, 900 Euclid Avenue, Cleveland, OH 44115

The glass-domed rotunda of this empty building became the bank where Captain America rescues the trapped citizens.

11. MANHATTAN
Rose Building, 2060 East 9th Street, Cleveland, OH 44115

Captain America falls on top of the car outside the Rose Building. Later, Thor (Chris Hemsworth) catches his hammer and Captain America catches his shield in front of the Rose Building before battling the aliens. The ornate Rose Building, built in 1902, is a designated city landmark.

12. SHAWARMA PALACE
Ohio Savings Plaza, 1801 East 9th Street, Cleveland, OH 44114

After flying through the leviathan, Iron Man crash-lands outside this restaurant, built by the filmmakers onto the Ohio Savings Plaza. The set no longer exists. Iron Man later flies around the south side of the high-rise.

SHOT ELSEWHERE

A SMALL BITE OF THE BIG APPLE

Iron Man flies under and over the double-decked Verrazano-Narrows Bridge, named for the Florentine explorer Giovanni da Verrazano and connecting Staten Island to Brooklyn. With a central span of 4,260 feet, the bridge was the longest suspension bridge in the world upon its completion in 1964. At the end of the movie, Thor takes Loki into custody at Bethesda Terrace, a scenic spot in Central Park overlooking Turtle Lake.

A Christmas Story

The 1983 movie *A Christmas Story* was based on humorist Jean Shepherd's 1966 book, *In God We Trust, All Others Pay Cash*—a collection of short stories based on Shepherd's recollections of growing up in Hammond, Indiana, during the Great Depression. In the movie, Ralphie Parker (Peter Billingsley) yearns for a Red Ryder carbine action 200-shot range model air rifle (with a compass in the stock and "this thing which tells time") for Christmas. Shepherd, who narrates the movie from the viewpoint of the adult Ralphie Parker, set the story in the fictional town of Hohman, Indiana, modeled after his hometown of Hammond, Indiana. Hohman Avenue is a main street running through downtown Hammond.

Director Bob Clark chose Cleveland for exterior filming because Bruce Campbell, then vice president of Higbee's Department Store, agreed to let the filmmakers shoot scenes inside the store, welcoming the publicity and offering to help build sets, provided he could personally edit out the profanity in the script to protect Higbee's family-friendly reputation. The producers agreed, and Ralphie's Old Man (Darren McGavin) grumbles scripted nonsense words rather than recognizable profanities.

In reality, Shepherd's hometown of Hammond contained no Higbee's department stores, and some filming took place in Toronto, Canada.

"Without Jean Shepherd, there would be no *Christmas Story*," wrote Chris Heller in the *Atlantic*, "and the movie resonates so strongly because he had a unique talent for making his audience feel like his stories were their own."

"You can tell a story about anything," Shepherd told an interviewer in 1971, "but the only stories that have any fidelity, any feeling, are stories that either did happen to you or conceivably could have happened to you."

1. THE PARKER FAMILY HOUSE ON CLEVELAND STREET
3159 West 11th Street, Cleveland, OH 44109

In 2004, San Diego entrepreneur Brian Jones, having founded the Red Rider Leg Lamp Company to manufacture replicas of the "major award" Ralphie's father wins in the movie, purchased this Victorian house, built in 1895. Jones restored the exterior to its movie appearance and, by watching the movie repeatedly, renovated the interior to match the movie set (built on a Toronto soundstage)—down to the fishnet-stocking leg lamp with "the soft glow of electric sex gleaming in the window." Original cast members attended the grand opening of A Christmas Story House in

2006, attracting some 4,300 visitors on opening weekend.

In the movie, Ralphie Parker's fictional boyhood home is on Cleveland Street, the name of the actual street where Shepherd grew up. At the beginning of the film, Ralphie and his friends run east along Rowley Avenue, across the street from the house. To get to school, the kids walk south along 11th Street.

A Christmas Story House is open 10 AM to 5 PM, seven days a week, year-round, except major holidays. For more ticket information, visit www.achristmasstoryhouse.com.

2. THE HIGBEE STORE IN DOWNTOWN HOHMAN
Horseshoe Casino Cleveland, 100 Public Square, Cleveland, OH 44113

On the south corner of Cleveland's Public Square stands the 12-story building that housed Higbee's, the department store where Ralphie first sees a Red Ryder BB gun in the window. Ralphie and his brother, Randy (Ian Petrella), visit Santa (Jeff Gillan) and his hostile elves (Patty Johnson and Drew Hocevar) on the second floor of the actual store. The man who tells Ralphie not to cut the line is author Jean Sheppard.

Opened in 1931 and named for company founder Edwin Converse Higbee, the 12-story Higbee Company building was the first department store in the greater Cleveland area. It became Dillard's in 1992 and went out of business in 2002. The Higbee building became home to the Horseshoe Casino in 2012. Higbee signs grace the corner of the building on Ontario Street.

The building is a part of Tower City Center (formerly known as Cleveland Union Terminal), a collection of buildings, including the landmark 52-story Terminal Tower (opened in 1928) and the central hub of Cleveland's rapid transit system. Terminal Tower was added to the National Register of Historic Places in 1976.

3. HOHMAN PUBLIC SQUARE
Public Square, Cleveland, OH 44113

From Public Square opposite Higbee's, the Christmas parade proceeds southeast along Ontario Street. In the esplanade stands the Soldiers' and Sailors' Monument, a Civil War memorial dedicated on July 4, 1894, and consisting of a 125-foot-tall column above a Memorial Room containing four bronze relief sculptures. For more information, visit www.soldiers andsailors.com.

4. FLICK SCHWARTZ'S HOUSE
3167 West 11th Street, Cleveland, OH 44109

Ralphie's friend Schwartz (R. D. Robb) lives in this house.

5. RANDY'S FALL
3171 West 11th Street, Cleveland, OH 44109

As the kids walk to school, Randy falls down and can't get back up in the front yard of this house.

ONTARIO

"I double dog dare you!" The showdown in the schoolyard of Warren G. Harding Elementary School, in which Flick (Scott Schwartz) gets his tongue frozen to the flagpole, was shot at the Victoria School (173 Niagara Street, St. Catharines, Ontario L2R 0A3, Canada). The school has since closed down and now operates as a woman's shelter. Townhouses and a parking lot now stand where the flagpole and monkey bars once were on the south side of the school, near Gibson Place. (Warren G. Harding Elementary School was author Jean Shepherd's alma mater in Hammond, Indiana.)

"Now this here is a tree." In the lot where Ralphie's family buys a Christmas tree, a food market now stands: Queen Live (238 Queen Street West, Toronto, Ontario M5V 1Z7, Canada).

On the southern end of the Cherry Street Bridge (Cherry Street, Toronto, Ontario M5A 3K8, Canada), the Old Man gets a flat tire, and Ralphie exclaims, "Oh, fudge!"

On a dead-end street in Toronto (end of Minto Street, Toronto, Ontario M4L Canada), Scut Farcus hits Ralphie with a snowball, provoking an attack.

Bo Ling Chop Suey Palace, the Chinese restaurant where the Parker family enjoys an eccentric Christmas dinner after the dog runs off with their turkey, is now Batifole (744 Gerrard Street East, Toronto, Ontario M4M 1Y3, Canada), "the best French restaurant in Chinatown."

Other Feature Attractions

A CHRISTMAS STORY HOUSE MUSEUM

1103 Rowley Avenue, Cleveland, OH 44109

Directly across the street from A Christmas Story House stands the official A Christmas Story House Museum, which displays original props, costumes, behind-the-scenes photographs, and memorabilia from the film, including toys from the Higbee's window, Ralphie's Red Ryder BB gun, Randy's snowsuit, and the chalkboard from Miss Shields's classroom. Next door at 3166 West 11th Street, the A Christmas Story House Gift Shop sells leg lamps, vintage Red Ryder BB guns, bunny-suit pajamas, and other collectibles. For more information, visit www.achristmasstoryhouse.com.

INDIANA WELCOME CENTER
7770 Corinne Drive, Hammond, IN 46323

Every November and December, the Exhibit Hall in the Indiana Welcome Center hosts "*A Christmas Story* Comes Home," featuring around six animatronic window displays from Macy's Department Store in New York that depict different scenes from *A Christmas Story*. The scene where Flick gets his tongue stuck to a flagpole on a triple dog dare has been immortalized in a bronze statue outside the Indiana Welcome Center in Hammond, Indiana, the hometown of author Jean Shepherd. Commissioned in 2013 to commemorate the 30th anniversary of *A Christmas Story*, the statue was created by artist Oscar Leon. For more information, visit www.southshorecva.com.

JEAN SHEPHERD'S CHILDHOOD HOME
Private Residence, 2907 Cleveland Street, Hammond, IN 46323

Born in 1921, author Jean Shepherd lived in this house during his formative years from 1928 to 1935. Please be respectful and do not loiter or disturb the residents.

THE CHIPPAWA VOLUNTEER FIRE DEPARTMENT
8696 Banting Avenue, Niagara Falls, Ontario, Canada

The 1938 Ford LaFrance fire truck used to rescue Flick from the flagpole can be viewed here every Sunday from 9 AM to 12 PM.

The Deer Hunter

Although the 1978 movie *The Deer Hunter* takes place in Clairton, Pennsylvania (ten miles south of Pittsburgh), director Michael Cimino shot the movie in Cleveland and several mill towns in Ohio to create a screen version of Clairton as an amalgam. Even the large sign reading "Welcome to Clairton, City of Prayer" at the beginning of the film was shot in Mingo Junction, Ohio.

The movie follows the story of three blue-collar friends of Eastern European descent (Robert De Niro, John Savage, and Christopher Walken) who work in the furnace of a Pennsylvania steel mill and how enlisting to fight in the Vietnam War alters their lives forever. Taken prisoner by the Viet Cong (filmed in Thailand), the trio is forced to play Russian roulette while their captors gamble on the outcome, emotionally damaging the three white American males. "It is not an antiwar film," wrote film critic Roger Ebert in the *Chicago Sun-Times*. "It is not a pro-war film. It is one of the most emotionally shattering films ever made."

"You have to think about one shot," says Michael (De Niro), while hunting deer in Pennsylvania. "One shot is what it's all about. A deer's gotta be taken with one shot."

"We've filmed *The Deer Hunter* right where it would have happened if the story wasn't fictional," said Christopher Walken in the production notes on the DVD. "We worked in steel mills, community halls, the most beautiful Russian Orthodox church I've ever seen, and in a tavern which we built as a composite of scores we visited while researching the film."

While reviewers lauded the film, former war correspondents denounced the movie's racism and historical inaccuracies. In the *Los Angeles Times*, Peter Arnett, who had won a Pulitzer Prize for his coverage of the Vietnam War, wrote, "In its 20 years of war, there was not a single recorded case of Russian roulette. . . . The central metaphor of the movie is simply a bloody lie." Despite the criticism, *The Deer Hunter* won five Oscars, including Best Picture and Best Director.

Said De Niro in an interview with *Vanity Fair*, "Whether [*The Deer Hunter*'s vision of the war] actually happened or not, it's something you could imagine very easily happening. Maybe it did. I don't know. All's fair in love and war."

1. CLAIRTON
Logan Avenue under the Ohio River Scenic Byway overpass, Mingo Junction, OH 43938

The truck heads east into town along Logan Avenue and makes a right onto Commercial Street.

2. THE STEELWORKS INTERIOR
US Steel Widowmaker Central Blast Furnace, 2199 East 28th Street, Lorain, OH 44055

The opening steel factory scenes show the molten orange metal of the blast furnaces.

3. THE STEELWORKS EXTERIOR
Mingo Junction Steel Mill, 454 Commercial Street, Mingo Junction, OH 43938

Michael (Robert De Niro), Steven (John Savage), and Nick (Christopher Walken) walk out of this steel mill after a hard day's work.

4. THE CHURCH
St. Theodosius Russian Orthodox Cathedral, 733 Starkweather Avenue, Cleveland, OH 44113

Steven marries Angela (Rutanya Alda) inside this replica of the Cathedral of the Annunciation in the Kremlin in Moscow.

5. WELCH'S LOUNGE
Empty lot, Commercial Street and State Street, Mingo Junction, OH 43938

Michael and his buddies drink, play pool, and sing "Can't Take My Eyes Off of You" by Frankie Valli in this tavern built for the film behind a storefront that is no longer standing.

6. EAGLE SUPERMARKET
Lilly Handmade Chocolates, 761 Starkweather Avenue, Cleveland, OH 44113

The grocery store where Linda (Meryl Streep) works, just west of the cathedral, was renovated into a chocolate shop.

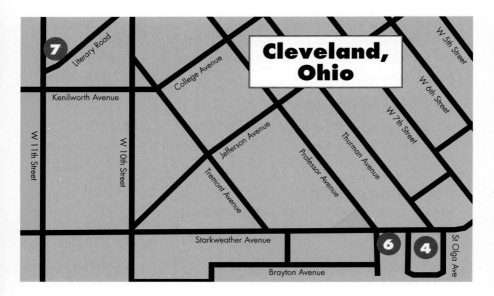

Cleveland, Ohio

Literary Road
College Avenue
Kenilworth Avenue
W 5th Street
W 6th Street
W 7th Street
Thurman Avenue
Jefferson Avenue
Professor Avenue
W 11th Street
W 10th Street
Tremont Avenue
Starkweather Avenue
St Olga Ave
Brayton Avenue

SHOT ELSEWHERE

NICK'S CABIN

The house where Nick lives, with used tires strewn on the roof, stood in Weirton, West Virginia (on what is now an empty lot on the northwest corner of the intersection of 2nd Street and West Avenue A). Across the street from the lot, Nick begs Michael not to leave him in Vietnam.

7. THE WEDDING RECEPTION

Lemko Hall, 1046 Literary Road, Cleveland, OH 44113

The festive wedding reception takes place inside this historic landmark. The word *Lemko* refers to a Slavic ethnic group from Lemkovyna, a region of southeastern Poland, with their own language, culture, and identity. At the end of the 19th century, Lemko immigrants settled in the Cleveland area in large numbers, and Lemko Hall, built in 1911 with a social hall and bar, became a community and cultural center for Lemkos. Sold in 1987, the building now contains condominiums, offices, and shops.

THE DEER HUNT AND VIETNAM

The deer hunt in the Allegheny Mountains was filmed along Glacier Creek and at Nooksack Falls in Mt. Baker–Snoqualmie National Forest in Whatcom, Washington. To get there, Michael and his friends drive across Diablo Dam in Rockport. "You have to think about one shot," says Michael. "One shot is what it's all about. The deer has to be taken with one shot."

For the scenes of rural Vietnam, the filmmakers used Sai Yok National Park in Thailand. On the River Kwai in Kanchanaburi, the filmmakers built the hut where the Viet Cong let Michael and Nick play Russian roulette with three bullets. "It's gonna be all right, Nickie," says Michael. "Go ahead, shoot. Shoot, Nickie." The Rajini School in Bangkok played the role of the Saigon Hospital, Patpong represented Saigon's red light district, and the restaged 1973 evacuation of Saigon took place at the US embassy in Bangkok.

8. WALKING TO THE GROCERY STORE

Southwest corner of McLister Avenue and Commercial Street, Mingo Junction, OH 43938

Mike and Linda walk east on McLister Street and turn right, walking south along Commercial Street.

9. THE BOWLING ALLEY

Bowladrome Lanes, 56 State Street, Struthers, OH 44471

At the town's bowling alley, Axel (Chuck Aspergren) gets stuck in the bowling-pin reset mechanism.

10. LOUIS STOKES CLEVELAND VETERAN'S ADMINISTRATION MEDICAL CENTER

10701 East Boulevard, Cleveland, OH 44106

Steven plays bingo in this VA hospital.

HOME AT LAST

Nick's burial takes place in McKeesport and Versailles Cemetery in McKeesport, Pennsylvania.

Rain Man

Slick-talking wheeler-dealer Charlie Babbitt (Tom Cruise) flies from Los Angeles to Cincinnati for his father's funeral and the reading of the will, discovers he has an autistic-savant older brother named Raymond (Dustin Hoffman) living in a nearby institution, and kidnaps him in the hopes of obtaining his share of the $3 million trust fund left to provide for Raymond. During the six-day drive from Cincinnati to Los Angeles in a 1949 Buick Roadmaster convertible, callous and egocentric Charlie stops calling his brother a "retard" and comes to see him as a very special person.

Dustin Hoffman portrays an autistic savant—a high-level functioning autistic person with savant syndrome—with exceptional accuracy and sensitivity. (Autism and savant syndrome are two distinct conditions; only 1 in 10 autistic people possess savant abilities.)

"Although it roams across expanses of America," wrote film critic Sheila Benson in the *Los Angeles Times*, "*Rain Man* is a small, mostly interior journey: the awakening of two walled-off souls." Just as their journey together transforms Charlie into a more compassionate human being, the time spent with his brother makes Raymond more comfortable with human contact.

Although Charlie and Raymond travel across the United States, a great deal of the movie was shot in Cincinnati, Ohio, and the surrounding area. The rest of the film was shot in Oklahoma (Guthrie, Cogar, Hinton, and El Reno), Nevada (Blue Diamond and Las Vegas), and California (San Pedro, Palm Springs, Los Angeles, and Santa Ana).

Rain Man won four Academy Awards, including Best Actor for Dustin Hoffman and Best Picture.

1. CEMETERY
Evergreen Cemetery, 25 Alexandria Pike, Southgate, KY 41075

Charlie (Tom Cruise) makes his girlfriend Susanna (Valerie Golino) wait in the car during his father's funeral at this cemetery four miles south of downtown Cincinnati.

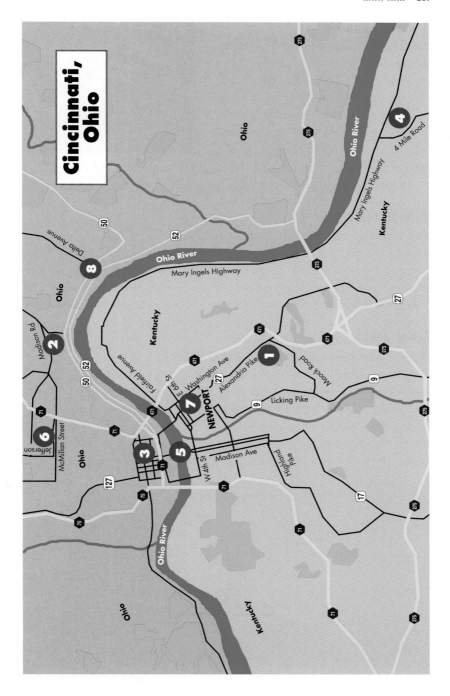

2. BABBITT MANSION

Private Residence, 2 Beech Crest Lane, East Walnut
Hills, OH 45206

At this Tudor-style mansion with
dying prize-winning hybrid rose
bushes and a drained swimming pool,
Charlie admires the 1949 Buick Road-
master convertible in the garage and
hears the reading of his father's will. Please be respectful and do not loiter
or disturb the residents.

3. CINCINNATI TRUST

Dixie Terminal, 120 East Fourth Street, Cincinnati, OH 45202

Charlie charms the receptionist inside the barrel-vaulted lobby of this
ornate 10-story building, opened in 1921. Aside from serving as a street-
car terminal, the building housed the Cincinnati Stock Exchange until
1995. The Roebling Suspension Bridge can be seen through the windows.

4. WALLBROOK

St. Anne's Convent, 1000 St. Anne Drive, Melbourne, KY 41059

"I'm an excellent driver." In the driveway of this fictional center for the
developmentally disabled, Charlie finds his brother, Raymond (Dustin
Hoffman). Built in 1919 by architect Howard McClorey and located just
across the Ohio River from Cincinnati, St. Anne Convent is the home
of the American Province of the Congregation of Divine Providence, a
community of Roman Catholic sisters.

5. THE BRIDGE
John A. Roebling Suspension Bridge, Cincinnati, OH 45202

Charlie, Susanna, and Raymond drive south across the John A. Roebling Suspension Bridge, opened in 1867 and designed by German American civil engineer John A. Roebling, who later designed the Brooklyn Bridge.

6. VERNON MANOR HOTEL
400 Oak Street, Cincinnati, OH 45219

Charlie, Susanna, and Raymond spend their first night in room 21 at this landmark hotel, opened in 1924. The hotel, which hosted President John F. Kennedy, the Beatles, and Bob Dylan, closed in 2009 and now houses offices for Cincinnati Children's Hospital.

7. POMPILIO'S BAR AND RESTAURANT

600 Washington Avenue, Newport, KY 41071

"You hungry?" asks Charlie. "Tuesday we have pancakes," insists Raymond. At this Southern Italian restaurant, opened in 1933, Raymond meets waitress Sally Dibbs (Bonnie Hunt) and immediately recites her phone number, which he read the previous night in the phone book. Later, he knocks over a box of toothpicks and immediately states the number of picks spilled on the floor.

8. ON THE ROAD

Columbia Parkway (OH-50, west of Delta Avenue), Cincinnati, OH 45226

As the two brothers head southeast toward Delta Avenue, Rays repeats the slogan, "97-X—*Bam!*—the future of rock 'n' roll!"

9. CINCINNATI/NORTHERN KENTUCKY INTERNATIONAL AIRPORT

2939 Terminal Drive, Hebron, KY 41048

Raymond sits watching television in front of two industrial mosaic murals in the now closed check-in area of terminal 2. The murals, which originally hung in Union Terminal's concourse, depict workers in the Cincinnati Milling Co.'s Oakley foundry and the American Laundry Machine Co.'s Norwood plant. In concourse C, Raymond recites airline crash statistics. "Quantas never crashed."

10. THE HIGHWAY

Interstate-275 West, Cincinnati, OH

Highway scenes, the accident, and Raymond walking ahead of the car were shot on the interstate that circles Cincinnati.

11. HONEYMOON HAVEN MOTEL

Hearthstone Restaurant, 18149 US 52, Metamora, Indiana 47030

Raymond refuses to leave this motel—supposedly on Route 60 somewhere in Missouri—until the rain stops. Located in Metamora, approximately 50 miles northwest of Cincinnati, the Hearthstone Restaurant rents cabins and serves country food.

The Shawshank Redemption

Although the 1994 prison drama *The Shawshank Redemption*, starring Tim Robbins as Andy Dufresne and Morgan Freeman as Red, takes place in Maine, the filmmakers shot the movie at the abandoned Ohio State Reformatory and at locations in and around Mansfield, Ohio, a town approximately 80 miles southwest of Cleveland.

Opened in 1896, the Ohio State Reformatory, a blend of Victorian, Gothic, Richardsonian, Romanesque, and Queen Anne architecture, housed more than 155,000 men before being closed in 1990 for inhumane living conditions. "You could feel the pain," Tim Robbins told *Vanity Fair* in 2014. "It was the pain of thousands of people."

"When I saw it, I knew it was going to be a sort of character in the film," actor Bob Gunton, who played the prison warden, told the *Indy Star* in 2013. "It is the embodiment of a hellacious place to spend your life, and it created a sense of dread and hopelessness that we could play into or play against."

Based on the Steven King novella *Rita Hayworth and Shawshank Redemption*, published in his 1982 book *Different Seasons*, *The Shawshank Redemption* did poorly in theaters, but after receiving seven Academy Award nominations, it became a hit in television reruns, video rentals, and DVD sales.

Ultimately, *The Shawshank Redemption* raises the hope that the freedom inside you can liberate you from whatever your prison might be. "I guess it comes down to a simple choice, really," says Andy Dufresne.

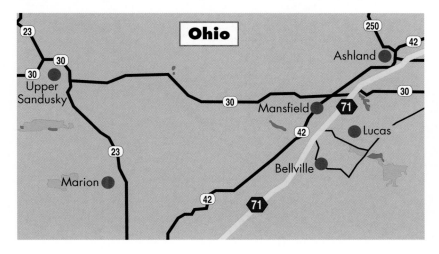

"Get busy living or get busy dying." A trip to Mansfield, where locals who worked as extras, playing prison inmates, eagerly share their stories and fondly recall meeting famous cast members, can help you get busy living.

1. THE CABIN
Pugh Cabin at Malabar Farm, 4050 Bromfield Road, Lucas, OH 44843

Andy Dufresne (Tim Robbins) sits outside this cabin in his Plymouth, drinking bourbon and fumbling with a revolver before confronting his cheating wife and her lover. In 1945, Humphrey Bogart and Lauren Bacall held their wedding and honeymoon at Malabar Farm.

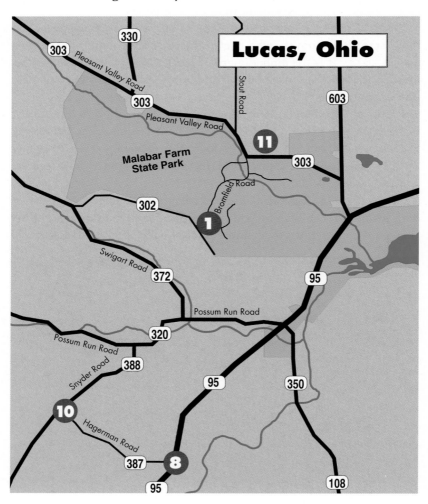

2. THE COURTHOUSE

Wyandot County Courthouse, 109 South Sandusky Avenue, Upper Sandusky, OH 43351

Inside this courthouse, Andy Dufresne is convicted and sentenced for the murder of his wife and her lover.

3. SHAWSHANK STATE PRISON

Ohio State Reformatory, 100 Reformatory Road, Mansfield, OH 44905

After 94 years of use, the massive Ohio State Reformatory on the outskirts of Mansfield closed its doors on New Year's Eve 1990. The state had planned to tear down the portentous prison, a combination of three architectural styles (Victorian Gothic, Richardsonian Romanesque, and Queen

Anne) after the filming of *The Shawshank Redemption* was completed, but a local group of preservationists intervened, and after demolishing the ancillary buildings, the state relented and sold the remaining main building to the Mansfield Reformatory Preservation Society for a dollar.

The reformatory houses the world's tallest freestanding steel cell-block—six tiers high. Approximately 600 cells, 7 feet by 9 feet, held two inmates each. Other well-known movies shot in the reformatory include *Air Force One* (1997), *Tango and Cash* (1989), and *Harry and Walter Go to New York* (1976).

Take the tour of the reformatory to see Andy's cell, the warden's office, the Parole Board room, the Brooks library (now a storage room), the showers, solitary confinement, and the fake sewer pipe that Andy crawls through to escape the prison. The Ohio State Reformatory hosts tours, conventions, trade shows, ghost hunts, concerts, proms, and even weddings. For more information, visit www.mrps.org.

4. PRISON WOODSHOP

Shawshank Woodshop and Museum, 228 South Eighth Street, Upper Sandusky, OH 43351

All scenes that take place in the prison workshop were shot in the Stephan Lumber Company building. When Andy locks himself in the warden's office and plays a recording of Mozart's *The Marriage of Figaro* over the public address system, Red (Morgan Freeman) and his fellow prisoners stop their work in the prison workshop to listen to the opera music. The workshop displays costumes, photographs, and memorabilia from the movie. Tours available by appointment. E-mail shawshankwoodshop@gmail.com.

5. THE BREWER HOTEL (AND THE PORTLAND DAILY BUGLE)

The Bissman Building, 193 North Main Street, Mansfield, OH 44902

"Brooks was here." In the movie, the Bissman Building became the Brewer Hotel, where Brooks (James Whitmore) resides after being paroled from Shawshank State Prison and later hangs himself. The building was also used as the set for the *Portland Daily Bugle*.

6. BROOK'S BENCH

West of the Gazebo in Central Park, Mansfield, OH 44902

A plaque marks the bench on which Brooks sits to feed the birds in the hope that his pet crow, Jake, will show up.

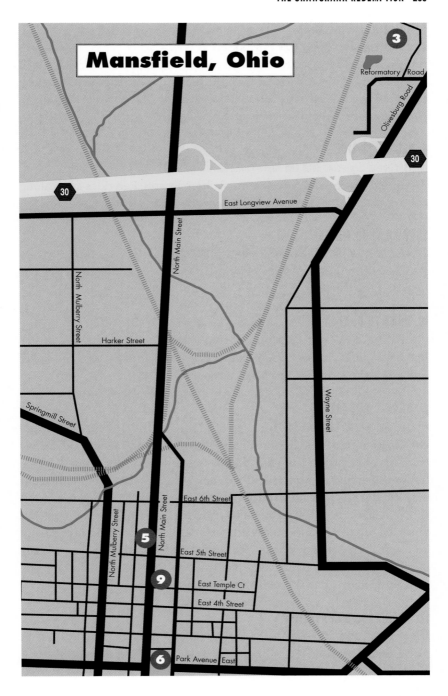

7. MAINE NATIONAL BANK

Crosby Advisory Group, 19 West Main Street, Ashland, OH 44805

Andy walks into the Maine National Bank, introduces himself as Randall Stevens, and closes his accounts. In the movie, we see the vault door, the teller line, and an upstairs office. Before leaving, Andy hands the teller a package addressed to the *Portland Daily Bugle*.

8. RED'S BUS RIDE

Intersection of Hagerman Road and Route 95 NE, Bellville, OH 44813

After being released from Shawshank State Prison, Red rides a bus along this road.

9. PAWN SHOP WINDOW

Carrousel Antiques, 118 North Main Street, Mansfield, OH 44902

Red looks through the windows of this shop at the compass he buys to help find the oak tree.

10. ROAD TO BUXTON

Intersection of Snyder Road and Hagerman Road, Bellville, OH 44813

Red hops out of the back of a pickup truck at this intersection and walks northeast along Synder Road to Buxton, Maine.

11. ANDY'S OAK TREE

Pleasant Valley Road, Lucas, OH 44843

On a private farm field on the north side of Pleasant Valley Road, across from Malabar Farm State Park, stands the remains of the giant oak tree under which Red digs up a metal box and reads a letter left by Andy. On July 29, 2011, high winds from a violent storm split the 175-year-old oak tree in half. Part of the tree remains standing. The tree's owner erected a fence to keep trespassers off the property, but you can still drive by slowly and see the tree from the road. The rock wall seen in the movie was built by the crew and no longer exists. Sadly, tourists who took rocks home as souvenirs dismantled the wall, piece by piece.

12. TRAILWAYS BUS STATION

Revivals 2 Thrift Store, 345 Orange Street, Ashland, OH 44805

At the counter inside this store, Red stands in a long line to purchase a bus ticket to Fort Hancock, Texas.

SOUTH DAKOTA

Dances with Wolves

Michael Blake's novel *Dances with Wolves*, published in 1986, revolves around the Comanche of Oklahoma and Texas. Needing a massive herd of buffalo to adapt the book into a film epic, and upon discovering that the Comanche language was nearly dead, director Kevin Costner changed the location to South Dakota, where the Triple U Ranch had a private herd of 3,500 buffalo and where the Lakota Sioux live on the nearby Rosebud reservation.

"I've always wanted to see the frontier . . . before it's gone," says Union soldier Lieutenant John Dunbar (Kevin Costner) in *Dances with Wolves*. Transferred to the edge of the Western frontier, he befriends and slowly assimilates into a Sioux tribe. "I've never known a people so eager to laugh," writes Dunbar in his journal, "so devoted to family, so dedicated to each other, and the only word that came to mind was 'harmony.'"

Filmed in 27 locations in South Dakota, the 1990 movie stars the American frontier. "Kevin wanted to offer a West so vast, so wild, so untamed, almost larger than life itself," production designer Jeffrey Beecroft told the *New York Times*.

After Costner used the original Pawnee and Lakota languages in the movie with English subtitles, the Sioux Nation inducted him, producer Jim Wilson, and actress Mary McDonnell (who plays Lieutenant Dunbar's love interest) into the tribe.

Treating the Native American culture with respect, *Dances with Wolves* won seven Academy Awards, including Best Picture. Box office sales surpassed $424 million, and in 2007 the Library of Congress selected *Dances with Wolves* for preservation in the United States National Film Registry.

1. ST. DAVID'S FIELD, TENNESSEE, FORT SEDGEWICK, AND INDIAN LAND
Huock Buffalo Ranch, 26312 Tatanka Place, Fort Pierre, SD 57532
Known as the Triple U Standing Butte Ranch when the film was made, the 55,000-acre Huock Buffalo Ranch is home to 3,500 buffalo, the world's largest privately owned herd.

Two miles east of the Missouri River, the ranch was the location of the Civil War battle in St. David's Field, Tennesse; Fort Sedgewick; and the buffalo hunt. The filmmakers built the two-story farmhouse and planted corn in the field for the movie. The real Fort Sedgewick was located in Colorado, approximately one mile west of Julesburg along the South Platte River.

2. FORT HAYS, KANSAS

Sanders-Olson Ranch (one mile south of Caputa General Store), Highway 44, Caputa, SD 57725

Seven miles southeast of Rapid City, the filmmakers built the Fort Hays major's quarters, the blacksmith shop, and the supply house. Several buildings were relocated as a tourist attraction to the Fort Hays Chuckwagon supper and show (see "Other Feature Attractions," page 213), including the major's quarters, complete with a hole where the bullet from Major Fambrough's (Maury Chaykin's) gun exited his office window.

3. WAGON JOURNEY

Sage Creek Wilderness Area, Badlands National Park, SD 57790

While most of the wagon ride from Fort Hayes to Fort Sedgewick was shot on Huock Buffalo Ranch, the filmmakers also used the spectacular scenery of the Badlands.

4. INDIAN SUMMER CAMP
Grubl-McNenny Ranch, 15252 Alkali Road, Sturgis, SD 57785
A Sioux village of 40 tepees stood and the wedding takes place in this grove of cottonwoods on the Belle Fourche River, about 35 miles east of Sturgis. The Grubl-McNenny Ranch did offer tours at one time, but no more.

5. THE BUFFALO HUNT
777 Bison Ranch, Fairburn, SD 57738
The Buffalo hunt took place at Huock Buffalo Ranch (see #1) and at 777 Bison Ranch.

6. INDIAN WINTER CAMP
Spearfish Canyon, Black Hills National Forest, Rapid City, SD 57754

Just south and west of the Spearfish Canyon Lodge (10619 Roughlock Falls Road, Lead, SD 57754) and north of Roughlock Falls sits Spearfish Canyon, where the Sioux camped in the winter. A sign marks the site, accessible by car on Forest Road 222 (Roughlock Falls Road), on the right, approximately 1.7 miles past the Roughlock picnic area. Less than a mile wide, Spearfish Canyon runs for 20 miles along Highway 14A, a designated National Scenic Byway. Standing atop a cliff, Wind in His Hair (Rodney A. Grant) bids farewell to Dunbar and Stands with a Fist (Mary McDonnell).

Other Feature Attractions

THE *DANCES WITH WOLVES* FILM SET
Fort Hays Chuckwagon Supper & Cowboy Music Show, 2255 Fort Hayes Drive, Rapid City, SD 57702
At the *Dances with Wolves* Film Set, you can visit the original major's quarters, supply house, and sawmill used in the movie, explore the South Dakota Film Museum, see blacksmith demonstrations, and enjoy a full chuckwagon dinner with musical entertainment. There is no admission fee to tour the buildings. Open mid-May to mid-October, 7 days a week, 7:30 AM to 7:30 PM. For more information, visit http://mountrushmoretours .com/fort-hays-old-town-square/.

1880 TOWN

Interstate 90, exit 170, 22 miles west of Murdo, SD

See props and memorabilia from *Dance with Wolves*, including a tent, wagons, and a replica of a sod house. The 1880 Town also boasts more than 30 buildings from the 1880 to 1920 era, authentically furnished with thousands of relics, historical accounts, and photographs. For more information, visit www.1880town.com.

MIDNIGHT STAR

677 Main Street, Deadwood, SD 57732

This restaurant, sports bar, and casino owned by Kevin Costner displays costumes, props, photos, and memorabilia from *Dances with Wolves* and other Costner movies, including *Field of Dreams*. For more information, visit www.themidnightstar.com.

TATANKA

100 Tatanka Drive, Deadwood, SD 57732

Kevin Costner owns this museum and buffalo statue tribute where Native American interpreters tell the story of the Lakota and the buffalo. The site also features 14 larger-than-life-size bronze sculptures of Lakota riders hunting bison. Open daily, 9 AM to 5 PM, from mid-May through September. For more information, visit www.storyofthebison.com.

How the West Was Won

How the West Was Won, a 1962 epic film advertised as "the movie Western to end all Westerns," takes place between 1839 and 1889 and follows four generations of the Prescott family as they migrate westward from Albany, New York. Narrated by Spencer Tracy, the movie stars a litany of Hollywood luminaries, including Carroll Baker, Lee J. Cobb, Henry Fonda, Carolyn Jones, Karl Malden, Harry Morgan, Gregory Peck, George Peppard, Robert Preston, Debbie Reynolds, James Stewart, Eli Wallach, John Wayne, and Richard Widmark. The star-studded cast was supported by 12,617 extras, including 350 Native Americans from five different tribes.

The film, divided into five chapters—"The River," "The Plains," "The Outlaws" (directed by Henry Hathaway), "The Civil War" (directed by John Ford), and "The Railroad" (directed by George Marshall), was the first and last feature film produced in Cinerama, a widescreen process that required three synchronized 35 mm projectors placed side by side to project the panoramic movie on an enormous curved screen.

In addition to the majestic scenery of South Dakota, locations included Kentucky (Paducah and Smithland), Colorado (Uncompaghre National Forest and Chimney Rock), Arizona (Oatman, Perkinsville, Tonto National Forest, and Tucson), Utah (Monument Valley), Illinois (Cave-in-Rock State Park, Battery Rock, and Shawnee National Forest), and California (Lone Pine, Inyo National Forest, and Courthouse Mountain).

As the title suggests, *How the West Was Won* depicts the conquering and settlement of the American West, which narrator Spencer Tracy tells us was a wilderness that "had to be won. Won from Nature and from primitive man." The film does show government duplicity in dealing with Native Americans and concludes with aerial shots of skyscrapers and busy freeways in Los Angeles, wryly showing how the white man transformed the wilderness into "civilization."

1. THE TRANSCONTINENTAL RAILROAD
Unknown location, Rapid City, SD 57701

To create the construction camp for the first transcontinental railroad, the filmmakers laid a stretch of track near Rapid City to run the Virginia and Truckee Railroad's Engine #11, better known as *The Reno*.

2. PONY EXPRESS RELAY STATION

Gordon Stockade, 25073 US-16A, Custer State Park, Custer, SD 57730

In the movie, a Pony Express rider changes horses at this cavalry fort. The Gordon Stockade, a replica of a log fortress built by the Gordon Party on the bank of French Creek as protection from Lakota attacks during the 1874 gold rush, stands on the site of the original stockade.

3. THE BUFFALO STAMPEDE

Wildlife Loop Road, Custer State Park, Custer County, SD 57730

In this valley known as "Movie Draw," home to a herd of 1,500 free-roaming bison, the Indians instigate a buffalo stampede to destroy a railroad work camp guarded by Zeb Rawlings (George Peppard) and Mike King (Richard Widmark) near the Game Lodge area at the northeast end of the Wildlife Loop Road. Park superintendent Les Price helped accomplish this feat,

enabling the filmmakers to shoot footage both above and beneath the thundering herd. In this same area, Jethro Stuart (Henry Fonda) hunts buffalo. The Wildlife Loop Road is an 18-mile scenic drive, and just southwest of the Buffalo Corrals, a yellow highway sign lists the films shot in the park. The park's annual buffalo roundup, held in September, draws thousands of visitors to Custer State Park, as cowboys and cowgirls drive a herd of approximately 1,300 bison. For more information, visit www.custerstatepark.com.

North by Northwest

In the 1959 movie *North by Northwest*, Communist spies mistake Manhattan advertising executive Roger Thornhill (Cary Grant) for a fictitious CIA agent and abduct him. Thornhill escapes, witnesses the murder of a United Nations official, and, wrongly accused of the crime, flees to Chicago, Indiana, and South Dakota, where he and his love interest (Eva Maria Saint) wind up hiding from enemy agents among the presidential faces at Mount Rushmore.

In 1951, director Alfred Hitchcock told columnist Earl Wilson that he had an idea for a chase scene over the presidential faces carved into Mount Rushmore. "I want to have one scene of a man hanging on to Lincoln's eyebrows," said Hitchcock. "That's all the picture I have so far." Years later, the director shared the idea with screenwriter Ernest Lehman, who decided to visit the national landmark to research the possibilities.

Lehman hired a forest ranger on his day off to guide him to the top of Mount Rushmore. "Halfway up, I looked down and thought, 'God, I'm just a screenwriter. What the hell am I doing up here? One slip and I'm dead!' So, I gave the Polaroid camera to the forest ranger, and I told him to go up to the top and take photos of everything."

Lehman realized the top of the monument did not offer adequate space to stage a movie scene. "Then the Department of Parks found out that we were planning to have people fall off the face of their famous monument," recalled Lehman, "and they banned Hitchcock from shooting up there."

"I wanted Cary Grant to hide in Lincoln's nostril and then have a fit of sneezing," said Hitchcock in a speech at the Screen Producers Guild in 1965. "The Parks Commission of the Department of Interior was rather upset at this thought. I argued until one of their number asked me how I would like it if they had Lincoln play the scene in Cary Grant's nose. I saw their point at once."

Although officials of the National Park Service and the Department of the Interior felt staging the script at Mount Rushmore (originally titled *The Man in Lincoln's Nose*) would desecrate the national monument, Hitchcock remained undaunted. He had, after all, set the climax of *Saboteur* (1942) at the Statue of Liberty, a climactic event in *Strangers on a Train* (1951) at the Jefferson Memorial, an assassination attempt in *The Man Who Knew Too Much* (1955) at the Royal Albert Hall, and a suicide attempt in *Vertigo* (1958) at the Golden Gate Bridge.

While Hitchcock did not film any chase scenes on Mount Rushmore, he did film still shots of the memorial, which he used as backgrounds to shoot the chase scene in the studio and on a replica of the monument built on MGM soundstages. The National Park Service and the Department of the Interior objected to these scenes in the finished film, claiming their violence desecrated the national memorial. Ironically, the controversy helped publicize the film, which in turn publicized the memorial.

SHOT ELSEWHERE

NEW YORK AND CHICAGO

Abducted from the Plaza Hotel at Fifth Avenue and 59th Street in Manhattan, Roger Thornhill (Cary Grant) is brought to the redbrick mansion at Old Westbury Gardens (Phipps Estate) in Old Westbury on Long Island, escapes his captors, visits the United Nations building in Manhattan, and flees New York City on the 20th Century Limited from Grand Central Station. Arriving in Chicago at LaSalle Street Station, he visits the Omni Ambassador East Hotel (1301 North State Parkway).

PRAIRIE STOP ON ROUTE 41, INDIANA

Thornhill takes a Greyhound bus to meet the mysterious "Mr. Kaplan" at this bus stop in the middle of nowhere—only to be attacked by a crop-dusting plane. Hitchcock filmed the scene just east at the intersection of Corcoran Road and Garces Highway (State Road 155) in Wasco, California (approximately 19 miles west of Delano).

---

1. THE MOUNT RUSHMORE CAFETERIA
The Buffalo Room, 13000 SD-244, Keystone, SD 57751

Carver's Café, the only cafeteria at Mount Rushmore, is not the cafeteria seen in the movie. The cafeteria with great close-up views of the carved presidential heads where Eve Kendall (Eva Marie Saint) shoots Roger Thornhill no longer exists. Demolished in the early 1990s, the Buffalo Room stood where the elevator to the amphitheater currently exists.

2. THE PARKING LOT

13000 SD-244, Keystone, SD 57751

The parking lot where the rangers carry away Thornhill in a station wagon exists no more. A $56 million renovation completed in 1998 altered the visitor's center at Mount Rushmore National Memorial, replacing the parking lot with a modern parking garage and creating a walkway lined with the US state flags.

3. MOUNT RUSHMORE

13000 SD-244, Keystone, SD 57751

Hitchcock shot a number of views of the memorial from various terraces. Mount Rushmore features the 60-feet-tall faces of US presidents George Washington, Thomas Jefferson, Theodore Roosevelt, and Abraham Lincoln, carved in granite between 1927 and 1941. The terrace where Thornhill looks out at the monument no longer exists. A broad stone terrace now overlooks an amphitheater where nightly presentations and light shows are held. Phillip Vandamm's futuristic house, built in the style of renowned architect Frank Lloyd Wright, does not sit near the top of Mount Rushmore. It was built on the MGM studio lot in Culver City, California. To plan your visit, see www.nps.gov/moru/index.htm.

WISCONSIN

Back to School

"Why don't you call me sometime when you have no class?"

Comedian Rodney Dangerfield stars as Thornton Melon, a crass self-made millionaire who enrolls at the fictional Grand Lakes University, home of the Hooters, as a role model to inspire his college-age son, Jason (Keith Gordon). "I don't have the background for this," says the elder Melon. "The high school I went to, they asked a kid to prove the law of gravity. He threw the teacher out the window."

The filmmakers used the University of Wisconsin–Madison for exterior shots of Grand Lakes University, where Thornton falls in love with his sexy English professor, Diane Turner (Sally Kellerman), clashes with his business professor, Philip Barbay (Paxton Whitehead), and hires Kurt Vonnegut to ghostwrite a paper on Kurt Vonnegut. Says Professor Turner, "Whoever did write it doesn't know the first thing about Kurt Vonnegut."

The sixth highest-grossing movie of 1986, *Back to School* "is a good-natured potpourri of gags, funny bits, populist sentiment and anti-intellectualism," wrote *New York Times* film critic Nina Darnton. The lovable slob and king of rapid-fire one-liners renovates his dorm room to create a luxury suite with a hot tub, sings "Twist and Shout" onstage at a local bar, and hires Oingo Boingo to entertain at a party in his dorm suite.

"It's a jungle out there," says Thornton during his college commencement speech. "My advice to you is: Don't go. . . . Move back with your parents. Let them worry about it."

SHOT ELSEWHERE

THE MELON MANSION

Thornton Melon (Rodney Dangerfield) lives in Beverly Hills, California, with his wife, Vanessa (Adrienne Barbeau), who has "six closets full of nothing to wear." Should you visit this private residence (9933 Shangri La Drive, Beverly Hills, CA 90210), please be respectful and do not loiter or disturb the residents.

1. GRAND LAKES UNIVERSITY
Bascom Hall, Lincoln Drive, Madison, WI 53706

From the steps in front of Bascom Hall, we look east over Bascom Hill and down State Street to the Wisconsin State Capitol Building.

2. GRAND LAKES UNIVERSITY BRIDGE
Bascom Mall Bridge, North Park Street (at State Street), Madison, WI 53706

As Thornton's limousine heads north on North Park Street, we see this walkover bridge, with Music Hall to the left and Geography Library in the distance.

3. VAN WISE HALL
1220 Linden Drive, Madison, WI 53706

The limousine heads north on North Charter Street and makes a left on Observatory Drive, passing Waters Residence Hall.

SHOT ELSEWHERE

PI NU SORORITY HOUSE

Although the University of Wisconsin–Madison is home to a dozen sorority houses, Thornton barges into the Delta Delta Delta sorority house at the University of Southern California in Los Angeles. "And just remember," Thornton tells the police officer who escorts him out, "the best thing about kids is making them." Please be respectful and do not loiter or disturb the residents.

---

4. WISCONSIN HISTORICAL SOCIETY
816 State Street, Madison, WI 53706

Jason Melon (Keith Gordon) walks east with his roommate Derek Lutz (Robert Downey Jr.) as they discuss Valerie Desmond (Terry Farrell). Says Derek: "I hate the whole bourgeois mentality of this school."

5. JASON'S DORMITORY
Slichter Residence Hall, 625 Babcock Drive, Madison, WI 53706

Thornton has a parking space reserved for his limousine in front of this building. Please be respectful and do not loiter or disturb the residents.

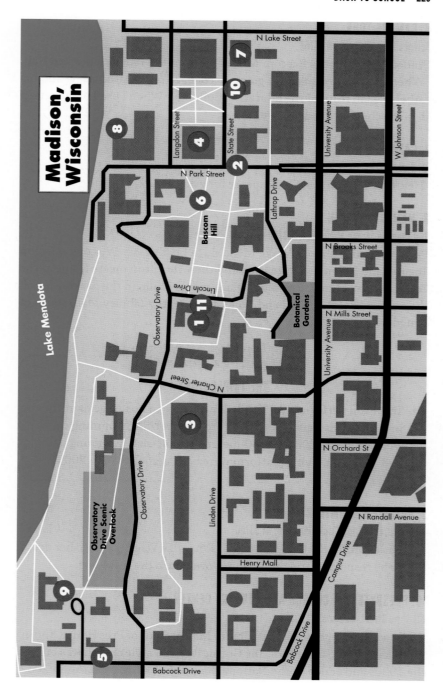

Madison, Wisconsin

Lake Mendota

N Lake Street

Langdon Street

N Park Street

Bascom Hill

Observatory Drive

Lincoln Drive

N Charter Street

State Street

Lathrop Drive

University Avenue

W Johnson Street

N Brooks Street

N Mills Street

University Avenue

Botanical Gardens

Observatory Drive Scenic Overlook

Observatory Drive

Linden Drive

Henry Mall

Babcock Drive

N Orchard St

N Randall Avenue

Campus Drive

Babcock Drive

6. CAMPUS TOUR
Science Hall, Madison, WI 53706

Students walk across Bascom Mall in front of the redbrick Science Hall. "When did you dream about going to college?" asks Jason as he and his father walk in front of the Education Building. "When I used to fall asleep in high school," replies Thornton.

7. CAMPUS BOOKSTORE
711 State Street, Madison, WI 53703

"Hey, folks, it's on me. Shakespeare for everyone."

8. MEMORIAL UNION
800 Langdon Street, Madison, WI 53706

From the south shore of Lake Mendota, a boat passes Wisconsin Union Theater and Helen C. White Hall, and then Thornton meets Diane at the Terrace at the Memorial Union. Diane meets Philip in the parking lot on the west side of Red Gym and walks south to the Library Mall, south of Langdon Street.

SHOT ELSEWHERE

THE TRIPLE LINDY

Thornton performs his "Triple Lindy" dive in Los Angeles at the Industry Hills Aquatic Center, a prominent USA Swimming club, which closed in 2005. The 50-meter Olympic-size swimming pool and 10-meter diving platform were both demolished in 2009.

9. VALERIE'S DORMITORY
Tripp Hall, 1510 Tripp Circle, Madison, WI 53706

After studying at the Observatory, Jason walks Valerie back to her dorm. Please be respectful and do not loiter or disturb the residents.

10. PRESBYTERIAN CHURCH AND STUDENT CENTER
731 State Street, Madison, WI 53703

While walking together across Library Mall in front of Pres House, Thornton asks Diane to tutor him. The Gothic Revival–style church was built in the 1930s and added to the National Register of Historic Places in 2002.

DIANE'S HOUSE

The Colonial-style house where Thornton's English professor resides can be found at 1530 North Orange Grove Avenue, Hollywood, CA 90046. This private residence also starred in the 1978 movie *Halloween* as the house where a young Jamie Lee Curtis babysits. Please be respectful and do not loiter or disturb the residents.

11. LINCOLN STATUE

Bascom Hall, Lincoln Drive, Madison, WI 53706

Thornton and Jason talk in front of this statue, unveiled in 1909. UW-Madison alumnus Richard Lloyd Jones, who purchased the farm where Lincoln was born in 1905, commissioned sculptor Adolph A. Weinman to create a replica of his original statue of Lincoln, erected in the president's

native town of Hodgenville, Kentucky. As president, Lincoln signed the Morrill Land Grant Act of 1862, allowing UW-Madison to purchase a 195-acre "experimental farm" for $28,000 in 1866.

THE FINAL FRONTIER

Thornton takes his oral final exams in Los Angeles in the Nimitz Room in Bob Hope Patriotic Hall (1816 South Figueroa Street, Los Angeles, CA 90015), where he recites "Do Not Go Gentle into That Good Night" by Dylan Thomas.

ACKNOWLEDGMENTS

*A*T CHICAGO REVIEW PRESS, I am grateful to my editor, Jerome Pohlen, for sharing my enthusiasm for this book, his wonderful photos, and his contagious enthusiasm for oddball travel. I am also deeply thankful to project editor Devon Freeny, cover designer Andrew Brozyna, interior designer Jonathan Hahn, my agent Laurie Abkemeier, and researcher Debbie Green.

For help with the photos in this book, my heartfelt thanks go to Brian Grams at Volo Auto Museum, David K. Staub, Payton Chung, Antoine Taveneaux, Daniel Schwen, the Library of Congress, Loyola University Chicago, Jyoti Srivastava, Ben Schumin, Lynae Sowinski, *Limestone Post Magazine*, Paul Browne at University of Notre Dame, Barbara Lindberg, Jacky Luetschwager, Robert Patterson, Denise Stillman at Field of Dreams Movie Site, Finney County Courthouse, Keith Stokes, Robert Maihofer II, Wayne Peacock at the Thunder Bay Inn, Jennifer Cosco, Mike Kinney, John Weeks III, Brenda Anderson, Tom Wilson, City of Delano, Dan Donovan, Megan Ketcherside at Fabulous Fox Theatre, John W. Ratcliff, Steve O'Loughlin at the St. Louis Union Station, David Hinkson, US Department of Transportation, Federal Highway Administration, Kara Pieraccini, C. Anderson, Boys Town Hall of History Archives, Boys Town curator Benjamin L. Clark, Matt Staub, NASA, Ohio Office of Redevelopment, Beth Ramsey, Sarah Feldt, US National Park Service, Beth Steinhauer, United States Forest Service, Kathryn Hester, Custer State Park, Josh Epstein, and Bob Epstein.

Above all, all my love to Debbie, Ashley, and Julia.

BIBLIOGRAPHY

Books and Articles

"Alfred Hitchcock's 'Expedient Exaggerations' and the Filming of *North by Northwest* at Mount Rushmore" by Todd Davis Epp. *South Dakota History* 23, no. 3 (Fall 1993): 181–196.

"Author Gillian Flynn Says Filming 'Gone Girl' Went Much Better Than Expected" by Robert W. Butler. *Kansas City Star*, September 27, 2014.

The Avengers review by Peter Travers. *Rolling Stone*, April 30, 2012.

"Back on the Trail of a One-Armed Man" by Janet Maslin. *New York Times*, August 6, 1993.

Back to School review by Nina Darnton. *New York Times*, June 13, 1986.

"Batman's Chicago Connection" by Luis Gomez. *Chicago Tribune*, July 22, 2014.

The Blues Brothers review by Gene Siskel. *Chicago Tribune*, June 20, 1980.

"The Book That Changed a Town" by Van Jensen. *Lawrence Journal-World*, April 3, 2005.

"Cameras Keep Rolling Through Iowa's Verdant Film Fields: Lights, Camera, Iowa!" by Diana Nollen. *Gazette* (Cedar Rapids, IA), April 5, 2015.

"Cinema: In the American Grain: The Untouchables" by Richard Schickel. *Time*, June 8, 1987.

Classic American Films: Conversations with the Screenwriters by William Baer. Westport, CT: Praeger, 2008.

"Classic American Road Movie: David Lynch's *The Straight Story*" by Jonathan Crocker. *Guardian*, April 26, 2013.

"Director Jason Reitman on Firing People, Recession and Film 'Up in the Air'" by Jen Chaney. *Washington Post*, December 3, 2009.

Escape from New York review by Vincent Canby. *New York Times*, July 10, 1981.

"For Reitman, the Best Characters Are 'Up in the Air'" on *Fresh Air* with Terry Gross. NPR, December 2, 2009.

The Fugitive review by Peter Travers. *Rolling Stone*, August 6, 1993.

The Golden Corral: A Roundup of Magnificent Western Films by Ed Andreychu. Jefferson, NC: McFarland & Company, 1997.

Gone Girl review by Peter Travers. *Rolling Stone*, September 23, 2014.

"'Gone Girl' Author Talks About Her Missouri Roots" by Keith Lewis. *Southeast Missourian*, October 20, 2013.

Grumpy Old Men review by Ty Burr. *Entertainment Weekly*, January 14, 1994.

"Highland Park Remembers 'Risky Business' 30 Years Later" by Greg Dorn. *Chicago Tribune*, May 6, 2013.

"*Home Alone* Breaks Away" by Gerald Clarke. *Time*, December 10, 1990.

"*Home Alone* Turns 25: A Deep Dive with Director Chris Columbus" by Amy Wilkinson. *Entertainment Weekly*, November 6, 2015.

"Home Movies: Alexander Payne, High Plains Auteur" by Margaret Talbot. *New Yorker*, October 28, 2013.

Hoosiers review by Paul Attanasio. *Washington Post*, February 27, 1987.

"In a Class All Her Own" by Amelia Wedemeyer. *Winona Post*, April 2, 2015.

"John Hughes's 'Breakfast Club'" by Janet Maslin. *New York Times*, February 15, 1985.

"John Hughes Wakes Up to Needs of Teens with 'Breakfast Club'" by Gene Siskel. *Chicago Tribune*, February 17, 1985.

"Kevin Costner Journeys to a New Frontier" by Richard C. Morais. *New York Times*, November 4, 1990.

"The Largely Forgotten, Cynical Genius Behind *A Christmas Story*" by Chris Heller. *Atlantic*, December 24, 2013.

"Marquette, Michigan Remembers 'Anatomy of a Murder'" by Dennis McCann. *Milwaukee Wisconsin Journal Sentinel*, November 7, 2008.

The Mighty Ducks review by Rita Kempley. *Washington Post*, October 5, 1992.

My Mother Was Nuts: A Memoir by Penny Marshall. Boston: Houghton Mifflin Harcourt, 2012.

"Omaha's Boys Town Has an Illustrious History" by Terry Turner. *Sioux City Journal*, December 1, 2014.

"On Location" by Robert Osborne. *Hollywood Reporter*, October 24, 1980.

"On Location with *Nebraska* Director Alexander Payne: Johnny Carson, Cowboy Hats, and an Awesome Saloon" by Jennifer M. Wood. *Condé Nast Traveler*, February 24, 2014.

"Paper Moon: The Making of a Classic Under the Midwest's Canvas Sky" by Thomas Arthur Repp. *American Road* 12, no. 3 (Autumn 2014).

"Penny Marshall Pitches 'League of Their Own' Agenda" by David Kronke. *Los Angeles Daily News*, July 2, 1992.

"Pick Flick: An Oral History of 'Election,' 15 Years Later" by Matthew Jacobs. *Huffington Post*, May 7, 2014.

Picture Shows: The Life and Films of Peter Bogdanovich by Andrew Yule. Winona, MN: Limelight, 1992.

Planes, Trains and Automobiles review by Hal Hinson. *Washington Post*, November 25, 1987.

Preminger: An Autobiography by Otto Preminger. New York: Doubleday, 1977.

"'Purple Rain,' with Prince" by Vincent Canby. *New York Times*, July 27, 1984.

"Q&A: 'Dark Knight' Director Christopher Nolan" by Devin Gordon. *Newsweek*, July 11, 2008.

"'Rain Man'—Not the Ordinary Buddy Film" by Sheila Benson. *Los Angeles Times*, December 16, 1988.

"Remembering 'Blues Brothers' 30 Years Later" by Christopher Borrelli. *Chicago Tribune*, June 16, 2010.

"Revisiting *Rudy*, 20 Years Later" by Liam Farrell. *ND Today*, 2013.

"'Risky Business' Director: 'Some People Like the Visibility. I Don't'" by Jake Malooley. *Salon*, September 2, 2013.

Roger Ebert's Four Star Reviews: 1967–2007 by Roger Ebert. Kansas City, MO: Andrews McMeel, 2007.

Rudy: My Story by Daniel "Rudy" Ruettiger with Mark Dagostino. Nashville: Thomas Nelson, 2012.

"Soul Men: The Making of *The Blues Brothers*" by Ned Zeman. *Esquire*, December 18, 2012.

"Stephen King's *Children of the Corn*" by Vincent Canby. *New York Times*, March 16, 1984.

"Superheroes, Super Battles, Super Egos" by A. O. Scott. *New York Times*, May 3, 2012.

"A Tale of Mice and Lens" by Colin Leinster. *Fortune*, September 28, 1987.

"25 Years Later, They Still Come to Iowa's Field of Dreams" by Kyle Munson and Rodney White. *Des Moines Register*, April 20, 2014.

Up in the Air review by Scott Foundas. *Film Comment*, November/December 2009.

"The Vietnam Oscars" by Peter Biskind. *Vanity Fair*, February 19, 2008.

"White Hot: From Rap to Riches" by Elvis Mitchell. *New York Times*, November 8, 2002.

"Why I Love . . . the Quarry in *Breaking Away*" by Xan Brooks. *Guardian*, August 22, 2013.

"With an Oscar in Tow, Writer Steve Tesich Finds His Career Is Finally Breaking Away" by Arthur Lubow. *People Weekly*, May 12, 1980.

Websites

www.bluesbrotherscentral.com
www.boystownmovie.org
www.cinematographers.nl
www.fast-rewind.com
www.filmscouts.com
www.itsfilmedthere.com
www.movie-locations.com
www.movielocationsandmore.blogspot.com
www.movielocationsguide.com

PHOTO AND MAP CREDITS

All photos and maps copyright © 2017 by Joey Green, unless otherwise noted below:

Illinois
The Blues Brothers: "Pilgrim Baptist Church," "Mrs. Tarantino's Boarding House," "South Shore Cultural Center," and "Bluesmobile" copyright © 2016 by Jerome Pohlen. Used with permission of the photographer and Volo Auto Museum.
The Dark Knight: "The Berghoff Restaurant" copyright © 2006 by David K. Staub. Used with permission. "Illinois Center" copyright © 2010 by Payton Chung. Used with permission. "Chicago Board of Trade Building" copyright © 2010 by Antoine Taveneaux. Used with permission.
The Fugitive: "Wells Street Bridge" copyright © 2009 by Daniel Schwen. Used with permission. "Chicago City Hall" by Hedrich-Blessing Ltd. Courtesy of the Library of Congress.
My Best Friend's Wedding: "Cuneo Mansion" copyright © 2016 Loyola University Chicago.
Planes, Trains and Automobiles: "Braidwood Motel" and "Gurnee Motel" copyright © 2016 by Jerome Pohlen. Used with permission.
The Untouchables: "Rookery" copyright © 2016 by Jyoti Srivastava. Used with permission. "Chicago Union Station" copyright © 2010 by Ben Schumin. Used with permission.

Indiana
Breaking Away: "Rooftop Quarry" copyright © 2016 by Lynae Sowinski, *Limestone Post Magazine.* Used with permission. www.limestonepostmagazine.com. "Stoller House" and "Sorority" copyright © 2016 by Jerome Pohlen. Used with permission.
Hoosiers: "New Richmond," "Knightstown Gym," and "Elizaville Church" copyright © 2016 by Jerome Pohlen. Used with permission.
A League of Their Own: "Huntingburg Stadium," "Huntingburg Outfield," and "Fitzgerald's" copyright © 2016 by Jerome Pohlen. Used with permission.
Rudy: "Notre Dame Main Quad," "Hesburgh Library," "Grotto of Our Lady of Lourdes," and "Basilica of the Sacred Heart," copyright © 2016 by University of Notre Dame. Used with permission.

Iowa
The Bridges of Madison County: "Francesca's House" copyright © 2000 by Barbara Lindberg. Used with permission. "Roseman Covered Bridge" copyright © 2016 by Jerome Pohlen. Used with permission. "Northside Cafe" copyright © 2015 by Jacky Luetschwager. Used with permission. http://dickybirdsnest.blogspot.com/. "John Wayne House" copyright © 2016 by Jerome Pohlen. Used with permission.
Children of the Corn: "Children of the Corn House" and "Flagpole" copyright © 2016 by Robert Patterson. Used with permission.
Field of Dreams: "Field of Dreams" copyright © 2016 by Iowa Memories, LLC, d.b.a. Field of Dreams Movie Site. Used with permission.
The Straight Story: "Alvin Straight's House" and "Grotto of Redemption" copyright © 2016 by Jerome Pohlen. Used with permission.

Kansas
In Cold Blood: "Finney County Courthouse," courtesy of Finney County, Kansas.
Paper Moon: "The Road" copyright © 2016 by Jerome Pohlen. Used with permission.
Picnic: "Riverside Park" copyright © 2016 by Keith Stokes. Used with permission.

Michigan

Anatomy of a Murder: "Cliffs Shaft Mine Museum" copyright © 2016 by Robert Maihofer II. Used with permission. "Thunder Bay Inn" copyright © 2016 by Thunder Bay Inn. Used with permission. "Lumberjack Tavern" copyright © 2016 by Jennifer Cosco. Used with permission. *8 Mile:* "Cow Head" copyright © 2016 by Jerome Pohlen. Used with permission.

Minnesota

Fargo: "Blue Ox" copyright © 2016 by Mike Kinney. Used with permission.
Grumpy Old Men: "John Gustafson House," "Max Goldman House," and "Ariel Truax House" copyright © 2016 by John Weeks III. Used with permission.
The Mighty Ducks: "Mickey's Diner" copyright © 2016 by Brenda Anderson. Used with permission.
Purple Rain: "First Avenue," "Orpheum," "The Kid's House," and "Crystal Court" copyright © 2016 by Tom Wilson. Used with permission.
A Simple Plan: "Delano Heritage Center," courtesy of the City of Delano.

Missouri

Escape from New York: "Fabulous Fox Theater" by Dan Donovan. Copyright © 2008 by the Fabulous Fox Theatre. Reprinted with permission. "Masonic Temple" copyright © 2016 by John W. Ratcliff. Used with permission. "St. Louis Union Station" copyright © 2016 by St. Louis Union Station. Used with permission. "Chain of Rocks Bridge" by David Hinkson. Courtesy of US Department of Transportation, Federal Highway Administration.
Gone Girl: "Downtown" and "Bar" copyright © 2016 by Kara Pieraccini. Used with permission.
Up in the Air: "Affton High School" copyright © 2012 by C. Anderson. Used with permission.

Nebraska

Boys Town: "Boys Town" copyright © 2016 by Boys Town. Courtesy of Boys Town Hall of History Archives. Used with permission.
Election: "Papillion–La Vista High School" copyright © 2016 by Robert Patterson. Used with permission.
Nebraska: "Mount Rushmore," courtesy of National Park Service. "Uncle Ray and Aunt Martha's House," "OK Auto," "Blinker Tavern," "Plainview News," and "Grants' House" copyright © 2014 by Matt Staub. Used with permission.

Ohio

The Avengers: "Plum Brook," courtesy of NASA. "Cleveland Trust Building," courtesy of Ohio Office of Redevelopment.
A Christmas Story: "Christmas Story House," "Kitchen Sink," "Leg Lamp," "Flick Statue," and "Jean Shepherd's Childhood Home" copyright © 2016 by Jerome Pohlen. Used with permission.
The Deer Hunter: "St. Theodosius Russian Orthodox Cathedral" copyright © 2016 by Jerome Pohlen. Used with permission.
Rain Man: "Babbitt Mansion," "St. Anne's Convent," "Roebling Bridge," "Vernon Manor," and "Pompilio's" copyright © 2016 by Beth Ramsey. Used with permission.
The Shawshank Redemption: "Mansfield Prison" copyright © 2016 by Jerome Pohlen. Used with permission.

South Dakota

Dances with Wolves: "Badlands" by Sarah Feldt. Courtesy of National Park Service. "Spearfish Canyon" by Beth Steinhauer. Courtesy of United States Forest Service.
How the West Was Won: "Gordon Stockade" copyright © 2016 by Kathryn Hester. Used with permission. "Buffalo Stampede," courtesy of Custer State Park.
North by Northwest: "Mount Rushmore," courtesy of National Park Service.

Wisconsin

Back to School: "Bascom Hall" copyright © 2016 by Josh Epstein. Used with permission.

ABOUT THE AUTHOR

*J*OEY GREEN IS THE AUTHOR OF more than fifty books. A former contributing editor to *National Lampoon* and a former advertising copywriter at J. Walter Thompson, Joey has written television commercials for Burger King and Walt Disney World, and he won a Clio for a print ad he created for Eastman Kodak before launching his career as a bestselling author.

Joey has appeared on dozens of national television shows, including *The Tonight Show with Jay Leno*, *Good Morning America*, and *The View*. He has been profiled in the *New York Times*, *People*, the *Los Angeles Times*, the *Washington Post*, and *USA Today*, and he has been interviewed on hundreds of radio shows.

A native of Miami, Florida, and a graduate of Cornell University (where he founded the campus humor magazine, the *Cornell Lunatic*, still publishing to this very day), he lives in Los Angeles.

Visit Joey Green on the Internet at www.joeygreen.com.